Decentralized Development in Latin America

The GeoJournal Library

Volume 97

Managing Editor:
> Daniel Z. Sui, College Station, USA

Founding Series Editor:
> Wolf Tietze, Helmstedt, Germany

Editorial Board: Paul Claval, France
Yehuda Gradus, Israel
Sam Ock Park, South Korea
Herman van der Wusten, The Netherlands

For other titles published in this series, go to
www.springer.com/series/6007

Paul van Lindert · Otto Verkoren
Editors

Decentralized Development in Latin America

Experiences in Local Governance and Local Development

 Springer

Editors

Paul van Lindert
Utrecht University
Faculty of Geosciences
International Development Studies
PO Box 80.115
3508 TC Utrecht
The Netherlands
p.vanlindert@geo.uu.nl

Otto Verkoren
Utrecht University
Faculty of Geosciences
International Development Studies
PO Box 80.115
3508 TC Utrecht
The Netherlands
verko053@planet.nl

ISBN 978-90-481-3738-1   e-ISBN 978-90-481-3739-8
DOI 10.1007/978-90-481-3739-8
Springer Dordrecht Heidelberg London New York

Library of Congress Control Number: 2009942533

Printed on acid-free paper

Springer is part of Springer Science+Business Media (www.springer.com)

List of Abbreviations

ACM	Asociación Chilena de Municipalidades
ADR	American Depository Receipt
AHMSA	Altos hornos de México
APEC	Asia-Pacific Economic Co-operation
APCG	Association of Pacific Coast Geographers
CBO	Community based organisation
CLAEH	Centro Latinoamericano de Economía Humana (Uruguay)
CMDRS	Conselho Municipal de Desenvolvimento Rural Sustentável (Brazil)
CEPAL	Comisión Económica Para América Latina (= ECLA)
CIFOR	Centre for International Forestry Research
COB	Central Obrera Boliviana
COECE	Organizaciones Empresariales de Comercio Exterior (Mexico)
CSO	Civil society organisation
ECLA	Economic Commission for Latin America
EIU	Economist Intelligence Unit
FDI	Foreign Direct Investment
FONATUR	Fondo Nacional de Fomento al Turismo (Mexico)
FSC	Forest Stewardship Council
FTAA	Free Trade Area of the Americas
GATT	General Agreement on Tariffs and Trade
GTA	Grupo de Tabalho Amazônico
GTZ	Gemeinschaft für Technische Zusammenarbeit
HDI	Human Development Index
INEGI	Instituto Nacional de Estadística, Geografía e Información (Mexico)
IADB	Inter-American Development Bank
IEP	Instituto de Estudios Peruanos
IHEAL	Institut des Hautes Études de l'Amérique Latine (Paris)
IIED	International Institute for Environment and Development (London)
IIRSA	Integración de la Infraestructura Regional en América del Sur
LA21	Local Agenda 21

LDA	Ley de Descentralización Administrativa (Bolivia)
LPP	Ley de Participación Popular (Bolivia)
MAP-initiative	Initiative for future regional integration, cross-border partnerships and local development in Southwest Amazonia, between the administrative entities Madre de Dios (Peru), Acre (Brasil) and Pando (Bolivia)
NAFTA	North American Free Trade Agreement
OECD	Organisation for Economic Co-operation and Development
OTB	Organización Territorial de Base
PDM	Plan de Desarrollo Municipal (Municipal Development Plan)
PMDRS	Plano Municipal de Desenvolvimento Rural Sustentável (Brazil)
PNUD	Programa de las Naciones Unidas para el Desarrollo (= UNDP)
PRA	Participatory Rural Appraisal
PRONAF	Programa Nacional de Fortalecimento da Agricultura Familiar (Brazil)
SBIF	Superintendencia de Bancos e Institutos Financieros de Chile
SECTUR	Secretaría de Turismo (Mexico)
SPTD	State Planned Tourism Destination (Mexico)
TNC	Transnational Corporation
UNAM	Universidad Nacional Autónoma de México
UNCED	United Nations Conference on the Environment and Development
UNDP	United Nations Development Programme
WTO	World Trade Organisation

Foreword

Much of the scholarly and professional literature on development focuses either on the 'macro' level of national policies and politics or on the 'micro' level of development projects and household or community socio-economic dynamics. By contrast, this collection pitches itself at the 'meso' level with a comparative exploration of the ways in which local institutions – municipalities, local governments, city authorities, civil society networks and others – have demanded, and taken on, a greater role in planning and managing development in the Latin American region.

The book's rich empirical studies reveal that local institutions have engaged upwards, with central authorities, to shape their policy and resource environments and in turn, been pressured from 'below' by local actors contesting the ways in which the structures and processes of local governance are framed. The examples covered in this volume range from global cities, such as Mexico and Santiago, to remote rural areas of the Bolivian and Brazilian Amazon. As a result the book provides a deep understanding of the diversity and complexity of local governance and local development in Latin America, while avoiding the stereotyped claims about the impact of globalisation or the potential benefits of decentralisation, as frequently stated in less empirically grounded analysis.

Appreciating the different ways in which globalisation impacts on different regions and social groups, and in which democratisation re-shapes local and national politics, is especially important at the present time in Latin America. Much of the region is now being framed as mineral and hydrocarbon 'concessions' and negotiations, and sometimes alliances, between national political elites and multi-national mining and oil companies are generating contrasting visions of what local development is, and of what it will mean, for those who live on concessions.

The chapters in this book demonstrate that while the sources of change in Latin American countries may be similar – globalisation and democratisation – their impacts on local livelihoods and processes vary greatly with context. On the positive side, economic growth rates in many localities have improved and extreme poverty has been reduced. However, there is also the negative side. Almost everywhere in the region economic inequality has been rising, socio-spatial fragmentation is becoming a norm (with gated communities segregates from city life) and deep pockets of chronic poverty remain, especially for indigenous groups, in countries that have reached middle income status (Chronic Poverty Research Centre

2008). Looking beyond such indicators, perhaps there is some room for optimism in the ways that socio-political processes have been gradually shifting. Democratisation at the national level may not have delivered fair societies but the capacity to demand change in local governance processes offers hope for the future. However, it remains to be seen whether the transfers in authority from central to local governments (i.e. legislative and administrative changes) will be matched by fiscal decentralisation.

While the book reveals the centrality of contests over material capabilities for understanding the changes that have occurred it also points to the influence of ideas. In the 1980s and early 1990s national governments and international agencies highlighted the need for 'local economic development' and, as a consequence, policies of infrastructural upgrading and small and medium enterprise promotion. However, over the last 15 years a broader idea, 'local development', has evolved with the prompting of civil society organisations, indigenous groups and small movements. This includes economic development but also embraces and promotes socio-political change.

Fascinatingly, the focus of these studies on the 'local' demands not only an examination of local-national relations but also of international relations. Sometimes this is pragmatic; many regions are distant from national capitals and main cities and need to envisage closer links (infrastructure, trade and perhaps more) with neighbouring municipalities in adjoining countries. At other times the international linkages are more ideational. This is revealed historically with the influence of the Tennessee Valley Authority (TVA) on regional planning across Latin America, and more recently with the import of US-based ideas about local economic development policies and urban regeneration. But Latin America is not only an importer of ideas. Participatory budgeting, an idea developed at Porto Alegre in Brazil, has been a source of experiment and innovation for more than 20 countries. Indeed the municipality where I work – Manchester City Council – has adopted participatory budgeting to help re-vitalise relations with its community and help Mancunians appreciate that they can influence local budgets and politics.

This book will not provide the reader with a 'silver bullet' policy to make local governance in Latin America more effective. It will, however, help the reader think through what is happening in specific contexts in the region and generate ideas about how progressive change might be fostered.

David Hulme
University of Manchester
Professor of Development Studies
Leverhulme Research Professor

Contents

1   **Local Governance and Local Development in Latin America:
Views from Above and Below**..   1
Paul van Lindert and Otto Verkoren

2   **From Polarization to Fragmentation. Recent Changes
in Latin American Urbanization**...   23
Axel Borsdorf and Rodrigo Hidalgo

3   **Territory, Local Governance, and Urban Transformation:
The Processes of Residential Enclave Building in Lima, Peru**   35
Jörg Plöger

4   **Global Cities and the Governance of Commodity Chains:
A Case Study From Latin America**   49
Christof Parnreiter, Karin Fischer, and Karen Imhof

5   **The Impact of Decentralisation on Local Development:
The Case of Bolivia**   69
Gery Nijenhuis

6   **Political Reforms and Local Development
in the Bolivian Amazon**..   87
Martina Neuburger

7   **The Changing Role of Farmers' Organisations in Rural
Development and Decentralisation in Bolivia**   101
Dicky de Morrée

8   **Constructing Regional Integration from Below:
Cross-border Partnerships and Local Development
in Southwest Amazonia**..   113
Cora van Oosten

9   Government, Governance and Governmentality in Pará,
    Northern Brazil 129
    Dörte Segebart

10 Changing Prospects for Sustainable Forestry in Brazilian
    Amazonia: Exploring New Trends 139
    Mirjam A.F. Ros-Tonen

11 Looking Back on NAFTA's Promises and Realities
    from a Local Perspective. The State of Coahuila, Mexico 155
    Leendert de Bell

12 Tourism and Local Development Strategies;
    The Mexican Case 171
    Ludger Brenner

About the Contributors 189

References 193

Index 213

Chapter 1
Local Governance and Local Development in Latin America: Views from Above and Below

Paul van Lindert and Otto Verkoren

Looking at Latin America in the twenty-first century, the subcontinent appears to have reinvented itself. Economies have been transformed under liberalization and globalisation, political environments have been modified by democratic transitions, and many social and cultural changes have brought about clear-cut modernization processes, with consequences such as, for example, the remodelling of the 'traditional role'-spatial pattern with its primate cities and weak peripheries. Undeniably, during the second half of the twentieth century, the manifold processes of decentralized development have had an impressive impact on Latin America's political, economic, social and spatial landscapes.

Over the past 2 decades, most countries of Latin America have consolidated their democracies, as witnessed by processes of state reform and administrative decentralisation. New social movements with strong ethnic and territorial components are claiming their rights. Typical examples are the creation of 'indigenous municipalities' *(municipios indígenas)* and the current practices of political representation of the 'ethnic voice' in the drafting of new constitutions through so-called *Asambleas Constituyentes*. Next, new spatial entities are coming into existence, within and across the traditional borders of regions and countries. Throughout the subcontinent, the inclusion of local and regional stakeholders in Latin America's development process is articulated through a variety of innovative initiatives in local governance and local development. At the same time, deeply ingrained forces and practices of traditional politics and policies, patronage and clientelism run counter to the inclusion and participation of local communities. And it still remains to be seen whether the many local development initiatives currently undertaken will lead to substantial improvements in the living conditions of the poor in their territories.

In Latin America, the current local governance and local development debates relate to very different levels of scale, ranging from small, rural communities, to fairly extensive (even international) spaces. At first, local development programmes started as 'occasional' initiatives of lower-tier governments, which were hardly embedded in national policy frameworks. Since the mid-1990s however, 'the state' has been catching up, without creating a new, centralized planning bureaucracy. In fact, it seems that local development processes have accentuated existing divisions, both territorial and socio-economical. Across Latin America, spatial and social fragmentation is on the rise.

The empirical studies presented in this volume clearly show the diversity in Latin America's ongoing processes of decentralized development. Before introducing these studies, this chapter first presents an overview of the changes that took place in the three relevant fields of study, *viz.* the transition from state-led toward market-led development; changing perspectives on local government and local governance; and the paradigm shift in regional and local development planning.

From State-led to Market-led Development

In the framework of the colonial mercantile system, Latin America had slowly but steadily become involved in the production of raw materials for export, such as silver, sugar, cacao, indigo etc. It was political independence, however, which really propelled the new states into the capitalist world economy and new forms of economic relationships (Kent 2006, p. 326). While Great Britain and – somewhat later – the United States were becoming evermore important in Latin America (e.g. by financing production and trade, building infrastructure, warehousing and shipping, etc.), the raw material exports became *the* driver of Latin America's economies. Over time, some Latin American countries specialized in mineral products; others 'did' tropical agricultural commodities, and yet others specialized in the export of agricultural commodities of the temperate zone (see e.g. Furtado 1970). Remarkably, the raw material exports took place without seriously involving the so-called export-valorising industries. For a long time, first- and second-stage processing activities were ill-developed in Latin America. The virtual absence of manufacturing in the Latin America meant that the region was over-whelmingly importing the manufactures it needed. Thus, a substantial part of Latin America's export earnings were destined to generate income for foreign exchange to pay for imports (Kent 2006).

Eventually, the national export commodity concentration ratios came to reach alarmingly high levels. Bulmer-Thomas (1994) showed that, in the early twentieth century, the Latin America's export sectors were already dominated by one or two commodities, with increasing trade-vulnerability as a result. Therefore it is not surprising that the international trade disruptions of the First World War, the depression of the 1930s and another round of trade-disruptions during Second World War caused huge set-backs for the Latin American economies. As a reaction, the outward-looking development models (the so-called *desarollo hacia afuera*) changed into inward-looking development models (*desarrollo hacia adentro*), aimed at the growth of the internal markets, with a keen eye toward import-substituting manufacturing development. Suffice it to say that the inward-looking development model blossomed in a bureaucratic-authoritarian context, also seasoned more often than not with nationalism and economic protectionism. At first, the inward-looking development did achieve (some) economic growth, while also fostering some industrialization. Eventually, though, the inward-looking development model was bogged down in economic stagnation.

A new development model came about, this time of neo-liberal cut. Its adoption was bolstered by the world's main multilateral institutions (such as the IMF and the World Bank), guided by the theoretical and ideological principles of the Washington consensus, and consolidated by Latin America's opening up to the world market, as a direct consequence of trade reforms (Gwynne 2004). While the Latin American states lost its hold on the process of economic development, the roles of market and private enterprise were strengthened. With the retreat of the state, state-led development transformed into market-led development, albeit often hesitantly and in fragmentary ways.

Thus, protection mechanisms were fading away and subsidies and surcharges were cut. Additionally, the functions and the size of the governments were trimmed down, which resulted in many thousands of civil servants losing their jobs (in central government and in lower tiers). Moreover, while attractive investment-packages were designed for foreign investors, many state-enterprises were privatised and sold to the highest bidder, a process which frequently went hand in hand with massive redundancies. Furthermore, the export-economy was 'restored' based on the 'traditional products' (if possible *with* some form of processing), the production of new, alternative mineral or agricultural exports, or on (assembly-based) types of manufacturing, via export-processing zones or other methods to attract foreign investors.

Though heralded as a mechanism that would transform Latin America from a continent of despair into a continent of hope, the changeover to neo-liberal policies brought about mixed results. With the exception of Chile, in general the reformed Latin American economies failed to show stable and high rates of investment and economic growth, which had a serious impact on the development process. As to the trade reforms, it turned out that they frequently boasted positive results in the larger, more industrialized, so-called middle-income Latin American economies, whereas in the small, less-industrialized and relatively poor countries of Latin America, the effects of trade liberalization were less clear or less advantageous. With respect to employment, income and poverty reduction, the neo-liberal model also shows a mixed track record, again with Chile as the positive exception. As Gwynne (2004, pp. 55) put it: '...the neo-liberal model has not provided the jobs required to reduce unemployment and has not generated the growth in wage employment required to reduce inequality and poverty'.

Unfortunately, the macro-economic results of the reforms proved heterogeneous and unstable, with growth figures frequently falling short of expectations. The regional and sub-regional effects were even more varied. For a long time, Latin American development was characterised by very large regional imbalances, in which huge socio-economic differences between the core regions and national peripheries stood out (as shown e.g. by Friedmann (1966), Odell and Preston (1973), Morris (1981), Gwynne and Kay (2004)). The neo-liberal reforms emphasized the growth of the core regions, a hardly surprising phenomenon given the competitive advantages and economies of scale and scope of the core regions.

Next, the growth of the (most important) secondary cities stood out, also as result of spatial decentralisation policies. Odell and Preston (1973) already observed this phenomenon (like the unstoppable expansion of the core areas). Finally, the revival of the export economy left its mark on spatial structures, through for example the exploitation of new mineral resources, the development of alternative agricultural production types, and the creation of (assembly-type) export-processing zones or other (manufacturing-based) export-enclaves.

The neo-liberal reforms seem to have had highly differentiated effects on spatial structures. For many years producers and other entrepreneurs could (under the umbrella of the inward-looking development model) rely on protectionist mechanisms, shielding them to some extent from foreign competition. Under the neo-liberal reforms and the opening up of markets, many national companies had to face serious competition from foreign imported goods and from newly entered foreign enterprises. Many national companies could not cope and closed shop, thus adding to the rapidly rising number of unemployed. And it is in this respect that the neo-liberal reforms have changed the spatial balance: following the neo-liberal reforms, a complex patchwork of regions and sub-regions came about, especially outside the national core regions. Regions that fared acceptably well under *desarrollo hacia adentro* faced painful (relative) declines, especially when it proved difficult to attract other investments. Elsewhere, regions that had shown little dynamism for a long time profited from their (re-defined) comparative advantages under neo-liberalism and went into amazing growth spurts (see e.g. De Bell 2005). Indeed, it became clear under the neo-liberal paradigm that prosperity and the development potential of a territory were frequently linked to the regional ability to attract (foreign) investment and produce for export markets. The current worldwide economic crisis, however, also painfully shows that such export dependent regions are extremely vulnerable to external shocks.

Decentralisation and the Role of Local Government

The shifts that have shaped Latin America's economic development over the past few decades were paralleled by equally important changes in the socio-political context. In association with region-wide decentralisation processes, the public sector in many Latin American countries was substantially restructured, which in turn led to new relationships between central, intermediate and local government, as well as between the public sector and civil society.

An important precondition for these decentralisation processes was the fact that popularly elected governments came to replace the once so powerful military-controlled bureaucratic-authoritarian regimes. In the year 1980, the crisis of state legitimacy was still reflected by the fact that out of the 18 countries in Latin America only six had regular elections. The democracies of three of these countries – Colombia, Mexico and Venezuela – were still based on one- or two-party systems (Lora 2007). In contrast, at the start of the new millennium, all nations of the region had elected governments and most had pluriform party structures put in place. Admittedly, during much of the 1980s and even in the next decade, armed conflicts, state repression and violation of human rights continued in too many parts of the region, especially in Colombia, Peru and in some of the poorest Central American countries that were still ruled by patrimonialist governments. In other countries, the transition to representative democracy had triggered the participation of marginalized social groups, albeit often channelled through new political movements with a notorious populist flavour. During the last decade, such populism caused high levels of political instability which in some cases – e.g. Bolivia, Ecuador – resulted in the deposition of consecutive presidents, whereas Venezuela presents an exceptional case by which the president gained almost absolute and indefinite power sanctioned through plebiscites. Thus, while it is a fact that as of the 1980s most Latin American nations have restored their representative democracies, many struggle with the challenges 'to reduce the democratic deficits' (Greig et al. 2007, p. 229).

An important step on the road towards a gradual consolidation of democracy in Latin America was the introduction of municipal elections. The link between the transition to democracy and the introduction of municipal elections is clearly established by Daughters and Harper (2007), p. 218–219; see Table 1.1). Between 1991 and 1995, Paraguay, Nicaragua, Chile and Panama were the last countries in the region to make the change from appointed to elected mayors and councillors. In addition to that – and depending on preceding municipal arrangements – new administrative and territorial municipal jurisdictions were defined through the promulgation and implementation of so-called 'organic laws'.[1] In some countries,

Table 1.1 Latin America: Year of democratic transition and first municipal elections (Daughters and Harper 2007, pp. 218–219)

Country	Year of democratic transition	Year of first municipal elections
Mexico	1917	1917
Costa Rica	1949	1949
Colombia	1958	1988
Venezuela	1958	1989
Ecuador	1979	1983
Peru	1980	1980
Belize	1981	1981
Bolivia	1982	1985
Honduras	1982	1982
Argentina	1983	1983
El Salvador	1984	1985
Guatemala	1985	1985
Uruguay	1985	1984
Brazil	1985	1985
Paraguay	1989	1991
Panama	1989	1995
Nicaragua	1990	1992
Chile	1990	1992

[1] A *'ley orgánica'* in Latin America creates a new institutional regime.

such as in Bolivia, these laws indeed tackled one of the traditional democratic deficits by directly incorporating the formerly excluded rural populations in the municipal political structures, which hitherto had always been dominated by the urban population. In the next step towards the consolidation of democratisation, the central governments transferred more political power to the sub-national governments and reformulated the respective public responsibilities for each of the various tiers of government.

Now that the reforms of the public sector have done away with the tradition of appointed mayors who might be tempted to act primarily in the interest of the president and the party, the 'new' local government is in many cases less authoritarian and exclusive than before. Under the current conditions of elected mayors and councillors, local political autonomy has increased *vis-à-vis* the central state. At the same time, there is more potential for local authorities to include a larger scope of actors in their decision-making and to open up spaces for social participation than there was under a centralist regime. This arrangement thus offers enhanced possibilities to establish multi-sector partnerships for local development, enabling and promoting participation of a wide range of stakeholders (Corrêa de Oliveira 2002).

On the other hand, even if there is increased political autonomy from the centre, this does not mean that decentralisation policies also have brought financial autonomy to the local governments. According to the principles of subsidiarity, the various roles and functions of the state at the different levels of government should be mutually complementary and decentralized to the lowest administrative level at which their implementation is the most effective. In many cases of service provision, the local/municipal level would be the most appropriate. In practice, however, the required transfer of fiscal resources from the national to the local governments, combined with measures to increase revenues from local taxes, did not keep pace with the delegation and devolution of responsibilities. As Nijenhuis (2008) shows, fiscal decentralisation in the countries with a federal state structure primarily focused on strengthening the intermediate levels, such as the provinces (Argentina) and the states (Brazil, Mexico and Venezuela). In the unitary states of the sub-continent, the main focus of decentralisation policies was on the municipal level. Whereas in the federal states sub-national spending varies between 32% and 42%, the average equivalent in the unitary states is quite modest. Even today, after roughly 2 decades of decentralisation in Latin America, the share of national resources that is reassigned to municipal budgets is in most nations still lower than 10% of the central state budget, while only a few countries show a fiscal decentralisation from the central to the local governments of 15–25% (IDB 2000; Nijenhuis 2008).

The analysis of the relative distribution of all governmental expenditure between national government, intermediate government (states, provinces) and local government (municipalities) presents an even bleaker picture for the latter (Table 1.2). For the first half of this decade, the table shows the performance of decentralizing expenditure in Latin American countries. While around 1980 the simple average decentralized expenditure in the region was some 12% of total government spending, this figure increased to an estimated 19% between 2002

Table 1.2 Latin America: Relative distribution of expenditure by National, Intermediate and Local Governments, 2002–2005 (UCLG 2008, p. 183)

Country	Percentage expenditure of total government by sub-national governments	Local government expenditure	Intermediate government expenditure	National government expenditure	Total government expenditure
Brazil	42.1	16.6	25.5	57.8	100
Argentina	41.6	7.8	33.0	59.1	100
Mexico	31.9	4.3	27.5	68.1	100
Colombia	29.8	17.0	12.8	70.2	100
Bolivia	29.5	8.5	21.0	70.5	100
Peru	26.8	8.5	18.3	73.2	100
Ecuador	22.1	17.2	4.9	77.8	100
Chile	15.0	13.2	1.8	85.0	100
Uruguay	13.2	13.2	–	86.8	100
Guatemala	13.0	13.0	–	87.0	100
El Salvador	8.7	8.7	–	91.3	100
Dominican Republic	7.0	7.0	–	93.0	100
Paraguay	7.0	5.2	1.8	93.0	100
Costa Rica	6.0	6.0	–	94.0	100
Honduras	5.6	5.6	–	94.4	100
Nicaragua	3.8	3.8	–	96.2	100
Panama	3.8	3.8	–	96.2	100

and 2005 (UCLG 2008, p. 182). These aggregate figures are undoubtedly influenced by the relatively high proportions of intermediate government expenditure in the federal states of Latin America. The relatively high figures for government expenditure by provinces and departments in Peru and Bolivia (both unitary states) may be explained by these countries' regimes for the redistribution of a percentage of the profits on natural resources (e.g. gold, gas, oil, etc.). On the whole, municipal expenditure in only six countries (Ecuador, Colombia, Brazil, Chile, Uruguay, Guatemala) exceeds 10% of general government expenditure. Then follow four countries (El Salvador, Peru, Bolivia, Argentina) with municipal expenditure over 7% of general government expenditure and the remaining countries range even lower on this indicator of financial decentralization. Evidently, the decentralisation of functions and responsibilities to the municipalities only occasionally coincides with the new distribution of resources, diverting resources from the central government to those municipalities.

In recent academic literature there has been quite some attention for the promising experiences of public management in for example Bogotá (Gilbert 2006), Monterrey

(Paiva 2003), Buenos Aires (de Luca et al. 2002), Montevideo (Canel 2001; Chavez 2004), and – perhaps most notorious of all – Curitiba (Schwarz 2004) and Porto Alegre (Abers 1998a,b, 2000; Fedozzi 2001; Souza 2001). These studies show that the large metropolitan areas frequently boast municipalities which demonstrate admirable planning and management performances in terms of efficiency and effectiveness. Still, the very existence of interlocking and overlapping administrative structures makes it a challenging task indeed to coordinate the efforts of the various local governments within the metropolitan area (Paiva 2003).

Many of these municipalities have also been successful in generating funds. They have been able to use their newly established or increased powers to raise local taxes directly, obtain funds from other sources, and attract national or foreign investment. After a thorough and systematic comparison of governments in some important capital cities of the region, Meyers and Dietz concluded that citizens become less resistant to paying taxes when they perceive that the municipal apparatus is likely to act in a fair and accountable way: 'in a few cases, elected municipal governments in capital cities have gained, at least momentarily, the reputation for collecting taxes honestly, impartially, and transparently – and for using tax revenues to fund needed urban improvements' (Meyers and Dietz 2002, p. 336).

Finally, some of these cities also stand out for their innovative ways to include citizen participation in their (budgetary) planning cycles. We will expand on the potential of such participatory budgeting experience in the next section, and maintain that overall assessment of its performance is very positive. Having said this, however, we should also add that tensions between the old-style centralized practices of clientelism and such more transparent forms of public management continue to exist in many of Latin America's major cities.

In the smaller towns of the region, not to mention the predominantly rural municipalities, the municipal balance sheets show quite a different picture. Here, the transfer of financial resources from the central government is vital for the local governments if they are to perform their new roles properly, if only to cover the expenses of services now provided to the citizens by them on behalf of the central government. This is even more important as many municipal authorities in Latin America lack the necessary capacities to raise their own revenues (Van Lindert and Verkoren 2004). By and large these local administrations suffer from a lack of competent staff, who would normally be held responsible for setting up and maintaining administrative information systems, analyzing local development opportunities, project planning, providing infrastructure and public services, collecting local taxes, development fees and user charges, etc. On top of that the small municipalities do not have the same opportunities as their big sisters to engage in debt financing (e.g. through municipal development funds) in order to contract additional means for investment. As the lion's share of the small local budgets is spent on personnel costs (in some cases up to 70–80%), it is hardly surprising that many of the tasks that were transferred from the central government to the local government cannot be carried out properly (Van Lindert 2005). A truly functioning subsidiarity principle calls for more than 'just' political decentralisation; it must be completed with a genuine and meaningful form of fiscal decentralisation.

Local Governance

One of the traditional primary roles of local government is to secure the smooth and efficient functioning of the public services, which are generally managed by its technical-administrative apparatus. As a matter of fact, this was one of the fundamental arguments of the first generation of decentralisation proponents, who also claimed that it would be easier to tailor local-level services to local needs and preferences. Implicitly, however, this raises the question as to how such local needs and preferences are to be identified. The current decentralisation doctrine firmly holds that 'the only feasible way is to have an inclusive process of local governance through which each segment of the population can express and fight over their preferences' (Osmani 2000, p. 6).

Parallel to the recognition that citizen participation is an essential prerequisite for local sustainable development, the vital role of the local government became also universally acknowledged. In the current international development debate, local government is held to be the key agent both with respect to local sustainability and to the eradication of poverty. The poverty reduction strategy papers of the most indebted countries, for example, generally include a strategic focus on local government, which is to become the main facilitator for the effective provision of social services and the creation of a productive environment. Also, capacity strengthening projects for local governments are now part and parcel of many international development aid programmes (UCLG 2008), including the so-called City-to-City partnerships that work through peer-to-peer approaches and exchanges (Bontenbal 2009a, b; Bontenbal and Van Lindert 2009; Campbell 2009; Van Lindert 2009). Most of such programmes focus on how local governments can become more effective agents for the improvement of local production and living conditions.

In this respect, it is revealing that the World Bank, in its 'Strategy for Urban Development and Local Government', highlights such concepts as liveability and good governance, together with notions of competitiveness and bankability (World Bank 2000). The notion of liveability includes the social and environmental dimensions of development, such as adequate housing, safety, security, health and education. The competitiveness of the local economy relates to the efficient functioning of factor markets (capital, labour, land); bankability refers to sound municipal finance, i.e. the competent and transparent management of municipal budgets (Van Lindert 2008). Together with an established integrity in local government, bankability and creditworthiness are important prerequisites for municipalities to be eligible for World Bank loans. Again, it is not surprising that such attributes and competences will be more readily available in the bigger cities (with larger tax bases and a more qualified staff) than in the rural municipalities.

As mentioned above, the new developmental role of the local governments implies that they really open up to their constituencies for participation in decision-making, not only during election times but especially when they have taken office. Latin America presents many interesting experiences which demonstrate how local government may become the prime mover for civil society to effectively participate in matters that concern their own living and production environments (Bontenbal and Van Lindert 2008). Such restructuring of the relationships between government and citizens is crucial to 'good governance'. According to Mitlin (2004, p. 3), governance 'encompasses the institutions and processes, both formal and informal, which provide for the interaction of the state with a range of other agents or stakeholders affected by the activities of the government'. Many authors, including Mitlin (2004), Gaventa (2001), Osmani (2000), and Schneider (1999), use the notion of participatory governance, which appears to carry a similar meaning as an earlier term: participatory democracy (as opposed to representative democracy). Both terms imply institutionalised processes through which stakeholders participate in activities such as needs assessments, agenda setting, decision-making, inspection and monitoring. Defined in this way, participatory governance is a necessary, but not a sufficient precondition for good governance. In addition to fostering participatory action, governance should also be transparent, accountable and contribute to equality before it would duly deserve the good governance certificate (UNDP 1998; Nijenhuis 2002). In this respect, Andrews and Shah (2005) use the concept of citizen-centred governance. They give the following three distinguishing features: citizen empowerment through a rights-based approach, bottom-up accountability for results, and evaluation of government performance (as the facilitator of a network of providers) by citizens (in their multiple roles as governors, taxpayers, and consumers

Box 1.1 The role of local government under the new vision of local governance (Shah and Shah 2006, p. 43)

'old view' (20th century)	'new view' (21st century)
➢ Based on residuality and local governments as wards of the state	➢ Based on subsidiarity and home rule
➢ Focused on government	➢ Focused on citizen-centered local governance
➢ Agent of the central government	➢ Primary agent for the citizens; leader and gatekeeper for shared rule
➢ Responsive and accountable to higher-level governments	➢ Responsive and accountable to local voters; assumes leadership role in improving local governance
➢ Direct provider of local services	➢ Purchaser of local services
➢ Intolerance for risk	➢ Innovative; risk taker within limits
➢ Depends on central directives	➢ Autonomous in taxing, spending, regulatory, and administrative decisions
➢ Bureaucratic and technocratic	➢ Participatory; works to strengthen citizen voice and exit options through direct democracy provisions, citizens' charters, and performance budgeting
➢ Coercive	➢ Focused on earning trust, creating space for civic dialogue, serving the citizens, and improving social outcomes
➢ Fiscally irresponsible	➢ Fiscally prudent; works better and costs less
➢ Exclusive with elite capture	➢ Inclusive and participatory

of public services). Box 1.1 presents the key elements of this new role of local government, as summarised by Shah and Shah (2006).

When applied to the role of the local government as to development and poverty reduction, participatory governance is seen to have considerably more potential than purely bureaucratic-technocratic forms of governance. Schneider (1999) emphasises that joint decision-making by politicians, civil servants and the relevant stakeholders (including the poor and other intended beneficiaries) leads to more efficient (and just) outcomes, since decisions and policies will be based on information that is more complete and of a better quality. A second rationale for citizen-centred governance that is stressed by Schneider is the fact that all actors are accountable *vis-à-vis* all stakeholders, and if effective mechanisms of sanctioning have been put in place, participatory governance will result in high levels of commitment to poverty reduction and development (Schneider 1999, p. 523).

The accountability issue, including the associated sanctioning mechanisms, is also identified by Blair (2000) as one of the major conditions for participatory governance to succeed. From an analysis of six countries with relatively successful track records of decentralisation and participation this author also stresses the importance of having a critical mass to participate in the political process. Participatory democracy only works if participation is general, and not limited to only a few interested stakeholders or the male segment of the population (Blair 2000).

Another important lesson learned from the Brazilian participatory budgeting experience is that the process of participatory democracy is not sustainable or irreversible by itself. One condition for irreversibility is that the population at large is aware of the importance of the process and its benefits (Cabannes 2004, p. 45). This is demonstrated in the case of Porto Alegre, where, contrary to what several other municipalities in Brazil have experienced, participatory budgeting proved to outlast a change in government. Here, in the cradle of the participatory budgeting (PB) experience, the Workers' Party which had introduced PB, had governed for an uninterrupted period of 15 years since 1989. The year-round PB-meetings involved ever-increasing numbers of participants who knew exactly what their entitlements were and also noticed that there had been a substantial shift in spending towards the poorest areas of the city (Wampler 2007). Remarkably, the conservative PMDB-led[2] municipal administration that took office in the year 2004 and prolonged its stay with a second term in 2008, carried on the PB process, initially perhaps also out of fear that it would otherwise lose legitimacy. Since then, the local government has restructured its urban management system and parallel to this it sustains a further institutionalisation of the PB process through the proposal for a Law on Participatory Budgeting,[3] although it is also pertinent to mention here that various observers report that considerable budget cuts have led the number of projects to drop and that citizen participation has watered down in latest years (Chavez 2008).

---

[2]PMDB: *Partido do Movimento Democrático Brasileiro*.

[3]*Projeto de Lei Orçamentaria* [www2.portoalegre.rs.gov.br/op/default.php?p_secao=1] and [www.portoalegre.rs.gov.br/portaldegestao].

Whereas in Porto Alegre the PB process was institutionalised following its successful practice – and not imposed by rules from above – Bolivia presents a different case. In Bolivia, the central government promulgated various laws in order to force participatory governance on to the local governments (Van Lindert and Nijenhuis 2002). After a hesitant start and some initial resistance from the organised peasants' segment in Bolivian society, the new legal and regulatory frameworks were soon followed by a massive transformation of the country's socio-political landscapes (Assies 2003; Kohl and Farthing 2008). Most importantly, the municipalities received relatively large amounts of money transferred from the central government, provided that they would follow the mandatory participatory planning procedures and follow up with formal municipal development plans. Some of the chapters that will follow will go into the role of local governments, citizen participation and development in Bolivia more specifically.

In sum, local governance ought to be intimately related with a well-defined decentralisation program which, apart from its local development goals, is specifically aimed to tackle democratic deficits (such as human-, gender-, democratic/political rights), to achieve a proper transition from a representative democracy to a participatory democracy and to bring about effective local decision making (see e.g. Gill 2000; UNDP 2002; Greig et al. 2007).

Planning for Regional Development in Latin America

Regional development planning has a notorious history in Latin America. Once national (economic) planning had become accepted, regional development and regional policy-making were also gradually embraced, to some extent a logical outcome of state-led development and enabling approaches. Mexico's early steps on the regional development trajectory (e.g. through large irrigation-based colonisation schemes or river basin development projects, which seems to echo the principles of the famous Tennessee Valley Authority Project), were followed by other Latin American countries in the 1950s and later, among which the grandiose resource frontier development projects (like Cd. Guayana in Venezuela, or the opening up of the Brazilian Amazon region) became well known examples. As the well-known studies of e.g. Friedmann (1966), Barkin and King (1970) and Stöhr (1975) became landmarks in the study of regional development, a vast array of regional agencies appeared in Latin America which became involved in the implementation of regional development policies and produced loads of regional development plans. In the 1970s and early 1980s, regional development in Latin America had achieved a prominent place in the development process. Small wonder that quite a few textbooks on the subcontinent – see e.g. Odell and Preston (1973), Gilbert (1974), Morris (1981) – reserved a prominent place for regional planning in Latin America.

Looking back, Latin America's planning-related, regional development efforts during the past few decades have fallen short of expectations. Admittedly,

Latin America's overall infrastructure is better today than it was in the 1950s and 1960s: urban and rural road networks have been upgraded and extended, ports and airports have been improved, flood controls have been built or reinforced, the range and delivery of electricity and piped water have developed, the number of schools and clinics has increased, etc. Next, it proved possible to slow down the sheer inevitable growth of the so-called primate cities and to boost the upsurge of secondary cities (and even smaller towns), a phenomenon that also resounds the effects of (decades of) spatial decentralisation-oriented, planning-related measures (see e.g. Aguilar et al. 1996; Ranfla Gonzalez 2000; Verkoren 2002; Palomares León 2003). The role of regional planning and its agencies seems to been a very modest one with respect to the realization of structural changes in Latin America's disadvantaged regions. As a result, many of the imbalances in economic development (once perceived as typical for the dual spatial economies of the 1960s and 1970s) are still very much recognizable (with huge pockets of (extreme) rural inequality and poverty as an unfortunate spin-off).

There has been a tremendous variation in planning policies and programmes, as well as in the agencies involved. In the early decades, much attention was paid to the so-called river basin programmes and to the colonization or settlement plans, both intended to attain higher levels of agricultural output by expanding the agricultural production areas and agricultural intensification. Next, attempts have been made to speed up the growth of secondary cities, to create the new urban centres and/or to improve the absorptive capacities of medium-sized and smaller cities. Frequently, these (planning-related, decentralisation) programmes possessed multi-purpose characteristics, combining the slowing down of the expansion of the primate cities, with economic improvements in the settlement structures of the intermediate and peripheral regions. To that end, growth-centre derived economic development measures were often combined with policies to improve public and private service-levels. Other planning programmes of the early days were related to improve the socio-economic situation of the so-called problem regions, or to create new agricultural regions on the settlement frontiers (to alleviate the quest for suitable, agricultural land and to step up agricultural production). In general, regional planning had a clear-cut top-down character. It was designed at the national and regional levels, popular participation was by and large absent, and local resources and capabilities were only seldom taken into account. When the Latin American states saw themselves compelled to tighten the belt under structural adjustment and neo-liberal approaches, regional planning efforts and their agencies were frequently among the first 'victims' of the budget cuts. In the words of Gilbert (1997, pp 181): 'The 1980s saw the withering away of most existing regional programmes and little in the way of policies to replace them'. In the 1990s, it became clear that decentralisation and democratisation called for different planning approaches: less top-down, more geared to local needs and resources, and allowing space for participatory decision-making and citizen empowerment.

Planning for Local Development

Interestingly, when the need for changes in planning in Latin America was acknowledged, an important shift in planning theory and planning paradigms took place. Slowly but steadily, the 'traditional' Latin American command-and-control approach with its design-based blueprint models gave way to more flexible proposals, with a regional/local orientation, in which a consensus had to be negotiated with the available stakeholders (see e.g. Carley et al. 2001). In the process, many lower-tier government institutions started to try to pursue policies of their own, seizing the opportunities offered by the political change from bureaucratic-authoritarian rule to more pluriform and democratic models. Pike et al. (2006) summarized the major differences between the 'traditional top-down approaches' and the 'bottom-up inspired' local/regional development strategies, which are in a slightly adapted form presented in Box 1.2.

Roughly from the 1980s onwards the notion of Local Economic Development (LED) developed and the LED-strategy had the original aim 'to stimulate local employment opportunities in sectors that improve the community, using existing human, natural and institutional resources' (Blakely 1994, p. xiv). Local economic development may provide the basis for regional policies which complement a market oriented macroeconomic philosophy (Cook and Hulme 1988, p. 228). It rapidly gained popularity, at first in the USA, and it was frequently applied in (small) urban contexts. In the USA, these LED-approaches were backed by regulation

---

Box 1.2 Local and regional development: old vs. new approaches (Pike et al. 2007, p. 17.)

Traditional (top-down) policies	*New (bottom-up) policies*
➤ Decisions as to areas and types of intervention are taken in the national centre	➤ Intervention initiatives come from below
➤ Managed by the national central administration	➤ Decentralized, vertical cooperation between different tiers of government and horizontal cooperation between the public and private sectors and civil society
➤ Sectoral approach to development	➤ Territorial approach to development
➤ Development of large (industrial) projects that foster economic development	➤ Based on the regional/local development potential, it is tried to stimulate the progressive adjustment of the local economic system, taking into account the changing economic environment
➤ Financial support, incentives and subsidies as the main factor of attraction of economic activity	➤ Provision of key conditions for the development of regional/local economic activity and -living conditions

defined at the national level and by legally prescribed stimuli for local economic development (e.g. the federal and state laws concerning Medium- and Small-Business Loans, Enterprise- or Empowerment Zones etc.). What is more, this local development process was to a very large extent implemented by professional 'Local Economic Development Corporations', themselves often public-private partnerships, many of which were operating under the auspices of, or in close association with, the Local Chambers of Commerce.

Of course, it was far from easy to adapt the US practice of local economic development to the Latin American contexts, as national (financial) regulations and stimuli were generally lacking, while many local governments struggled with huge resource-deficiencies, including human capacity and experience (Verkoren 2002). Nevertheless, quite a few Latin American local governments took up the gauntlet, exploiting the niches in the national political and economic structures (often supported by ongoing processes of (financial) decentralisation and/or participatory decision-making).

A quick-scan of today's literature on local development in Latin America shows that the term 'local development' is used in highly different ways.[4] To some, local development is a relatively narrow concept: for example, Meyer-Stamer (2002) takes a business-oriented view, seeing local development in a strict relation to local enterprise. For others, (e.g. Abastoflor and Rivero 1999) local development is a community-based phenomenon, that is clearly embedded in the rural areas; thus, they stress the role of livelihoods as well as non-economic factors. For again others (such as Bustamante 2004; Altschuler 2006) local development has a clear-cut, locality-based orientation, with the aim to improve the quality of local life by improving the local economic, social, and political situation.

While the original (U.S.-based) LED-policies were fairly urban-oriented and emphasizing sectoral approaches (see e.g. Blakely 1994; Helmsing and Guimaraes 1997; Helmsing 2002; Pike et al. 2006), the Latin American local development debate, which took place in a context of apparent political and economic change, unfolded over time in a different way. Here, local development soon referred to municipalities with urban *and* rural spaces, which not only reflected the importance of Latin America's rural population, but also the need for rural poverty reduction. The Bolivian concept of the *municipio productivo* (i.e. productive municipality) is an interesting example of a planning strategy which also focuses on the smaller centres in the rural areas, trying to offer opportunities for endogenous development (Pader/Cosude 1998; Abastoflor and Rivero 1999). And through the so-called community approaches it was even tried to spur development in places at the very bottom of the settlement-hierarchy, which were even less

---

[4] In a relatively early stage of the Latin American local development debate interesting theoretical contributions came from e.g.), De Mattos (1989), García Delgado (1997), Corragio (1998), Albuquerque (1999), Boisier (1999), and Marsiglia (1999). Among the early contributions with a more practical point of view, one finds e.g. sources such as Asociación Chilena de Municipalidades (1996), Pader/Cosude (1998), and IFAM (1999).

endowed; it proved a strategy however which resulted in the creation of (a few) social or cultural facilities, simply because sufficient support for local *economic* development was virtually absent. Moreover, the ongoing discussion about territorial development in Latin America (spearheaded by well-known scholars such as Francisco Albuquerque, Sergio Boisier, or José-Luís Corragio) caused the local development debate to become evermore territorial, while paying less attention to sectoral development. Finally, the Latin American local development debate became – already in a relatively early stage – clearly tied to (local) politics, to governance-issues and to participatory decision-making. Latin American thinking about local development quickly reflected the trend towards democratisation and popular participation, which led to the creation of partnerships with clear civil society involvement, as well as to a rapidly growing need for (development-related) capacity-building at the local level (see e.g. Burin and Heras 2001; Carpio Benalcázar 2006; Rofman 2006; Villar 2007). Over time, voices were heard among the participants in Latin America's local development debate that local development was a strategy to achieve political change and (eventually) to arrive at a more democratic, more participatory and more just society (see e.g. Cravacuore 2006; Corragio 2006). Thus the role of local development as a tool to achieve socio-political change came to be more emphasized (Gallicchio 2006).

Meanwhile, Helmsing (2002) has come up with an interesting attempt to cut through the hedges that separate the various approaches to local development in Latin America. Helmsing perceives local economic development as a mechanism that should 'mobilize actors, organizations and resources, and develop new institutions and local systems through dialogue and strategic action' in the control and use of local physical, human and institutional resources (Helmsing 2002, p. 81). Local economic development is thus defined as 'a process in which partnerships between local governments, community-based groups, and the private sector are established in order to manage existing resources, create jobs, and stimulate the economy of a well-defined territory' (Helmsing 2002, p. 81).

As such, many definitions emphasize the economic dimension of local development. However, this 'narrow' definition may easily be broadened and opened up for other components such as civic society, wellbeing, etc. In our view, local development is aimed at improving local production structures *and* local living conditions. This means, that measures to improve the delivery of collective services (e.g. piped water, sanitation, electricity, education, health, public transportation) or measures to prevent natural hazards (like erosion, floods, landslides), may well be part of 'local development'. Also, pro-poor measures that aim to redress local poverty and inequality may be incorporated in local development planning. Hence, local development aims to stimulate both the economy and the society of a well-defined territorial entity, through a process in which participatory approaches and partnership formation are essential. However, local development is not a jack-of-all-trades, capable to combat widely differing economic, social, political and other desires. Local development plans must therefore be well crafted and based on sound analyses of local situations and local opportunities. The local development process is thus unfit for blanket approaches, which do not recognize the possibilities and drawbacks of locations, local resources, local interest groups, local capabilities, etc.

Another tendency among the Latin American local development approaches is to engage in cross-border development efforts, based on cooperation between adjacent local governments to achieve commonly formulated goals, e.g. river basin management, water provision, garbage collection and waste processing, or collectively attracting investments, businesses, tourists etc. The so-called *mancomunidades* (associated municipalities) typically represent this type of inter-municipal development cooperation, by which the participating municipalities seek to solve their problem of having a too small size and capacity to respond to the demands of their citizens. Such *mancomunidades* have been set up successfully in Argentina, Bolivia, Ecuador, and Guatemala, while Colombia and Chile present examples of local government associations which have been established with the special aim to carry out administrative functions for their members and to facilitate a joint provision of public services by the municipalities (UCLG 2008, p. 182). In recent years, other local development efforts that embrace associative arrangements between local governments, provincial and regional entities on a larger spatial scale have become more common. Cravacuore et al. (2004) and Altschuler (2006) even connect ongoing processes of local development-related, inter-municipal cooperation with the creation of larger, development-oriented micro-regions. Some of these micro-regions already cross international borders. In this respect, Vieira Posada (2008) discusses the opportunities and perspectives of trans-border integration zones between Colombia-Venezuela and Colombia-Ecuador. Van Oosten (2009; Chapter 8 in this volume) deals with a tri-national partnership in South West Amazonia, the so-called MAP initiative (between Madre de Dios in Peru, Acre in Brazil, and Pando in Bolivia).

Generally, regions and localities show huge differences in resource endowment, in political, social and economic structures, in institutional strength, in development potential, etc. In other words: contexts matter. Hence, it is of utmost importance to clearly contextualize experiences in local governance and local development. Also, one should realize that the implementation of local development strategies in different (political, institutional, economic, social, geographical) contexts may well lead to completely different outcomes. Quite a few authors already emphasized the importance of spatial (i.e. territorial) differentiation in the development process (e.g. Wiggins and Proctor 2001; Schejtmann and Berdegué 2004; De Janvry and Sadoulet 2004). As such, it is remarkable that most of current decentralization studies focus on aggregate state levels (or comparisons of states) while hardly paying attention to the phenomenon of spatial differentiation within or between countries (see e.g. Segovia 2003; Saito 2008; Kauneckis and Andersson 2009).

Finally, the ongoing local development debate in Latin America shows, quite interestingly, a 'return of the state' – albeit in a supportive role. With the growing importance of local development projects, the need emerged to clearly lay down the relationships between the local, provincial and national levels in the process, for example to specify responsibilities, to develop guidelines, to diagnose local bottlenecks and opportunities for development, to produce (participatory) planning manuals, etc. Thus local development, the execution of which clearly remained in the hands of lower-tier governments, is gradually becoming embedded in nationally defined frameworks for spatial, economic and social development.[5]

The Contributions to This Book

This volume, based on empirical research, echoes the current debate on local governance and local development in Latin America from a geographical – i.e. spatial – perspective. The book is organized in three parts. The first section zooms in on development processes in the context of Latin America's metropolitan areas, which – as the very nodes of globalization – mirror highly conflicting development tendencies. Here, the growth of global productive networks and opulent gated communities goes hand in hand with the, seemingly perpetual, reproduction of inequality. As a consequence, the metropolitan spaces are becoming ever more contested and fragmented. The huge spatial differentiation within Latin America's metropolitan areas and the highly varied outcomes of local governance and local development processes fully warrant separate consideration.

In Chapter 2, Borsdorf and Hidalgo add a very interesting dimension to the ongoing debate on the changing Latin American metropolitan areas, by concentrating on the multi-scalar and multi-actor policy processes which have come about since the 1980s. Faced with new challenges, intimately related to the privatisation of public space, the unstoppable emergence of gated communities, the dilapidation of inner city areas (etc), the urban governments were compelled to reconsider their policies. The fragmentation of the urban structures is reflected in new patterns, as a consequence of which the resulting new urban spaces become an assembly of socio-spatial and functional-economic cells. The formation of residential enclaves such as gated communities and enclosed neighbourhoods is one trait of this process. Consequently, the urban community, once clearly perceived as a unified organism, has evolved into a collection of highly fragmented urban spaces. This phenomenon calls for new types of urban governance, regulation and control, as well as for more (spatially) differentiated local development strategies.

In Chapter 3, Jörg Plöger takes on the effects of polarisation and fragmentation in the structure of metropolitan Lima. He uses the concept of 'condominisation', i.e. the privatisation and fortification of (residential) spaces through legal, physical and social means of spatial control. As a response to the growing feeling of insecurity in Lima's challenging urban environment, the residents of more and more neighbourhoods are opting to protect themselves by e.g. gates and security guards. Since state institutions appear to be incapable of providing adequate infrastructure and (security) services, residents are organizing their security needs themselves, as

---

[5]The *Programa de Desarrollo Productivo Local* of the Argentine *Instituto Federal de Asuntos Municipales* (2003) and the *Plan Nacional de Desarrollo Local y Economía Social* of the Argentine *Ministerio de Desarrollo de la Nación* (2005) are appealing examples of such national frameworks for local development.

a consequence of which the system of local governance is shifting towards a highly complex constellation of actors. The findings in Lima indicate that the emerging security geography correlates with socio-economic status and thus reproduces existing levels of inequality.

In Chapter 4, Christof Parnreiter, Karen Fischer and Karen Imhof focus on the relationship between global city formation, the deepening of global integration and the governance of commodity chains. For as far as yet, the literature on the topic consists of two different research strands on global commodity chains and on the formation of global cities, respectively. In their contribution, the authors combine both approaches into an interpretative framework for the analysis of the global economy and its impact on territorial developments. The authors focus on the intersections between the spaces of flows stretching between global cities and the spaces of flows created through global commodity chains, using Mexico City and Santiago de Chile as prime examples.

The second section of this volume contains three contributions on the local governance and local development processes in Bolivia, as one of the frontrunners of decentralized governance in Latin America. In 1994, the Bolivian government introduced a highly ambitious decentralisation programme. This Bolivian model of decentralisation had three main components: firstly, the creation of 314 new municipalities; secondly, the transfer of responsibilities and funds from the central to the local, municipal level; and thirdly the involvement of the local population in local decision-making through participatory planning through the Law on Popular Participation (LPP). The objectives of the Bolivian decentralisation model were twofold. Firstly, it sought a more effective way of public policy implementation, in order to foster local development. Secondly, it set out to increase the popular participation in local planning and decision-making processes, especially as to the rural populations who had been neglected for such a long time.

Gery Nijenhuis, who closely followed the Bolivian decentralisation effort from its first years of implementation, considers in Chapter 5 the effects of LPP and related legislation on local development in the rural context. Her analysis, based on a comparison of six municipalities in highland Chuquisaca, shows that the implementation of decentralisation did result in an increased municipal investment capacity, as well as in growing numbers of local projects and slight increases in local employment. However, the results also show important differences between the studied municipalities, which were strongly related to the administrative capacities of local government and the quality of their project designs. Moreover, since the opportunities and the capacities to raise local revenues were severely limited, the municipal capabilities to acquire external funds proved to be vital for successful local development planning.

Martina Neuburger links up with this discussion in Chapter 6, shifting the focus to the effects of institutional reforms in Bolivia's Amazon lowlands. The various institutional reforms created 36 new municipalities in the region, which henceforth could administer their territories, manage municipal finances and design and implement local development plans. In comparison to the Chuquisaca region of the

previous chapter, state presence in the Amazon lowlands is very weak, while mana-
gerial and planning capacities of the local administrations are almost completely
lacking. On top of this, the municipalities also show incipient, weak organisational
structures in local civil societies as well as a dominant role of local elites. Small
wonder, that the author questions the claim that decentralization and popular participation did actually strengthen local governance and development in the region.

In Chapter 7, Dicky de Morrée elaborates on the different forms of peasant
organisation in the highland communities of Chuquisaca and Potosí. Three different
organizational types were encountered: informal networks for resource exchange,
such as land, labour and capital; peasant unions (*sindicatos*) and village authorities;
and the more modern economic farmers' organisations, such as producers' associations and cooperatives. The author then links up with the decentralisation debate in
Bolivia that started in Chapters 5 and 6 and shows how the institutional reforms
impacted peasant organisation in different ways. Before the municipal reforms, the
'traditional' peasant and community organizations operated outside the municipal
structures, fulfilling their roles almost autonomously. The new (administrative)
situation sometimes clashes with the old one, which weakens the traditional organisations. However, in municipalities where mayors and/or a fair proportion of the
municipal council members have an outright farming background, the traditional
organisations experience fewer problems.

The third section in this volume concentrates by and large on Brazil and Mexico.
Both countries are federal states which, in comparison with Latin America's unitary
states, show highly different decentralization experiences. Moreover, both countries
have a strong heritage as centralized developmental states. The chapters in this section focus on a divergent development approaches, some of which date from the era
of outright sectoral state intervention; others emphasize more people-centred
approaches.

Chapter 8 takes up the issue of cross-border development and regional integration
in Latin America, focusing on the regions of Madre de Dios in Peru, Acre in Brazil,
and Pando in Bolivia. Through the creation of cross-border partnerships, local
stakeholders from these three peripheral regions are trying to jointly face the
development challenges within a rapidly changing international context. In this
chapter, Cora van Oosten analyses the major processes of socio-economic and
political change in the three regions and explains how and why the cross-border
partnerships emerged in recent years. She also elaborates on the importance of
these partnerships for local economic development and local governance in the
Southwest Amazon and their role in the process of regional integration. Despite
potential threats of renewed nationalism, the author anticipates continued regional
cooperation which may lead to innovative forms of transboundary governance, with
a strong involvement of local stakeholders, and directly related to the management
of the region's natural resources.

In Chapter 9, Dörte Segebart addresses participatory planning processes in rural
development, more especially in the Federal State of Pará (Brazil). She focuses on
the experiences with participatory monitoring in two municipalities in Pará's
Northeast and identifies the major factors relevant for local governance. The moni-

toring tools help to improve municipal transparency and accountability and to strengthen public administration.

In Chapter 10, Mirjam Ros-Tonen analyses the recent processes that have led to major changes in the supply patterns of the timber industry in Brazil's Amazonia. Among the processes that have contributed to these changes are the dynamics inherent in the frontier-related nature of logging in upland forests; the decentralisation of forest management; the devolution of land rights to local communities; a greater role for civil society organisations in forest policy; and globalisation and global environmental governance. The author explores what new supply patterns and trends are emerging in response to increasing timber scarcity, increased control of forest land by small-scale producers and market- and donor-driven incentives for sustainable forest management. Whereas the expansion of external markets provokes increasing deforestation, the author expects that decentralisation and democratisation of forest governance and global preoccupation about the loss of environmental services and livelihood opportunities for local people will create new incentives for sustainable forest management.

In Chapter 11, Leendert de Bell focuses on the role of globalization on local development in the state of Coahuila, Mexico. This state, situated in the northeast of Mexico, appears to be one of the more successful examples of Mexico's economic liberalization policies. Coahuila's impressive economic growth rates over the past one-and-a-half decade are the direct result of a spectacular increase in foreign direct investments, which strongly emphasized export manufacturing. However, ongoing market liberalization also tended to polarize existing inequalities, both between and within (sub)regions, economic sectors, and social groups. The analysis focuses in particular on changes in the local socio-political structures as a result of processes of international economic restructuring.

Ludger Brenner, in Chapter 12, looks at the role of state-sponsored tourism development strategies. It is often perceived that tourism development provides ample opportunities for the local and regional populations to participate in the sector, both directly and indirectly. However, Brenner's cautious analysis of coastal resort development curbs overall enthusiasm on the (potential) role of this sector in local development. Even small-scale and technically well-planned luxury resorts do not automatically lead to sustainable, inclusive development. The growth of the tourist resorts in Mexico is even related with burgeoning shantytowns, social segregation and the marginalization of the local population and the formation of economic enclaves.

Taken together, the chapters in this volume offer a diverse panorama of decentralization, local governance and local development in Latin America. They show that it is far from easy to achieve tangible local development, especially in the lower ends of the urban hierarchy and in the (peripheral) rural areas. They also demonstrate how difficult it is to create viable and inclusive forms of local decision making, which bring about more local prosperity, well-being and liveability as a greater good for all. Deep-rooted practices of traditional politics, of patronage and clientelism are persistent and they are often running against the inclusion and participation of the poor. Certainly, one has to acknowledge that the new approaches still contain quite a few blind spots and blank spaces and that their outcomes are often contradictory. Still, there are also signs that improved local governance may lead to more democratic and inclusive results. Precisely because of the huge contextual variations and the differences between spatial scales, the relationships between decentralization, local governance and local development are difficult to grasp. For as far as yet, there still is an urgent need to study, compare and analyze real-life examples. This will make it possible to develop a conceptual framework of decentralization, local governance and local development which might help to find out how to replicate successful approaches to other contexts, or even to scale them up.

Chapter 2
From Polarization to Fragmentation. Recent Changes in Latin American Urbanization

Axel Borsdorf and Rodrigo Hidalgo

In most Latin American cities the polarization between rich and poor quarters in the urban fabric (*ciudad rica* and *ciudad pobre*) is – although still visible – weakening. New rich quarters rising in formerly poor neighbourhoods seem to suggest that the texture of society is changing and that rich and poor are beginning to mix. Yet, on closer inspection, it immediately becomes obvious that socio-spatial segregation has become more pronounced. The millionaires in the hermetically closed off luxury quarters mostly do not care less about the social environment beyond the walls of their communities They are islands of the rich located within an ocean of poverty. Accordingly, Janoschka (2002a) called contemporary Buenos Aires a 'City of islands', and the islanders are the ones who have won. Indeed, they are 'los que ganaron', as Svampa (2001) has pointed out.

Nevertheless, it would be too simple to blame only the rich for spatial segregation. Contemporary Latin American cities abound with walls. Middle class neighbourhoods are walled off and even marginal quarters tend to construct fences. Walls and gates protect leisure clubs, shopping centres, office towers, business districts, industrial estates, and even some quite normal public streets. Polarization thus has been superseded by fragmentation, not only in the urban structure but also in the social fabric, the functional pattern , and the infrastructure of the agglomeration. Two decades ago, modern malls, copies of the U.S. American model, were only to be found in the 'rich city' (Bähr and Mertins 1995, p. 107); nowadays they are found in towns everywhere.

Urban researchers have taken a while to notice the significance of these structural changes in Latin American cities. Even recent monographs (see e.g. Wilhelmy and Borsdorf 1984, 1985; Gilbert 1994 Bähr and Mertins 1995) contain only few hints on new segregation tendencies. Furthermore, none of the above authors have recognized the implications of these developments for the urban structure. Neither did those few studies published in the early 1990s that focus on upper class quarters (Achilles 1989; Köster 1995). Only the latest publications on Brazilian towns deal with the intensification of segregation and the rise of gated communities (Lopes de Souza 1993; Pöhler 1999; Wehrhahn 2000; Coy and Pöhler 2002), following Brazilian academic research results (Viera Caetano O'Neill 1986; Caldeira 1996). Subsequently, the first studies on the new trends in the Spanish cultural subcontinent

P. van Lindert and O. Verkoren (eds.), *Decentralized Development in Latin America:*
Experiences in Local Governance and Local Development, GeoJournal Library 97,
DOI 10.1007/978-90-481-3739-8_2, © Springer Science+Business Media B.V. 2010

have appeared (Borsdorf 1998, 2000, 2002a; Janoschka 2002a, 2002b, 2002c; Meyer and Bähr 2001; Rovira 2002; Sabatini et al. 2001). Supported by young scholars working on their diploma theses (like Evangelisti 2000; Kanitschneider 2004; Kohler 2002; Goumas 2002), an Austrian research team (Borsdorf, Parnreiter, Fischer, Jäger, Kohler) carried out field work in Argentina, Chile, Ecuador, Mexico, and Peru. The results of these studies form the basis of this chapter.

The changes observed in the socio-spatial structure of Latin American cities brought about a discussion of the so-called 'model of the Latin American city'. Meyer and Bähr (2001) presented a new model for Santiago de Chile, Janoschka (2002b) for Buenos Aires, and Borsdorf (2002b) modified his model of urban development in Latin America. Joining forces, Borsdorf, Bähr, and Janoschka integrated their results and published a new model of the Latin American city structure and development in 2002. Drawing on these reflections, this chapter deals with the conditions, procedure, and results of the restructuring of the urban fabric in Latin America in order to find out whether these developments justify a modification of the traditional 'model of the Latin American city structure'.

Changing Economic and Social Conditions in Latin America

Massive changes have been taking place in Latin American societies since the early 1980s, when re-democratization processes started to replace the military regimes installed 1 decade before. Regardless of whether the orientation of the new democratic governments was left-wing or conservative, the politics they implemented were capitalist and neo-liberal without exception. These political changes coincided with the crisis of the development strategies that had prevailed since the end of WWII. Promoting the substitution of imports by internal industrialization, these policies had been accompanied by restrictions on imports and active economic intervention by the state (Parnreiter 2004). Since the 1980s this development strategy has steadily been replaced by a model that tends towards integration in the world market and involves the reduction of tax barriers. State-owned companies and formerly state-organized services were privatized. The ensuing attractiveness of the market radically transformed the economic activities in Latin America. Foreign Direct Investment and the subjugation to open market laws diminished the importance of the state. Furthermore, fierce competition from imported products induced a de-industrialization process in many countries. This neo-liberal economic path seems to have had a serious impact on the social structure of Latin American societies. Social polarization has increased substantially (cf. Ciccolella 1999) and unemployment has risen markedly, despite the high economic growth rates which most Latin American countries have experienced in the 1990s.

Since the crisis of the financial market in the late 1990s, Latin America's economic panorama has changed enormously. With the exception of Chile and Mexico, the latter country profiting from the NAFTA integration process with the USA and Canada, the growth of the Latin American economies has markedly slowed down.

The Latin American countries slid from boom to bust. Capital flows reversed in 1998 and have been negative ever since. Economic growth has been low and the income per capita has been decreasing slowly. Some countries such as Argentina, Uruguay, or Venezuela fell into serious economic depression accompanied by internal political problems. As a consequence social polarization has surged (cf. Ocampo 2003; Ruiz 2003).

The political and economic changes have also left their mark on the cities. Especially in the last 15–25 years, urban structures have been going through a rapid modernization process. Mainly driven by foreign investment, this process was on the one hand concentrated on basic urban services such as telephone lines and water provision. These are now owned by international companies that provide services conforming to international standards for the middle and upper classes. However, more investments went into urban elements that exemplify the globalization of urban spaces and illustrate the growing importance of a new imported lifestyle oriented towards leisure activities. These include the expansion and privatization of motorways, the establishment of private industrial parks, international hotel chains with integrated business facilities, shopping malls and hypermarkets, urban entertainment centres, multiplex cinemas and, last but not least, gated and access-restricted residential quarters both in urban and suburban areas. These infrastructural novelties are signs of post-modern urban development which finds expression in their exclusive architecture and social target (cf. Janoschka 2002b). As the state did not intervene in urban planning processes, and private investment to a large extent neglected public means of transportation, a new, car-based lifestyle has flourished, causing an even greater degree of fragmentation and spatial segregation.

The changed lifestyle has also become the motor of urban expansion. Before the 1980s urban growth was primarily driven by lower class migration from rural to urban areas. These patterns have changed. While migration declined strongly, the space needed per capita has increased, chiefly driven by changes in residential areas of the upper and middle classes, and this has become the main driving force of urban expansion in the last 2 decades.

Additional Causes for Socio-spatial Segregation and the Rise of Gated Communities in Latin America

Although globalization is a major driver of urban segregation and fragmentation, it is not the only relevant force in this process. This becomes obvious if we take a quick look at the distribution of gated communities in Latin America. These are not limited to the regions heavily incorporated into the global market system, such as the Central Zone of Chile, the Mexican border region with the U.S., or the metropolitan areas of the Iberian nations. Barrios cerrados have also been established in very conservative regions like the Ecuadorian or Peruvian sierra, the extreme South of Chile, and the Yucatán peninsula, as well as in medium sized Brazilian towns

(Lima Ramires and Ribero Soares 2002), in Rosario (Bragos et al. 2002) or in Puebla y Toluca (Rodriguez Chumillas and Mollá Ruiz-Gómez 2002).

The economic transformation towards neo-liberal models enforced privacy and generated deregulation policies that have liberated the real estate market, weakened urban planning and undermined the norms and rules of previous habitat policies. These economic factors have facilitated the rise of neighbourhoods outside the public space.

Another factor in this development is the changing understanding and organisation of governance. New liberal tendencies and the orientation towards individualism and private initiatives are perceived to be important drivers of fragmentation and segregation. Moreover, the economic crisis, growing poverty, terrorism, and the increase in criminality in many Latin American countries have enhanced the demand for safe enclaves providing protection from a dangerous social environment. Finally, we should not neglect basic human demands, such as the desire for a quiet and safe place to live, for a safe environment for children, in other words for a life without fears and horrors. Moreover, the upper classes search exclusivity, individuality and the possibility to realize their own lifestyles.

The changing conditions on these three levels, the global, the national and the private, explain the rise of gated communities all over the world. It really is a global phenomenon as well as a phenomenon of globalization. However, while in many cultures gated communities are limited to the upper classes, Latin America has a wide spectrum of forms and structures and a great variety of types of fenced neighbourhoods.

The global phenomenon produces various forms that depend on local specificities. As demonstrated by Rovira (2002) and Borsdorf (2002a), Latin American cities have been pervaded by trends of privatization and exclusion from the beginning of urban history. The patio house and the monastery cities were early expressions of these demands, whereas modern tugurios, conventillos and vecindades that are closed off from the road by strong doors are striking examples of their persistence. Figure 2.1 demonstrates the causes for the rise of gated communities in Latin America.

Types of Gated Communities

Latin American city regions are currently experiencing a phase of strong increase in gated residential neighbourhoods. A typology of these developments would first of all have to deal with the variety of names that are used to refer to the different types of gated housing complexes in Latin America. Condomínio fechado (Brazil), Barrio Privado (Argentina), Urbanización Cerrada or Conjunto Cerrado (Ecuador), Condominio, Coto or Fraccionamiento Cerrado (Mexico) describe various products of the real estate market in the different countries. Furthermore, the meanings of the same word can vary substantially between the different countries. The term Barrio Cerrado (closed neighbourhood), which is used as an overarching term in recent publications (Borsdorf et al. 2002; Borsdorf 2003a), refers to a wide variety of gated communities. Generally speaking, Barrio Cerrado serves to describe a dwell-

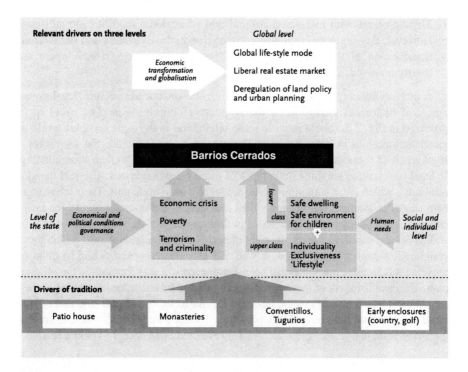

Fig. 2.1 Drivers for gated community development in Latin America (Modified from Borsdorf 2003a)

ing complex that contains more than one unit, has a common infrastructure, and is separated from the public by gates and fences or walls. The infrastructure may include anything from playgrounds, kindergartens, and swimming pools to tennis and golf courts and club houses. Thus a secured apartment building is a gated community if it is fenced off and equipped with a common infrastructure.

Considering only aspects such as structure, location and size, we can differentiate between three main types of gated neighbourhoods.

- *Urban gated communities* are usually groups of attached houses or even towers or skyscrapers that only offer a limited number of facilities. These developments cater for either middle or lower middle class families in intermediate locations (they could even be social housing projects) or upper middle to upper class families in central areas. This concept also involves the massive enclosure of existing areas, in most cases high standing single-family housing areas in central or intermediate locations.
- *Suburban gated communities* predominantly cater for the middle and upper classes. They offer oversized single detached houses and share wide areas for common sports facilities. However, suburban gated communities that are located in the periphery and do not include common facilities may be oriented toward lower middle class income groups.

- *Mega-projects* with integrated cultural and educational facilities are still rare. However, this segment is rapidly growing due to the dynamics and the internationalization of the real estate market, as new transnational developers are mostly involved.

A more detailed typology needs to take into account social structure, legal status, age, and historical evolution of the respective communities. The mind map, provided in Fig. 2.2, should provide some orientation in the quite complex world of gated communities in Latin America. However, it does not include the – invisible – legal status of these developments, a key element with regard to their sustainability. In legal terms, there are three main types of gated neighbourhoods. The real 'condominiums', which are common property, are legally one single unit. Their inhabitants own shares or interests but not individual elements of the community. As the infrastructure, such as roads etc., is included in these properties, they may be fenced in or walled off and gated. However, the right of access to the individual units within these communities cannot be restricted. A wall and gate hindering the public freedom of movement is in this case somewhat semi-legal, even if it was foreseen in the original plan. The establishment of these fraccionamentos and urbanizaciones cerradas, as they are called in Mexico and Ecuador, has been facilitated by neo-liberal rule that diminished the power of the state. This is even truer for the ex-post facto road closures by gates, the so-called 'calles cerradas', which restricted open access to public roads.

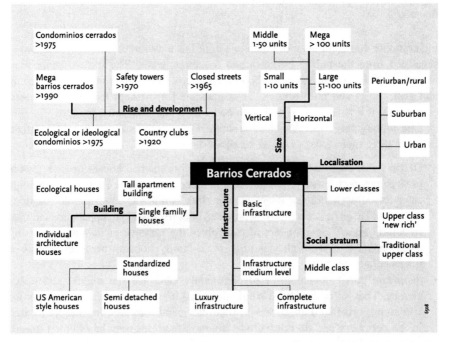

Fig. 2.2 Kinds of gated communities in Latin America. A mind map (Modified from Borsdorf 2003a)

The Distribution of Gated Communities

There has been a boom in gated communities all over Latin America in recent years. In Mexico City alone around 750 new gated neighbourhoods with almost 50,000 housing units were thrown on the market between 1990 and 2001 (Parnreiter 2004). The Argentinean capital Buenos Aires has more than 450 suburban gated communities; a dozen of them reach a size of more than 5,000 inhabitants each (Janoschka 2002a). The exact number of the urban gated communities, called garden towers in Argentina (Torre Jardín, cfr. Welch 2002), is unknown. However, more than 130 of these garden towers offered new apartments in the local Argentinean newspapers in 2002. Estimations of their total number of inhabitants range between 300,000 and 600,000 people. Pöhler (1999) states that more than 100,000 people live in condomínios fechados in Rio de Janeiro's upper class and beach-oriented city expansion area called Barra da Tijuca. Brazil's biggest megacity São Paulo also counts on a mega-project, 'Alphaville', with around 35,000 inhabitants and more than 100,000 people working inside the gates. Gated communities have also diffused to secondary cities such as Córdoba, Argentina (1.3 million inhabitants). This city has more than 50 gated residential developments, with one of them (Valle Escondido), promoted as 'the new city', offering a cluster of different gated communities for a total population of approximately 25,000 inhabitants (Roca 2001). Curitiba in Brazil has approximately 300 gated communities. Thus gated communities pervade in most big Latin American cities and are becoming more and more common in medium size cities (< 500,000 inhabitants) and in some cases even in small towns (for example Gualeguaychú, Entre Rios in Argentina; Valdivia, Temuco, Rancagua in Chile).

Unfortunately, it is extremely difficult to estimate the exact market share of gated housing complexes in these cities, not only due to the substantial differences between the countries. Statistical data on the construction sector is poor and in most cases the differentiation between the products is not clear. In Buenos Aires, the number of units in suburban gated communities amounts to about 100,000, while the whole number of dwellings reaches approximately three million. So suburban gated housing represents no more than 3% of the housing stock. However, if we look at the total of suburban housing, the market share of gated communities rises to 10%. Furthermore, if we limit the calculation to the demand group (which are the upper 15–20% of the population, equivalent to 450,000 households), these 100,000 units represent between 20% and 25% of the market share. These calculations exclude the number of 'quasi' gated communities (streets and neighbourhoods with strong vigilance and closure of access during the night or posterior enclosed neighbourhoods) which are not marketed as gated communities in the open real estate market. They also neglect gated housing at the other end of the social pyramid, for example social housing projects from the 1970s which nowadays are walled and gate-guarded, or the whole range of areas that are inaccessible due to the predominance of criminal structures. To resume, it is a fact that in Buenos Aires, the market for single detached houses and the construction of detached houses in suburban locations are situated predominantly in gated communities. The expansion of gated communities accounted for 80–90% of the urban expansion during the period of macroeconomic stability from 1991 to 2001.

Modelling the Fragmented City

Before the crisis of internal development strategies in the 1980s, one of the basic principles of Latin American cities was the strong polarization of urban spaces. Differentiation in social status was heavily bound to location within the city. Urban space fell into polarized sectors such as the rich and the poor city (cf. Gilbert 1994). This tendency has changed during the last 2 decades. The strict urban frontiers between the rich and the poor have become blurred. High-income members of the population have started to occupy suburban areas that used to be poor whereas poor families have settled in abandoned middle and upper class spaces. This process has been accompanied by a new and strict delimitation of small areas, often by way of private security services. These novel homogeneous, highly segregated and protected islands within the urban neighbourhoods promote the physical fragmentation of urban space (Sabatini et al. 2001; Parnreiter 2004). This change is of fundamental importance for the development of a new model of the Latin American urban agglomeration.

From a geographical or urban point of view, the term 'model' has three different meanings. First, city models can be a constructive utopia – a vision or *Leitbild* for further urban development, such as the modern city in its time or the garden city movement. Second, a city model can be the result of theoretical studies based on deductive logic, as presented by Christaller or Thünen. Finally, a model may reduce the complexity of urban life in order to provide a better understanding of a certain type of city (cf. Borsdorf et al. 2002). The last approach constitutes the basis of regional city models that try to analyse social behaviour through the modelling of city structures, from the early urban models of the Chicago school up to the latest works of authors such as Dear (2000) or Soja (2000). Latin American city structures and the question whether models can ever do justice to the complex reality have been heavily debated in the US as well as in Europe from the 1970s up to the present (Griffin and Ford 1980, 1993; Gormsen 1981; Deler 1989; Crowley 1995; Bähr and Mertins 1981; Borsdorf 1982). Starting point of these intense discussions were two models of the Latin American city structure published independently by the German geographers Bähr and Borsdorf in 1976.

The dramatic transformations of the Latin American city regions from the 1980s onwards have only recently generated new theoretical approaches by Ford (1996), Meyer and Bähr (2001) and Borsdorf (2002b). Drawing on the latest empirical data, these authors either redesigned the traditional models or developed new ones (Janoschka 2002b, c). Joining forces, Bähr, Borsdorf and Janoschka updated their individual investigations and produced a new joint model which integrated the different arguments of the three authors (Borsdorf et al. 2002;

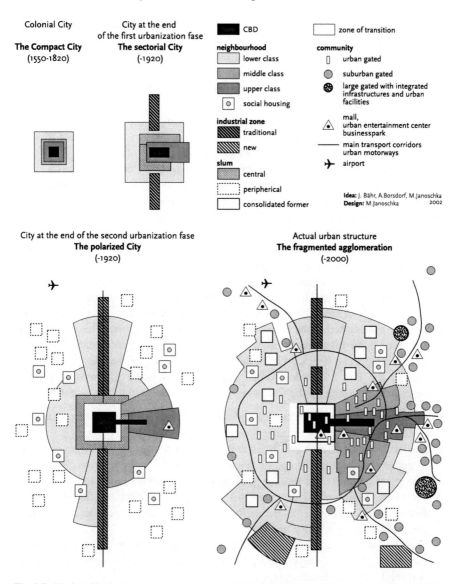

Fig. 2.3 Model of Latin American urban structural development (Adapted from Borsdorf et al. 2002)

see Fig. 2.3). According to this model, city development in Latin America falls into four phases which correspond to different degrees of state intervention (urban planning) in the real estate market.

The model departs from the observation that these different phases of urban development are each characterized by specific structural principles and urban policies. In the early phase, the colonial time, the urban body was compact and the social status of the inhabitants decreased with the increasing distance from the central plaza where the central social and political functions were located. This compact urban model was a realization of the royal instructions for the foundation of cities in Spanish America. The central plaza and its immediate surroundings were reserved for the most important functions which in turn attracted the colonial elite.

After independence, linear structures began to intersect this compact city. The upper classes moved into new houses along a main street – the Prado. Vegetable growers and craftsmen settled along the most important roads to the countryside. Later on some industrial sectors were established. These sectoral patterns did not dissolve the ring structure but strongly transformed the cities.

From 1930 onwards the flight from rural areas to urban centres caused a strong increase in the population. The ensuing agglomeration process was accompanied by the polarization between rich and poor areas – a phenomenon that is typical of the modern industrial city (Marcuse 1989). The upper classes abandoned their central locations for suburban areas. At the same time the poor areas in the cities grew enormously. Political guidelines for urban development became obsolete – not only due to the high growth rates but also because corrupted and polemic policies alternated with authoritarian regimes during phases of dictatorships. The main characteristic of urban development was the growing polarization, superimposed on the sectoral principle of urban growth. Only some time later, a process of cell-type growth came to be established in the peripheries. Social housing communities were built in suburban or outer urban areas, as well as illegal marginal settlements. Hence the cellular principle can be traced back to this earlier phase of urban development.

During the last 2 decades, urban expansion has again followed a different scheme, mainly driven by the following principles (Janoschka 2002a, p. 65).

- Gated communities for the upper and middle classes have spread throughout the metropolitan area, undermining the sectoral class structures.
- Malls, shopping centres and urban entertainment centres are no longer restricted to upper class sectors but can be found in the whole agglomeration.
- The gated communities tend to get larger and to include more and more urban functions. Major gated communities in large cities such as São Paulo and Buenos Aires and even smaller cities such as Córdoba, Argentina now surpass small cities in complexity and size.
- Transport infrastructure has come to play a key role in urban development. Thus proximity to a motorway entrance determines the attractiveness and price of detached suburban housing areas.
- Industrial production has been transferred to suburban areas and is located in peripheral industrial or business parks or centres of logistic activities.
- The access to poorer communities and marginal areas has been restricted by walls or informal ways of separation.

These changes demand new theoretical approaches which are mirrored in the new scheme of the Latin American city structure. The fragmentary and urban nodal structure has been facilitated by the transformation of the transport infrastructure. Private investment has turned the insufficient and congested motorways into a modern and effective system. The ensuing major reduction in commuting time has been decisive for attracting middle and upper classes, whose time is restricted, to suburban locations. In this way private and privatising urban development in the neo-liberal political and economic system is driven by private interventions which respond to the demands of the real estate market.

The second important structural change also follows the principles of post-modern urban development. The cellular elements in the periphery (in former times predominantly marginal areas) have been integrated into the market sphere and have become increasingly interesting for investment by real estate enterprises. Furthermore, fragmentation cannot only be observed for housing but also for func-tional spatial units, such as the retail sector. Although the urban centres gain new importance due to renovation programs and other upgrading interventions, they cannot compete with suburban malls, which represent a north-American lifestyle of rising popularity. These islands of consumption and leisure do not restrict access by walls, but exclude anyone who does not have private transport. The first malls were clearly oriented towards the upper class market in the urban upper class sector. However, due to the dispersion of the upper and middle class population, they can now be found in the whole urban area.

Poorer areas have also changed during the last decades. Some marginal areas have been integrated into the urban space – and in a number of cases were upgraded. Others were kept apart and now are almost inaccessible nodes of criminality. The transformation of the Latin American city structure shows that the desire for dif-ferentiation through enclosure and restriction of access is not reserved to the popu-lation with high income, but represents a general societal principle. This should have become clear in the historical account of the rise and diffusion of gated resi-dential neighbourhoods.

Whether the structural changes in the contemporary Latin American city are a symptom of the transformation in mobility (Borsdorf 2004) or whether they reflect an even more fundamental shift in global social and urban systems remains to be discussed.

Consequences for the Social Contract in Latin America

In the last couple of decades the internal structure of cities has changed rather markedly throughout Latin America. Concomitantly multi-level and multi-actor policy processes have unfolded in Latin America during the 1980s and 1990s. Authorities at urban levels have been faced with new challenges and new ideas about privatisation of public space, enclosuring, and new social ghettos. The urban community – once seen as a unique and, from a governance point of view, unified organism – is now divided in different spaces with different underlying norms, structures, and also control. Urban governance involves actors at different scales, following their respective interests and objectives. It may be too early to give an evaluation of this change, but there are first indicators of a loss of community conscious-ness, social responsibility, and socio-spatial coherence under the new conditions.

The physical fragmentation processes have thus had a serious impact on the quality and the understanding of urban life. Inhabitants of gated communities change their lifestyle rapidly and the access-restricted areas accommodate their daily demands. Public spaces lose their basic role as points of interaction between different classes, as each class develops its own homogeneous space. The growing size of these spaces and their integration of complex urban functions further accentuate this tendency. As a consequence inhabitants live in bubbles which are detached from the local political and social environment. As put forward in this article, the Latin American elites never did show any interest in their own society, but rather followed lifestyles imported from Europe and later from the US. The life behind walls in gated neighbourhoods removes these elites even further from the social reality of their 'home' society. Yet, neither the Latin American media (press and broadcasting), nor politicians, urban planners, or architects have interpreted the gates as a severe problem for society in the past 2 decades. This is hardly surprising since all of these groups, relevant for urban and economic progress, directly or indirectly benefit from the gated communities. There is an urgent need for more research and an objective assessment of the new and accelerated segregation trends in the urban world of Latin America. Will we have to tear down gates in the heads in order to undermine the perceived necessity of physical ones, as some authors contend, or are these gates an indicator of the basic human need for safety, transparency, privacy, and personal realization?

Chapter 3
Territory, Local Governance, and Urban Transformation: The Processes of Residential Enclave Building in Lima, Peru

Jörg Plöger

Since the 1990s, Latin American metropolises in most of the countries throughout the region have changed considerably due to the effects of globalisation and the implementation of neo-liberal politics (de Mattos 2002). According to Pradilla (1998, p. 195), the contemporary neo-liberal Latin American metropolis is a highly contradictory version of the capitalist city, with all of its vices and without most of its limited virtues.

The traditional spatial structure of the Latin American city is being transformed by a process that scholars from different academic disciplines have called fragmentation (e.g. Cariola and Lacabana 2001; Díaz 1997; Prévot-Schapira 2001; Scholz 2000). Fragmentation is regarded as the spatial outcome of urban disarticulations such as increasing socio-economic inequality, socio-spatial polarisation and segregation, social disintegration, and the loss of public spaces. The emerging 'fragmented city' can be characterised as a heterogeneous collage of socio-economically homogeneous and mono-functional cells (Borsdorf et al. 2002). These spatial units are often privatised micro-scale territories. They can be interpreted as the expression of deeply unequal urban societies, where the service provision by the public sector is regarded as insufficient, crime has become a major concern and the urban environment increasingly hostile.

This chapter introduces the concept of 'condominisation'. The term derives from *condominium*, which – in the context of housing – describes a residential complex that consists of private residential units and internal spaces designed for communal use. In Latin America security is a common feature of such complexes. In the metropolises of the region many residents now employ some form of socio-spatial control mechanism to protect their neighbourhoods and properties from perceived urban threats.

The general conceptual framework of the process of 'condominisation' and the main research questions will be laid out in the following paragraphs. The theoretical considerations will then be applied to analyse the specific characteristics of residential enclave building in Lima. The Peruvian capital provides several interesting insights into the appropriation, control and fortification of spaces.

P. van Lindert and O. Verkoren (eds.), *Decentralized Development in Latin America: Experiences in Local Governance and Local Development*, GeoJournal Library 97, DOI 10.1007/978-90-481-3739-8_3, © Springer Science+Business Media B.V. 2010

The Concept of 'Condominisation'

The urban landscapes of the cities in Latin America can be interpreted as a reflection of the polarisation of their societies and the unequal distribution of material resources (Pradilla 1998). Threat scenarios and discourses about crime, social disintegration or dangerous places are being reproduced through the media and interpersonal communication. According to Sibley (1995, p. 69), the increasing trend towards 'boundary erection' can be understood as a response to the changing urban environment. This results in the emergence of what he calls 'dominant landscapes'. These are characterised by a collage of territories that – through the implementation of various place-bound strategies – are more regulated, privatised and physically closed-off than their precursors (ibid., p. 81). Harvey (1996, p. 294) offers a similar interpretation. He argues that residents are responding to the penetration of 'their' neighbourhood through external forces with attempts to secure the permanence of these places. When an individual or a group is exercising control over a particular part of physical space for a longer period, this results in the establishment of a territory (Madanipour 2003, p. 50). The formation of access-controlled and walled-off residential areas in Latin America can thus be understood as a spatial manifestation of these practices. In urban environments where these territories are contested or where boundaries between them are not clearly defined, people seem to show heightened levels of spatial stress, whereas clearly defined boundaries tend to have a stabilising effect (ibid., p. 52; Suttles 1972). Behavioural models in environmental psychology show that rising levels of stress in cities are caused by increasingly challenging urban environments and that constant adjustment is therefore required to feel comfortable (Bell et al. 1996, p. 375).

The questions underlying the study presented here were the following: 'Which process is currently transforming many neighbourhoods in Lima?'; 'which measures and strategies are used to achieve residential enclave building?'; 'what are the spatial consequences of these practices?'; and 'what are the underlying causes for this process?'. Another aspect of consideration is the relationship between public-sector authorities and alternative, non-institutional actors in the system of local governance such as homeowner or neighbourhood associations or other forms of private micro-governments. While the authorities in many cities are struggling to provide adequate services in their respective jurisdictions on the one hand, organised groups at the neighbourhood level are representing specific, localised interests on the other.

By introducing the concept of 'condominisation', this chapter attempts to present a possible framework for further research about processes of enclave building in Latin American cities (Plöger 2006b). It should be regarded as an addition to existing studies about gated neighbourhoods, socio-spatial segregation, exclusion and related topics. The concept is used to illustrate different forms of spatial intervention in residential areas, although 'condominisation' can also be observed in non-residential areas, e.g. shopping malls or office complexes. The concept of 'condominisation' is used to describe various practices of spatial intervention.

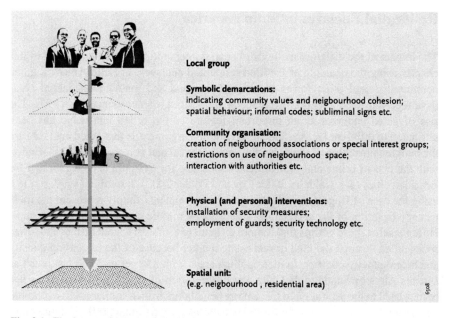

Fig. 3.1 The layers of 'condominisation'

The key aspect is that a group, occupying a specific area, is articulating spatial power through the appropriation, control and fortification of the immediate surroundings. A number of different practices with spatial implications, both formal and informal, are being used to achieve greater control over space.

Three categories or layers of 'condominisation' can be identified (Fig. 3.1). The intensity of each of these layers can however differ considerably. The first or 'physical' layer consists of the most obvious interventions such as walls, fences, gates or surveillance technology and alarms. It also includes the employment of security guards. The second or 'organisational' layer is less obvious for outsiders, but nevertheless has important spatial implications. It comprises the activities by the local community aiming at achieving greater control over their neighbourhood. One of the main and fundamental steps towards enclave building is the formation of local micro-governments such as neighbourhood associations or other groups with specific place-bound interests. This layer may also include the establishment of internal regulations about the use of neighbourhood space. Another objective of organisation is to enable a more effective and coordinated interaction with the authorities. The third or 'symbolic' layer encompasses any cultural or symbolic activities with a spatial impact. These practices are more subliminal and less coordinated. Space is equipped with signs, which can send messages to, both, residents and outsiders. Examples for this layer include class-related forms of habitus, local traditions or cultural codes. In reality, the use of the layers of 'condominisation' varies widely across neighbourhoods and a mix of different approaches is applied in most cases.

Residential Enclaves in Latin America

The impact of the different methods of spatial intervention will be addressed in this chapter using the example of fortified residential enclaves. In Latin America, gated communities and other forms of access-controlled and guarded residential areas have received wide attention from social and spatial sciences since the 1990s. The rise of gated enclaves as an important feature of the urban landscape has been attributed to different factors. The most common argument is that gated enclaves are the built manifestation of rising insecurities, both real and perceived. This association with the fear of crime and 'dangerous classes' has for example been elaborated for Brazilian cities (e.g. Caldeira 2000; Coy and Pöhler 2002). Jaramillo (1999, p. 119), using the case of Bogotá, argues that gated developments simply represent the most recent adaptation of the segregation strategies by middle and upper income groups. He argues that these groups find it more difficult to establish spatial distance to lower social strata through the land or real estate market because of the increasing density and heterogeneity of cities. In metropolitan areas with a larger middle-class, such as Buenos Aires or Santiago de Chile, the proliferation of gated residential areas has been related to the aspiration to live among neighbours from a similar socio-economic background, as well as to new lifestyles patterns (e.g. Svampa 2001; Hidalgo et al. 2003). For Buenos Aires, Janoschka (2002) and Pírez (2002) among others have also linked the move into private residential enclaves with their own infrastructure to the unsatisfactory services provided by the public sector.

The variety of different forms throughout the region renders the attempt to establish a general typology of residential enclaves for Latin America difficult. Various authors have identified typologies for single cities, but each of these approaches is usually based on different sets of criteria (Meyer et al. 2004). In his analysis of the metropolitan area of Buenos Aires Janoschka (2002) has mainly drawn on the factor location. Using the case of Santiago de Chile, Meyer and Bähr (2001) have used a combination of socio-economic indicators, location, and architecture. For the same city, Hidalgo (2003) has distinguished three types based on a legal definition: (1) Private residential communities planned as such; (2) formal transformation of residential areas into privatised neighbourhoods or condominiums; and (3) informal and arbitrary closing and control of streets and neighbourhoods.

Residential Enclave Building in Lima

Lima is a mega-city with a population of more than eight million. The Peruvian capital has received considerable attention by scholars in previous decades. Their interest was mainly related to the particular characteristics and consequences of rapid urban growth driven by migration towards the primate city. Due to a lack of affordable housing, a large proportion of the poor has been absorbed by the growing number of marginal settlements (*barriadas*) on invaded land outside of the consolidated core (Kross 1992; Matos Mar 2004; Calderón 2005).

More recent processes of urban transformation have received far less attention however. According to Ludeña (2002, p. 46), Lima has become a 'strange *barri-ada*-metropolis' that resembles nineteenth century cities of wild capitalism on the one hand, and is already 'practising on the backyard of an omni-present global city' on the other. The implementation of neo-liberal politics of structural adjustment during the presidency of Alberto Fujimori in the 1990s has left its imprint on the urban landscape of Lima (Ugarteche 1998; Gonzales 1998). According to Joseph (2004) the emerging urban structure is characterised by new patterns of micro-scale segregation and a pronunciation of socio-spatial inequality. One particular outcome is the increasing number of residential enclaves.

Historically, private residential complexes in Lima can be traced back to the early Republican phase. *Quintas*, for example, are ensembles of residential units built around a private dead-end street, whose only entrance is often equipped with a gate. Nevertheless, the recent expansion of socio-spatial security measures took place relatively late in comparison with other Latin American cities. There are some similarities to countries struggling with armed internal conflicts at the same time, such as El Salvador or Colombia. During the mid-1980s *Sendero Luminoso* expanded its guerrilla-warfare towards the cities and the capital, which confronted the – until then – relatively undisturbed middle- and upper classes with the immediate threat of terrorist activities. As a reaction many households moved into guarded apartment complexes or private residential developments, often equipped with their own infrastructure to avoid dependency on the unreliable public service provision. The massive spread of gated residential enclaves did however not occur until the 1990s and must be regarded as a reaction to the increasingly unequal socio-economic structure and the widespread fear of becoming a victim of crime or violence (Plöger 2006b).

Two general types of residential enclaves that can be identified in Lima Metropolitana (Fig. 3.2), subsequently enclosed neighbourhoods and private residential developments. The main differentiation is their legal status. The first type is far more common in Lima and will be elaborated below.

Private residential developments or 'real condominiums' are already planned and developed including security measures a mix of private and communal spaces. This type subdivides into horizontal and vertical developments. The horizontal developments resemble the 'typical' US-American gated community (Blakeley and Snyder 1997). In Lima, gated communities are relatively few. They are usually designed for middle- and upper-income groups and located in wealthier suburban areas (e.g. La Molina, Santiago de Surco). Gated leisure developments are located further out in areas with attractive natural features. Several of these have been developed along the beaches south of the metropolitan area since the late 1990s. Usually they are not inhabited permanently, but used as second homes by the affluent.

Apartment complexes (*condominios de edificios*) have emerged as a housing option for middle- and upper-income groups since the 1970s and normally provide some common amenities as well as guarded entrances. They are clustered in traditional upper-income areas such as San Isidro and Miraflores that have experienced densification and functional diversification. More recently, numerous apartment complexes targeting the (lower) middle-class segment have been built, offering

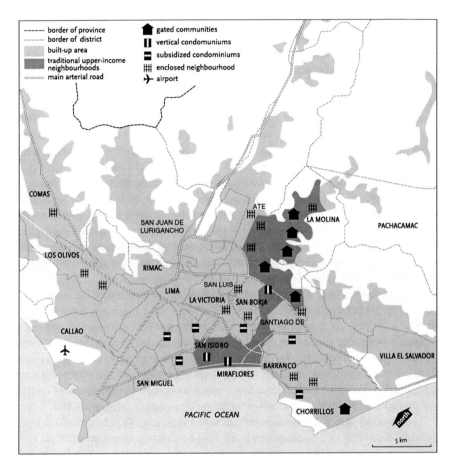

Fig. 3.2 Types of residential enclaves in Lima Metropolitana

subsidised owner-occupied housing through the national *MiVivienda* programme. These typically medium-sized developments with standardised architecture are especially located in older middle-class districts such as San Miguel or Jesús María. Although they often lack common amenities, they do provide enclosure and security services.

Subsequently Enclosed Neighbourhoods

An important aspect of the enclave building process in Lima is that 'typical' gated communities planned and constructed as such are relatively rare in comparison with other Latin American metropolises. Subsequently enclosed neighbourhoods are the most widespread type of residential enclave. These are existing neighbourhoods that are transformed through the appropriation, control and fortification of space. They resemble the US-American *security zone communities* identified by Blakeley and Snyder (1997).

The spatial interventions are planned and implemented by a group of residents, organised in some form of local association. The quality and quantity of the security measures depends on three main factors: the cohesion of the local community; the socio-economic status of the area; and the relevance of the local security discourse (Plöger 2006b). Gates are the most common security measure. They are usually installed at the entrance to the area to restrict its accessibility. Security guards are employed through monthly contributions paid by the residents. Apart from the physical interventions some neighbourhood associations have ratified their own regulations regarding the use of the neighbourhood space. These can prohibit certain activities such as loitering, gathering in groups or practicing sports in the public spaces. Sometimes these regulations are phrased in a patronising way, revealing underlying social prejudices. The process of residential enclave building will be illustrated further below using the examples of two subsequently enclosed neighbourhoods.

At the beginning of this investigation, almost no information was available about the number and geographic distribution of residential enclaves in Lima Metropolitana.[1] Only in very few cases had district authorities collected information about the security measures installed in their jurisdictions. The estimate presented here, is based on two main sources: the review of newspaper articles on the topic and extensive mapping carried out by the author.[2] According to this, approximately 3,000 security measures had been installed in about 300 residential enclaves in Lima Metropolitana until 2005 (Plöger 2006b). Apart from some denser inner-city areas, access-controlled residential enclaves can be found in most of the 49 metropolitan districts. The most gated district is by far the wealthy, suburban La Molina, where around 80% of the residential areas have installed some form of access-control. Several other districts such as San Luis, Los Olivos, Santiago de Surco, San Miguel or Chorrillos also have significant concentrations. Yet, the spread of fortified neighbourhoods is not limited to middle- or upper-income areas. A proliferation of residential enclaves has also been observed in various neighbourhoods of marginal origin in poorer districts, e.g. in Comas, San Juan de Lurigancho or Villa El Salvador (Plöger 2006a).

Regulation of Security Measures

The authorities have responded to the spread of security measures obstructing the free access to public streets and spaces with a regulatory framework. Throughout the 1990s the metropolitan authority of Lima held the remit. However, limited resources constrained its ability to control compliance with existing regulation.

---

[1] For the purpose of simplification, the term residential enclave will be used here synonymously with subsequently enclosed neighbourhood.

[2] See Plöger (2006b) for a more detailed account of the spread of residential enclaves in Lima Metropolitana.

It was during this phase that the 'security landscape' in Lima became increasingly informalised. Most district authorities are not interested in confronting their residents (and voters) with unpopular measures such as the removal of gates, especially when they do not dispose of appropriate means to guarantee sufficient levels of security in their jurisdictions. Nevertheless, several local authorities – predominantly in districts with a high number of informal street closures (e.g. La Molina, San Borja, Los Olivos, Ate) – published their own regulations. In 2004, the Peruvian office of the ombudsman presented a study that not only documented the irregularity of the situation and the negative impact on constitutional rights such as free movement and access to public spaces but also acknowledged the demand for improved security and the inefficiency of the responsible institutions (Defensoría del Pueblo 2004). Soon afterwards, the metropolitan authority has responded to the recommendations with a new regulation; ordinance 690 presents the guideline for the formalisation of existing and the procedure for new security devices. The ordinance has however been implemented very slowly by the district authorities. Only a few consolidated districts have made serious efforts to enforce the legal guidelines, while the informal status quo persists elsewhere (El Comercio 26/07/2005).

Informalisation of the Security Landscape

According to ordinance 690, the installation of security measures on public streets is only permitted in exceptional cases. Yet, the impact of the relatively strict regulation on the security landscape in Lima has been minimal. In reality, gates and other physical security devices remain a widespread and mainly unregulated feature of the urban landscape. The informality and arbitrary nature of the security measures is possibly the most characteristic feature of gated neighbourhoods in Lima. Evidence from 21 case study areas clearly shows the extent of informal practices during the process of enclave building. This correlates with a general lack of control from most of the district authorities. Only two neighbourhoods had authorisation for the implemented measures. The interviews with the representatives of the neighbourhood organisation that was responsible for the implementation of the security measures reveal the range of reasons for informality. The following arguments were mentioned for not having official authorisation:

- *Bureaucratic obstacles*: In four neighbourhoods the procedure to obtain a permit for the measures was described as too costly, bureaucratic, complicated or protracted.
- *Informal agreements* or a 'good relationship' with the district administration were given as a justification for not having an authorisation in four neighbourhoods.
- *Waiting game*: Three of the areas were conscious of the informal nature of the installed measures, but did not do anything about it because the local authorities did not enforce the regulation.
- *Incomplete formalisation*: Four neighbourhoods obtained legal authorisation for some but not all of the implemented measures.
- *No action* at all has been taken to formalise the situation in four areas.

The Framework for 'Condominisation' in Lima Metropolitana

The process of 'condominisation' in Lima Metropolitana can be interpreted as a physical manifestation of the pronounced levels of socio-economic inequalities within Peruvian society. It can be argued that the practices leading towards the appropriation, control and fortification of neighbourhood spaces are a reaction by the population to two complementary and highly interwoven sets of factors. According to this logic, residential enclave building in Lima is driven by (a) the increasing threats of crime and violence, and (b) the inability of public authorities to provide adequate services, including public safety.

Local Crime and Security Discourses

Local security discourses are a key factor in the production of urban insecurities. On a daily basis, print and television media feature dramatic reports on crime, violence, and social disintegration. Even the respected newspaper El Comercio has regular sections on these topics such as *zonas de temer* ('zones to fear'), *radiografía urbana* ('urban X-ray') or *zonas de alto riesgo* ('high-risk zones') that portray dangerous places and a chaotic urban environment. For many Limeños, districts like La Victoria, El Agustino or Callao have become de-facto 'no-go-zones' on their 'mental maps of urban risks'.

The lack of reliable data on crime makes it difficult to analyse and compare crime patterns and to prove the validity of such scenarios. This reinforces the significance of perceptions on crime and violence. A further problem is that crimes, especially property offences are chronically under-reported. Only an estimated 10% of all crimes are actually reported to the police (INEI 1998), reflecting the lack of trust in the institution. The most comprehensive evidence of the actual impact of crime on society is provided by two, albeit outdated, surveys about victimisation in Lima (INEI 1998; Apoyo 1999). According to these, the majority of Limeños perceive urban life as insecure and more than a third of the respondents had been a victim of some sort of crime (ibid.). More recent surveys reveal that insecurity has now become the prime concern of Lima's population.

Weakness and Inefficiency of Public Authorities

In Peru, the public sector is widely criticized for delivering insufficient protection. The police and the judicial system, the institutions responsible for law enforcement, are the least trusted of all public institutions (Basombrío 2003, p. 62). Several authors have elaborated on the issue of institutional weakness in Peru and argued that it results from a history of incomplete nation building and inherent social inequalities (e.g. Figueroa et al. 1996; Matos Mar 2004; Crabtree 2006).

The proliferation of informal practices – including those used to appropriate residential areas – can be interpreted in this context. The marginal influence of local authorities on shaping and regulating space is also evident in districts where the administrations do not actively enforce regulations, such as ordinance 690, to avoid confronting residents with this contested issue.

In the realm of security, it can be argued that the insufficient service provision by the State has caused a 'protection gap'. A complex constellation of additional public, private and community-based security-providing actors has emerged as a result of this. Since the 1990s, the number of private security guards has increased strongly in Lima and now exceeds public-sector security forces. The majority of these guards are employed on an informal basis (Joseph 2004, p. 54). Although some responsibilities have been devolved to the district level, insufficient budgets and a lack of professional administration restrict most municipalities of Lima Metropolitana in their actual ability to provide comprehensive services (Dietz and Tanaka 2002). Nevertheless, three quarters of all metropolitan districts have responded to the growing demand for citizen security by establishing a so-called *serenazgo*. This municipal security force is basically a 'quick-response unit' aimed at closing gaps in the provision of security and reinstalling public order.

The distribution of security services reflects and reinforces socio-economic inequalities in Lima (Plöger 2006b). There is a close relationship between the quality and quantity of the protection of an area, and its location and socio-economic status. More centrally located and consolidated areas benefit from a higher police presence, while peripheral and predominantly poorer areas often remain under-protected (Pereyra 2003). The ability of district authorities to provide services, including those related to security, depends on their budgets. Higher incomes from local taxes enable those districts with wealthier neighbourhoods to provide better services. Several larger districts on the poor periphery were on the other hand not able to implement a *serenazgo*. On the neighbourhood level, much of the ability of the residents to organise security measures depends on the available financial resources and thus socio-economic status.

Residential Enclave Las Flores

With its population approaching one million, San Juan de Lurigancho has become the most populous district of Lima Metropolitana. Much of its growth can be attributed to informal modes of urbanisation. The residential area of Las Flores de Lima was built by a developer on former *hacienda* land in the first half of the 1970s. Most households of this predominantly lower-middle class area have expanded their original houses over the years. The selected study area comprises the first of three construction phases. The area has 180 properties and approximately 900 inhabitants.

In the mid-1970s, soon after the houses were first occupied, the residents established the homeowner association that still exists today. The main reason for creating this organisation was dissatisfaction with some of the features promised by the developer.

The area was not properly connected to basic infrastructure networks, some houses showed construction deficiencies and there were concerns about obtaining the property titles in the future.

From the late 1990s onwards, security has become a major concern. According to the president of the neighbourhood association, burglaries and assaults have become increasingly frequent. Some of the busy streets in the vicinity were also described as dangerous. The inhabitants of nearby marginal settlements were blamed for most of this insecurity. As a response to this situation, the neighbourhood has been equipped with gates at each of its five street and two pedestrian entrances since 2003 (Fig. 3.3).

In order to install these measures the association asked all households to contribute the equivalent of 16 Euros. Most of the households paid this special fee. The importance of the measures is illustrated by the fact that a small celebration was organised every time one of the gates was installed. In addition, the neighbours are asked to contribute the equivalent of 5 Euros monthly to support a security service. Six guards are currently employed, three each during the day and night shifts. Fewer households pay for this service on a regular basis. The president of the homeowner association was complaining about the 'free riding' of some households on the back of those contributing to the community security.

The street closures were installed without obtaining a permit beforehand. The association did however inform the district administration about these measures afterwards. The president of the neighbourhood association justified this as follows:

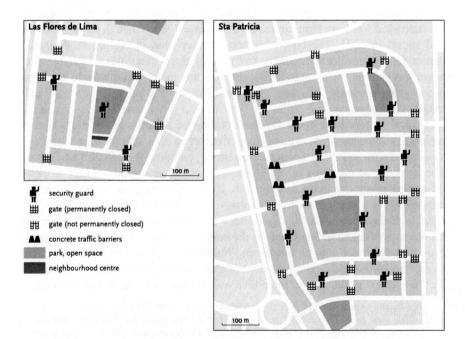

Fig. 3.3 Map of security measures in Las Flores and Sta. Patricia

"Of course it is prohibited to close off streets without authorisation. But the procedure to obtain it takes far too long. Therefore we had to act before actually getting the permit. If we had waited any longer, the robberies would have continued. Due to our bad security situation this was not possible." (President of homeowner association, Las Flores)

The homeowner association was surprised to receive a fine from the district administration as a result of their actions and rejected to paying it. By the time of the interview, the issue had escalated and the residents had drafted a statement to the district mayor, which highlights the emotionality attached to the security issue in Lima:

"Apart from the fact that we are forced to provide our own security, although this should be your responsibility, you now fine us for our actions [...]. This is unbelievable! This is the reason why nobody has trust in the public administration anymore. The only time you ever approach us is before the elections."

Residential Enclave Sta. Patricia

In the middle and upper class district of La Molina the majority of neighbourhoods are gated. A good example to illustrate the process of 'condominisation' is the larger neighbourhood of Sta. Patricia, also located on former *hacienda* land. The study area is the first of three construction phases. It consists of approximately 1,500 households and roughly 6,000 inhabitants. The owners who had purchased the individual lots have built houses on them since 1980, although a few lots were still vacant in 2005. The type of housing ranges from individual single-family homes for more affluent residents and two- or three-storey terraced housing to apartment buildings with up to five floors. This mix indicates a relatively heterogeneous socio-economic structure. Yet, most households belong to the 'typical' middle-class segment.

Several factors have caused a deterioration of security in the area. Lima's rapid growth has confronted this formerly suburban area with problems typically associated with inner-city areas such as traffic, commercial activities and crime. The interviewed members of the homeowner association reported that property crimes became more frequent in the late 1990s. The situation was further exacerbated when a new football stadium was opened in the vicinity in 2000. The *Estadio Monumental* immediately became a security hazard for Sta. Patricia and other surrounding neighbourhoods as the hooligans of local football clubs (*barras bravas*) carried out acts of vandalism, violence and assault on match days (El Comercio 26/06/2002). The president of the homeowner association mentioned that in addition to this threat, the police was not providing sufficient security:

"The barras bravas were all over the [adjacent] major roads. They destroyed everything crossing their path. They robbed pedestrians, car drivers, everybody. The police did not intervene. All neighbourhoods in this part of La Molina were affected by this." (President of homeowner association, Sta. Patricia)

In the late 1990s, the residents responded to the earlier problems by employing security guards. This service was organised on the micro-level of street-blocks. Thirty-six guards divided into two shifts are currently employed throughout the area. Less than half of the households actually pay for this service. The residents became worried again about the status of the area and the safety of their properties with the opening of the new stadium. A homeowner association was founded in 2001. The main purpose was to organise the financing and implementation of gates on all entrances leading to the neighbourhood. Between 2001 and 2003 all 11 access roads were equipped with gates (Fig. 3.3). The necessary financial contributions of approximately 20 Euros were paid by only one third of the households. While the representative of the homeowner association claimed that an official authorisation had been obtained for the measures, the district authority denied having issued this.

Although all exterior entrances were equipped with gates, the security landscape of Sta. Patricia is uncoordinated. Some areas within the neighbourhood have installed additional security devices without coordinating with the homeowner association or the residents of nearby street-blocks. The residents in these internal enclaves benefit from double protection but pay only once. Another problem arises from the incoherent use of private security guards on the street or block level. With varying degrees of micro-level organisation and different attitudes towards the handling of security, the result is ambiguous. In those areas where not enough funds were collected to employ a guard, the gate often remained permanently closed, while other areas only close them during the night. The low degree of neighbourhood cohesion was also mentioned by the president of the homeowner association:

> "I think this is part of the process of social decomposition. For a number of reasons the people have decided to isolate themselves in their homes and to only resolve their particular problems [...] and that's it. They have absolutely no interest in the problems faced by their neighbours [...]." (President of homeowner association, Sta. Patricia)

Conclusion

Residential enclave building constitutes an important aspect of the more recent transformation of Lima's urban landscape. In many neighbourhoods, the residents have responded to the exposure to urban insecurities, and insufficient security provision by the authorities by imposing additional layers of control. As a detailed study about the emergence of residential enclaves in Lima has shown, these practices are not only a reaction to crime, but also a strategy aimed at keeping out unwanted social groups, creating physical barriers to nearby 'marginal' or 'dangerous' areas, reducing the impact of traffic, as well as restricting informal commercial activities. The concept of 'condominisation' was introduced to identify and differentiate the different levels of socio-spatial intervention on the neighbourhood level. It is also intended to provide a framework for the changing structure of spatialised governance systems.

With the increasing appropriation, control and fortification of neighbourhoods the residents aim to recover a sense of 'spatial comfort' by securing the permanence of their immediate surroundings (Harvey 1996). The widespread informality of this process is related to the weakness of the Peruvian State (Crabtree 2006). Informal activities have long been ingrained into urban development. In a situation where existing regulations are rarely enforced, the informal status quo is first tolerated and later legalised, as in process of residential enclave building. Although friction may occur, as shown in the example of Las Flores, the measures are rarely being contested by the authorities. The continuous expansion of informal security devices throughout Lima Metropolitana is thus a spatial manifestation of a problematic relationship between State and society. As the system of local governance is transformed by these practices, the residents themselves – organised in some form of group representing local interests – emerge as important place-building actors. In some cases, as shown by the example of Sta. Patricia, the joint effort is based on just one specific task and does not necessarily imply that the security topic is translated into higher levels of neighbourhood cohesion.

The particular characteristics of residential enclave building in Lima add further detail to existing theories about the spatial fragmentation and social disarticulation in Latin American cities. The micro-scale spatial practices reflect increasing levels of social inequality. They also correspond with an increasingly challenging urban environment. The emerging urban structure is influenced by a deficit of spatial control and consists of a collage of heterogeneous spatial units, each equipped with its individual degree of spatial appropriation. More affluent areas generally have more resources at their disposal to implement additional layers of security. They also receive a higher level of security provision by public-sector security forces such as the police or the *serenazgo*. Socio-spatial inequalities are therefore reproduced through the emerging 'security geography'.

Chapter 4
Global Cities and the Governance of Commodity Chains: A Case Study From Latin America[1]

Christof Parnreiter, Karin Fischer, and Karen Imhof

Analysis of contemporary globalisation processes has generated two major strands of literatures that focus on the spatial organization of the world economy. In the global commodity chains literature (see, for example, Gereffi and Korzeniewicz 1994; Dicken et al. 2001; Gereffi et al. 2005) attention is paid (a) to the creation and distribution of value within transnational chains or networks of production, and (b) to the control of value creation and distribution along the different nodes of a commodity chain – from raw material exploitation through stages of trade, services and manufacturing processes to final consumption.

Concerned with the question of how value is transferred from periphery to core, the global commodity chain approach necessarily deals with the issue of how uneven relations between core and periphery are organized, sustained and controlled. The focus is, thus, on the governance structure of global production chains or networks, defining governance as the "authority and power relationships that determine how financial, material and human resources are allocated and flow within a chain" (Gereffi 1994, p. 97).

The second major literature on the spatial organization of the world economy is the research on the formation of global cities and a world city network (see, for example, Sassen 1991; Taylor 2004). Departing from the observation that advanced producer services are becoming both more and more important for the organization of the world economy and ever more concentrated in leading cities, the main argument of this approach is that globalisation processes give rise to a new form of centrality – the global cities. Global cities are the nodes, where the worldwide flows of money, information, commodities and migrants intersect. More importantly, global cities are, according to Sassen, the places wherefrom these flows are managed and controlled. In this understanding, producer services represent both the technical tools to make global production processes feasible (e.g. the management and handling of a global assembly line), and the means of

---

[1] The empirical part of this chapter was elaborated in the scope of the project "Transformation and Urban Processes in Latin America", financed by the Austrian Science Fund (FWF), No. 14883. We thank Peter Taylor for making the GaWC database available to us.

control: Producer services are the necessary instruments to command trans-state economic processes. It is in this sense that Sassen argues that global cities function "as highly concentrated command points in the organization of the world economy" (Sassen 1991, p. 3). Because firms inputting advanced services into global production processes are assumed to exercise governance functions in commodity chains, we contend that global cities have emerged as the key places for the governance of commodity chains.

However, although sharing a common world-systems analysis progeny, and despite their common concern with the governance of the uneven development in the world economy, the literatures on global commodity chains and global cities have developed independently with little or no cross-referencing (Parnreiter 2003, 2010; Brown et al. 2010). Despite the merits of each approach this mutual unawareness causes some shortcomings.

The strength of the global commodity chain approach lies in providing a non-state-centric framework for the analysis of global production and trade. A particular focus has been on the organisational changes in global production and trade since the 1970s. These are, first, new modes of industrial outsourcing of previously integrated components of TNCs' activities, i.e. the spatial distribution of production. Second, trade is increasingly organised in sub-components and services and is consequently more complex than in earlier times. Third, a major part of global trade (up to two thirds) is now conducted within TNCs or through systems of governance that link firms together in a variety of sourcing and contracting arrangements (see e.g. Dicken 1998). By tracing all inputs required to bring a product from conception, through the intermediary phases of production, to the consumers, the global commodity approach stresses linkages and co-ordination between economic agents and sites. Despite its important conceptual contributions and a growing number of empirical case studies on different commodities, a serious limitation must be asserted: research in this field lacks an understanding of the crucial role of producer services. This deficit is astonishing because cross-border networks of production require sophisticated forms of logistics, coordination and control. These inputs are provided by service intermediaries. Producer service firms supply a range of financial, professional and creative services, which are essential in order to insert firms all over the world into a global division of labour. Despite an initial call to explore the service sector as a key link within global commodity chains (Rabach and Kim 1994), this has remained an under-researched field (but see Parnreiter 2010).

Global city research, on the other hand, is strong in conceptualising the relationship between globalisation and cities, paying much attention to the role of advanced producer services. A main limitation of the world city literature is, however, the concentration on relatively few large metropolitan centers. While the role and dynamics of the highest ranking cities of the world city network have been studied in depth, cities below these leading cities have remained relatively un-explored (see Robinson 2002, 2005 for the critique; for recent attempts to analyse the world city network beyond the leading cities see for example Brown et al. 2002; Parnreiter

2002). Though these studies have extended our understanding beyond a limited number of leading cities, they still fail to explain the connection of major global cities to cities on other scales.

For the purpose of this chapter, the most important omission resulting from the mutual unawareness of the two approaches discussed is that global commodity chains research on the whole took little notice of the specific geography of governance (wherefrom is it exercised?), while global city research paid little attention to the "demand side" of governance (which economic processes are governed by advanced producer services in global cities and where are they located?). If, however, a basic premise of the global city literature is that global cities integrate local, regional and national economies into the world economy, then both issues – the geography of governance and the ramifications of operations across different scales through macro-regional and national to local – are on the research agenda. In other words: there have to be intersections between the spaces of flows stretching between global cities and the spaces of flows created through global commodity chains. Given that service intermediaries have already been identified as crucial actors in global city formation (Sassen 1991) and in tying the world city network together (Taylor 2004), we will argue in this chapter that the intersections between the networks of cities and of production are established through producer service firms located in global cities. In particular, we seek to specify the relationship between global city formation and the governance of commodity chains by accomplishing a case study on financial service providers in Mexico City and Santiago de Chile. Using stock-market transaction data, we have analysed the involvement of (local and global) finance institutions in bond and share issues of the 50 top ranked Mexican and Chilean enterprises. With our initial empirical investigation on financial service intermediaries that provide services to leading corporations in Mexico and in Chile we take a first step to specify how the two firm-based, trans-state networks – global city and production networks – relate.

Global City Formation and the Deepened Integration of Mexico and Chile in the World Economy

In previous articles we have posited that both Mexico City and Santiago have been taking on global city functions since the 1980s (Parnreiter 2002, 2003). In order to confirm the hypothesis of global city formation in Mexico and in Chile, three assumptions must apply. First, it has to be shown that the two economies have become increasingly integrated into global chains of production and trade. Second, the globalisation of the Mexican and Chilean economies must, at least partly, be organised, managed and controlled from their capital cities. This requires a substantial number of advanced producer service providers in the cities in question. Third, the cities must be linked with other global cities through the flows of producer services, capital, information, etc. Let us exemplify each argument in turn.

The deeper integration of Mexico and Chile in the world economy is shown by a rapid increase of exports, which is fostered through free trade agreements of the two countries, most notably with the United States and the European Union (and, additionally, APEC in the case of Chile). But not only did the annual value of exports grow; they also show a significant change in their structure. In Mexico, manufacturing exports made up more than 80% of all exports in 2008. These exports are generally organized via global commodity chains, which is revealed by the fact that about 85% of all Mexican exports are comprised of tax-free imports that are processed in Mexico and then re-exported (Dussel Peters 2000). Chile based its export orientation on the country's abundant supply of natural resources. While copper still remains the most important export commodity, non-traditional exports (agricultural goods and processed "industrial commodities" such as fish meal, canned fruit, bottled wine, and wood products) have steadily gained importance since the mid-1980s. The agro-food export sector has become progressively integrated into global commodity chains that are controlled and managed by transnational corporations (TNCs) (Gwynne 1999).

This fact leads us to a second characteristic of the shift towards a world market oriented economy. Due to privatisation and widespread industrial restructuring, TNCs have gained increasing influence. In Mexico, TNCs spearhead global commodity chains in the automotive, electronics, computer, and garment industry as well as the financial service sector. In Chile, TNCs dominate the agro-food export sector. Telecommunication, energy, and financial services are by and large transnationalised, with global providers of services seeking access to the regional market. Conglomerates owned by private Chilean capital still assert their position, although joint ventures with foreign investors have become a standard practice (Fazia 2000). The strong presence of TNCs is reflected in the volume and the direction of foreign direct investment. In Mexico, annual foreign direct investment grew ninefold between 1980 and 2007 with the manufacturing, the transport, the telecommunication, and the financial service sectors as main recipients. According to the World Investment Report report, the stock of FDI in Chile reached 55.4% of GDP in 2006, up from just 30% in 1990. The first recipient sector is mining followed by electricity, gas and water and services (UNCTAD 2007).

The increasing orientation towards the world market of the Mexican and the Chilean economies is, at least partly, organized from the two capital cities. Mexico City experienced a deep transformation of its productive base under the new development regime. The city ceased to be specialized in manufacturing, developing a high coefficient of local specialization in services. In 2003 Mexico City's producer services accounted for more than a third of urban production, while the city's share in the national production of these services had risen to 76 per cent. The concentration of companies' headquarters further strengthens the argument for global city formation. An analysis of the regional distribution of headquarters of main companies operating in Mexico not only shows that Mexico City is the place where most companies have their command centre. Moreover, the interesting finding is that the greater a firm's sales volume and the stronger its links to the global economy in terms of exports, imports, and foreign capitalisation, the higher the probability that its headquarter is located in the inner part of Mexico City, the Federal District. Regional distribution of FDI points in the same direction. It is remarkable that the Federal District maintained a very high level of 60% of all FDI for the last twenty years, despite the end of important privatisations and regardless of the significant growth of FDI directed at the export processing zones in the North, the so-called maquiladora industry (Parnreiter 2007, 2010).

Changes in the economic structure of Santiago de Chile began in the early 1970s. Between the 1960s and 1990s, employment in manufacturing suffered severe losses, while services substantially increased their participation. A look at production, however, shows that from the mid-1980s manufacturing was able to maintain its share in the urban GDP. That points to a recovery of industry that began with the implementation of more flexible, heterodox policies. It is, however, striking that financial services (including insurance and producer services) contribute more to the urban GDP than manufacturing, being the second sector behind trade. The spatial concentration is even higher than in Mexico: 78% of national GDP in financial services is produced in Santiago, representing the strongest concentrated sub-sector in Chile (Banco Central de Chile 2001). Regarding headquarter locations, only two of the top 50 enterprises – both shipping companies – are not headquartered in Santiago. Examining the regional distribution of FDI reveals that the metropolitan area of Santiago is by far the region where most capital is flowing in (INE 2002).

Empirical evidence on the third condition for global city formation – linkages to other global cities through nets of advanced producer services firms and other critical flows – is provided by studies of the "Globalization and World Cities Study Group and Network" (GaWC), which prove that Mexico City is well embedded in the cross-border grid of global cities (Taylor 2004). Among 55 world cities identified by the GaWC, Mexico City ranks 20th, being the highest ranked Latin American city. It has 12% of world city formation (measured in terms of the level of service provision of the producer service sector relative to the top scoring city), ahead of São Paulo (with 11%), Buenos Aires, and Caracas (both 6%). Mexico City can be compared to cities like Zurich, Johannesburg, Milan and even Los Angeles. Santiago is in fifth place in Latin America with 5% of world city formation.

Globalisation and the Role of Financial Service Intermediaries in Mexico and Chile

To this point, the argument has been that the three conditions stated above (the deepening of trans-state processes, the concentration of command and control functions in both capitals, and their embeddedness in the global city network) must be met in order to prove global city formation. The crucial point is that though each of these findings may be well documented individually, the links between them are still not proven. It is, however, precisely the *connection* between the deeper integration into world economy, growing importance and concentration of advanced producer services as well as cross-border links between cities, that makes the notion of global city formation sound. A way to achieve a better understanding of how transnationalised economic activities, centralised services, and cross-border networks are coming together is to integrate two bodies of literature: global city research and global commodity chain research (Brown et al. 2010; Parnreiter 2010).

With our empirical investigation we take a first step in this direction, i.e. to identify the producer service firms as interlockers of global commodity chains and urban networks. By drawing on financial institutions which provide services to top ranked companies in Mexico and Chile, we want to establish a better understanding of how spatially dispersed production, centralized services, and cross-border networks come together. In other words, by identifying the involved financial service firms (be they local or global companies) we expect to grasp how and by whom connections between production and urban networks are established and sustained.

We concentrate on the financial sector because it represents a major form of economic activity in which globalisation can be observed. Globalisation has led to a deeper degree of financial integration of Latin American countries into the world market. Accordingly, the internationalisation of financial services is an important development linked to globalisation (Eichengreen 1996). This internalisation is achieved through two channels (Schmukler 2004). The first channel is an increased presence of international financial service providers, mainly foreign banks, in local markets. The second channel involves the use of international financial intermediaries that are located outside the country by local firms, borrowers, and investors. One feature of the latter is the trading of bonds and shares, mostly in the form of depositary receipts (ADRs), on major stock exchanges. The internationalisation of financial institutions is stimulated, first, by gains in information technology which offer the opportunity to provide a wide range of financial products and services in different markets and countries. Second, banks and financial firms sought to meet the increased competition by expanding their market shares into new businesses and markets in order to diversify risk. Third, the liberalisation of regulatory systems along with the privatisation of public financial institutions has opened the door for international firms to enter local markets. These general trends found their way into the financial systems of Mexico and Chile.

The Financial Service Sector in Mexico and Chile

In Mexico, the financial system underwent severe reforms following the so-called "Peso-Crisis" in 1994/95, but even more so in 1998/99 when the remaining barriers to foreign ownership in the financial sector were eased. The role of foreign capital in the consolidation process of the financial sector was significant: with full liberalisation the foreign stake increased to more than three quarters of the banking assets in 2001. At present, the five largest banks, which represent 85% of the nation's bank assets, are owned by foreign banks (OECD 2002; Krebsbach 2003). In Chile, a rapid consolidation process of the finance industry took place during the 1990s. The number of banks dropped from 40 in 1992 to 26 in 2003, with four banks reaching almost

70% market share. In 1997 and 2001, the government lifted several restrictions on the banking system, opening new business activities to banks (such as international investment in banks, derivative activities, and investment banking). The liberalisation of capital markets significantly increased the participation of foreign institutions. At present, seven foreign-controlled banks – headed by Spain's Santander Central Hispano – dominate the sector with a market share of 45%, followed by eight locally-controlled banks, the State Bank, nine branches of foreign banks, and a finance company (Latin America Monitor 2004; EIU 2004; SBIF 2004).

The increased presence of foreign banks and the resulting internationalisation of financial services have shaped the way Mexican companies have access to investment capital. Global financial giants like BBVA, Citigroup, HSBC and Santander Central Hispano have made large investments (an estimated US$ 25 billion) in the Mexican banking system in the last 10 years (OECD 2004, p. 14). These investments were not made to foster private sector lending but can be seen as a sign of a shift in banks' revenue formulas. The largely under-banked retail market (consumer and mortgage loans) and workers' remittances payments generate high fees and therefore promise higher profits for international banks than interest on loans. Hence, international banks operating in Mexico have largely concentrated on this more profitable segment of the market. While non-bank financial intermediaries have become a source of credit for small and medium-sized enterprises, the high end corporate loan business has benefited from the easier access to international capital due to the presence of international financial service firms. Because of the high cost of borrowing, national and international bond issue and the participation of companies in the U.S. equity markets using ADRs have increased significantly. The average ratio of ADR trading in New York over the total value traded in the Mexican markets has risen from around 30% (1990–1995) to 70% (1996–1999) (Schmukler 2004, p. 47).

In Chile, consumer credit and mortgage loans of banks register considerable growth rates, whereas corporate lending has grown by only one percent (all figures 2003, EIU 2004). The large and foreign banks in Chile make loans almost exclusively to large firms and multinationals and concentrate on capital market activities. Measuring the different sectors of the financial system, Gallego and Loayza (1999, pp. 18–21) come to the conclusion that the liberalisation process has been related to a shift in the financial structure of the economy, in such a way that the stock market and other capital markets have gained importance relative to the banking sector. By the end of the 1990s, the local equity and bond markets had surpassed the credit market in activity, size, and efficiency (OECD 2003).

Empirical Basis and Method

In order to grasp the importance of financial institutions operating in Chile and Mexico we rely on two sources of data. The first set of data which was compiled by the GaWC group in 1997/98, consists of a matrix of the "service values" of 100 global service firms in the sectors accountancy, advertising, law, insurance, management consultancy, and financial services. The service values are estimates of the importance of a city within a firm's global office strategy, taking into account features such as size and function of offices. Because of the multifarious nature of the data, drawn largely from the web sites of firms, service values are based on a simple coding ranging from zero (no presence) to five (headquarters). This research defines the relations between cities through the differential presence of global service firms within each city, using the plausible conjecture that the larger a firm's service value (the level of service offered by that firm) in a city, the greater the number of the firm's flows of information, knowledge, instruction, ideas, strategies, plans, etc. that will emanate from that city to connect with offices in other cities (for details, see Taylor 2004). We draw on the results regarding financial service providers.

The second source of information is the Bloomberg database. This financial information network was launched in 1982 and provides information on the way companies finance themselves by listing equities and bonds issued by companies, the stock exchange(s) on which these instruments are listed, and in most cases the name(s) of the financial service firm(s) that were involved in the deal. This enables us to draw a direct relationship between companies and the financial service firm involved.[2] Drawing on the Bloomberg database, we analysed the bond and stock issues of the top 50 financial and non-financial companies in Mexico and Chile ranked by sales (Expansión 2002; El Diario 2003). After having identified the financial service providers that service the top 50, we ranked them by frequency of occurrence. At a second stage, we compared our Bloomberg findings with the results of GaWC. Besides presenting topic information on the presence and significance of financial service providers in Mexico and Chile, we are able to establish changes over time by comparing our results with those from the GaWC group.

Empirical Findings

Regarding the Mexican sample, in 26 out of the top 50 companies we were able to identify in the Bloomberg database the financial service firm(s) that were involved in either a stock or a bond issue. In the case of 12 foreign companies that were listed as part of the top 50 companies, the Mexican subsidiary did not appear on the national stock/bond market. This leads to the assumption that they financed themselves internally (e.g. stock/bond emissions of the headquarters located outside Mexico). In some cases the foreign mother company appeared listed on the Mexican stock exchange but not the Mexican branch. These companies were subtracted from the sample because we were looking for the relationship between a service provider and enterprises operating in Mexico only. Additionally, three financial institutions that have been de-listed from the Mexican stock market after their foreign takeover and the State Bank were excluded. Regarding Chile, in 20 out of the top 50 companies we were able to identify the financial institutions that service their stock-market transactions. In the other cases the Bloomberg database did not reveal information about the involved service intermediaries.

---

[2] For detailed information, see http://www.bloomberg.com

Ranking of Asset Managers in Mexico and Chile[3]

The ranking of financial service companies by the frequency of their occurrence in the Bloomberg database is shown in Table 4.1 for Mexico and in Table 4.2 for Chile (the GaWC ranking is used by way of comparison).

In the case of Mexico, Citibank/Citigroup (to which we added Salomon Smith Barney and Banamex because of its acquisitions in 1998 and 2001 respectively) appears as the leading financial service firm, followed by JP Morgan Chase and the Bank of New York, the latter mainly because of its leading role as ADR depository. Looking at the detected financial service firms, one main characteristic stands out: a majority is foreign owned. Only four out of 34 financial service providers are owned by private Mexican capital; they are *italicised* in Table 4.1.

As far as the presence of foreign financial institutions is concerned, the picture in Chile is similar to the one in Mexico. Only four out of the 26 detected financial institutions are owned by private Chilean capital (they are *italicised* in Table 4.2.); IM Trust became 100% Chilean after exiting the partnership with Bankers Trust in 1992. Service providers with global reach are heading the ranking: Citigroup shares the top position with JP Morgan Chase Manhattan, followed by Spain's Banco Santander and Morgan Stanley Dean Witter. Unlike Mexico, some foreign institutions with a high frequency of occurrence do not run a local office, even if they are more important than their counterparts in Mexico (this applies to Morgan Stanley, the Bank of New York and Dresdner Kleinwort Wasserstein).

Empirical Assessment: Comparing Bloomberg and GaWC data

A comparison of the Bloomberg and the GaWC data reveals substantial changes regarding the presence of banking and finance companies in Mexico and Chile as well as the structure of the banking sector itself. In order to complete the picture, the GAWC results are presented below (the tables also involve the global service firms which show the service value 0 for no presence in the respective capitals) (Tables 4.3 and 4.4).

In the case of Mexico, most noticeable is that the Japanese banks seem to have lost ground. Our set of data revealed that they were not involved in share or bond emissions of Mexican companies at all. Even with regard to their presence in the Mexican market only three out of the five banks that were included in the GaWC list still have branches in Mexico. When it comes to the German banks, our results are opposed to the GaWC ranking, too. Deutsche Bank/Bankers Trust

---

[3] Since empirical research was conducted in 2005, the names of the banks refer to the status quo of that time.

Table 4.1 Mexico – Ranking of Financial Service Providers

Financial Institution	Ranking Bloomberg (transactions by frequency of occurrence)	Ranking GaWC (0-5)	Client (national company rank by sales)	Office in Mexico (2004)
Citibank/Citigroup (with Salomon Smith Barney and Banamex added)	15	2 Citibank – Salomon	Petroleos Mexicanos (1), Teléfonos de México (3), Grupo Carso (6), Walmart de México (8), Cemex (12), Controlada Comercial Mexicana (19), Savia (21), Vitro (25), Grupo Televisa (34), Gruma (38), Kimberly Clark de México (42), El Puerto de Liverpool (43) Grupo Bimbo (20), Grupo IMSA (33), Coca-Cola Femsa.(40)	Yes
Bank of New York	12	–	Carso Global Telecom (2), Grupo Carso (6), Walmart de México (8), Fomento Economico Mexicano (13), Controlada Comercial Mexicana (19), Vitro (25), Grupo Gigante (26), Grupo Televisa (34), FEMSA Cerveza (37), Coca Cola Femsa (40), Grupo Casa Saba (44), Hylsamex (49)	Yes
JP Morgan Chase (merged in 2000)	12	3 JPM 2 Chase	Petróleos Mexicanos (1), Teléfonos de México (3), Walmart de México (8), Cemex (12), Grupo Bimbo (20), Savia (21), Grupo Financiero Banamex Accival (Nassau Branch) (29), Grupo Televisa (34), Gruma (38), Coca-Cola Femsa (40), Grupo Casa Saba (44), Nadro (45)	Yes
ING Bank	9	–	Petróleos Mexicanos (1), Teléfonos de México (3), Volkswagen de México (9), Cemex (12), Controlada Comercial Mexicana (19), Grupo Bimbo (20), Grupo IMSA (33), Grupo Televisa (34), Savia (21)	Yes

Deutsche Bank	7	0	Petróleos Mexicanos (1), Teléfonos de México (3), Walmart de México (8), Cemex (12), Savia (21), Grupo Financiero Banamex Accival (29), Grupo Televisa (34)	Yes
Credit Suisse First Boston	5	2	Petróleos Mexicanos (1), Teléfonos de México (3), Vitro (25), Grupo Financiero Banamex Accival (29), Grupo Televisa (34)	Yes
Bear Stearns	4	–	Petróleos Mexicanos (1), Gruma (38), Coca-Cola Femsa (40)	No
Inversora Bursatil	4	–	Teléfonos de México (3), Grupo Carso (6), Grupo Alfa (14), Grupo Televisa (34)	Yes
Lehman Brothers	3	–	Petróleos Mexicanos (1), Gruma (38), Aerovias de México (47)	Yes
Merryll Lynch	3	–	Teléfonos de México (3), Grupo Financiero Banamex Accival (29), Grupo Televisa (34)	Yes
Santander Serfin	3	–	Vitro (25), Cemex (12), Hylsamex (49)	Yes
Dexia Banque International á Luxembourg	2	–	Grupo Televisa (34), Kimberly Clark de México (42)	Yes
Kredietbank Luxembourgeoise	2	–	Teléfonos de México (3), Savia (21)	No
Morgan Stanley Dean Witter	2	–	Grupo Alfa (14), Grupo Financiero Banamex Accival (29)	Yes
Scotia Inverlat	2	–	Vitro (25), Kimberly Clark de México (42)	Yes
UBS	2	0	Petróleos Mexicanos (1), FEMSA Cerveza (37)	Yes
ABN AMRO	1	2	Petróleos Mexicanos (1)	Yes
Afin Casa de Bolsa(Grupo Financiero Banorte)	1	1	Gruma (38)	Yes
Banca Nazionale de Lavoro	1	–	Petróleos Mexicanos (1)	No
Banco Commerciale Italia (banca intesa)	1	–	Petróleos Mexicanos (1)	No

(continued)

Table 4.1 (continued)

Financial Institution	Ranking Bloomberg (transactions by frequency of occurrence)	Ranking GaWC (0-5)	Client (national company rank by sales)	Office in Mexico (2004)
Bank of America Mexico	1	–	Grupo Bimbo (20)	Yes
Barclays Capital	1	3	Petróleos Mexicanos (1)	No
BMO Nesbit Burns International	1	–	Savia (21)	Yes
Caboto SIM Spa (Banca Intesa)	1	–	Petróleos Mexicanos (1)	No
Cassa di Risparmio	1	–	Petróleos Mexicanos (1)	No
Dresdner Kleinwort Wasserstein SEC	1	–	Grupo Televisa (34)	No
Goldman Sachs	1	–	Petróleos Mexicanos (1)	Yes
HSBC	1	2	Petróleos Mexicanos (1)	Yes
IBJ Schroder Bank & Trust (now IBJ Whitehall Trust Company)	1	–	Controlada Comercial Mexicana (19)	No
Lazard Freres Luxembourg	1	–	El Puerto de Liverpool (43)	No
Multivalores Casa de Bolsa	1	–	BBVA Bancomer (36)	Yes
Standard Bank London	1	–	Vitro (25)	Yes
US Bank Trust	1	–	Cemex (12)	No
Value Casa de Bolsa	1	–	Vitro (25)	Yes

Table 4.2 Chile – Ranking of Financial Service Providers

Financial Institution	Ranking Bloomberg (transactions by frequency of occurrence)	Ranking GaWC (0–5)	Client (national company rank by sales)	Office in Chile (2004)
Citibank/Citicorp Chile (with Salomon Smith Barney added)	6	– Salomon 3 Citibank	Codelco (1), Endesa (10), Telefonica CTC Chile (12), Minera Escondida (18), SQM (24), Citibank (49)	Yes
JP Morgan Chase Manhattan (merged in 2000)	6	2 JPM 2 Chase	Codelco (1), ENAP (5), Banco Santander (6), Endesa (10), CTC (12), CMPC (16)	Yes
Banco Santander/Santander Investment Bank/Santander Corredores	5	–	Banco Santander (6), Endesa (10), Banco de Chile (14), Entel (15), CorpBanca (48)	Yes
Morgan Stanley Dean Witter	5	–	Codelco (1), Enersis (2), Banco Santander (6), Endesa (10), CMPC (16)	No
Banco Bice/Bice Corredores de Bolsa	4	–	CTC (12), Sodimac (21), CCU (30), Gasco (43)	Yes
Deutsche Bank Securities	4	3	Enersis (2), ENAP (5), Endesa (10), AES Gener (28)	Yes
BBVA (Banco Bilbao Vizcaya Argentaria)	4	–	Codelco (1), Enersis (2), Endesa (10), Cencosud (17)	Yes
Bank of New York	3	–	Cencosud (17), BBVA (41), CorpBanca (48)	No
IM Trust & Co/IM Trust Corredores	3	–	CTC (12), Sodimac (21), CorpBanca (48)	Yes
Dresdner Kleinwort Wasserstein Securities	2	–	Codelco (1), Endesa (10)	No
Merrill Lynch	2	–	Codelco (1), BBVA (41)	Yes
BNP Paribas	2	2	Codelco (1), Endesa (10)	Yes
American Express Bank	1	–	CTC (12)	Yes
Banca IMI	1	–	Endesa (10)	No

(continued)

Table 4.2 (continued)

Financial Institution	Ranking Bloomberg (transactions by frequency of occurrence)	Ranking GaWC (0–5)	Client (national company rank by sales)	Office in Chile (2004)
Banca Nazionale del Lavoro	1	–	Endesa (10)	No
Banco de Chile	1		Banco de Chile (14)	Yes
Bank of America Securities	1	–	Endesa (10)	Yes
BCI	1		BCI (22)	Yes
Credit Lyonnais	1	–	Endesa (10)	Yes
Credit Suisse First Boston	1	0	CorpBanca (48)	No
DF King	1	–	Banco Santander (6)	No
Goldman Sachs & Co	1	–	BBVA (41)	No
HSBC	1	2	Endesa (10)	Yes
ING Barings	1	3	Endesa (10)	Yes
RBC Capital Markets	1	–	Codelco (1)	No
UBS	1	0	Endesa (10)	Yes

Table 4.3 The GaWC Sample and Ranking of Global Financial Service Providers in Mexico City

Financial Institution	Service Value (0–5)	Office in Mexico City (2004)*
Barclays	3	No
JP Morgan	3	Yes
Sumitomo Bank	3	No
ABN AMRO	2	Yes
Bayerische HypoVereinsbank	2	Yes
Bayerische Landesbank Girozentrale	2	No
BNP Paribus	2	Yes
BTM (Bank of Tokyo-Mitsubishi)	2	Yes
Chase	2	Yes
Citibank	2	Yes
Commerzbank	2	Yes
Credit Suisse/First Boston	2	Yes
DKB (Dai-Ichi Kangyo Bank)	2	Yes (as part of Mizuho)
Dresdner Bank	2	Yes
Fuji Bank	2	Yes (as part of Mizuho)
HSBC	2	Yes
Rabobank International	2	Yes
Sanwa	2	No
WestLB (Westdeutsche Landesbank Girozentrale)	2	Yes
Deutsche Bank , ING, Sakura Bank, UBS	0	Yes (except Sakura Bank)

* Source: GaWC database and own investigation

Table 4.4 The GaWC Sample and Ranking of Global Financial Service Providers in Santiago de Chile

Financial Institution	Service Value (0-5)	Office in Santiago (2004)*
Dresdner Bank (sold to Grupo Security in 2004)	3	Yes
Deutsche Bank	3	Yes
ING	3	Yes
Citibank	3	Yes
WestLB	2	Yes
Chase	2	Yes
BNP Paribas	2	Yes
Rabobank International	2	Yes
Barclays	2	No
JP Morgan	2	Yes
BTM (Bank of Tokyo-Mitsubishi)	2	Yes
HSBC	2	Yes
Commerzbank , ABN AMRO, Credit Suisse/First Boston, UBS, Fuji Bank, Bayerische Hypo Vereinsbank, Bayerische Landesbank Girozentrale, Sakura Bank, Sumitomo Bank, Sanwa, DKB (Dai-Ichi Kangyo Bank)	0	ABN AMRO and UBS yes; rest no

* Source: GaWC database and own investigation

(service value 0 in the GaWC list) is very present and comes in fifth in regards to stock/bond emissions. All other GaWC-listed German banks have become less important; the Bayerische Landesbank Girozentrale even closed down its local branch. U.S. American and Spanish financial institutions, however, have significantly extended their engagement.

In the case of Chile, one out of the four banks with the highest service value in the GaWC study recently disappeared as an independent entity: Dresdner Bank restructured its business in Latin America and sold its subsidiaries to the Chilean Group Security in April 2004. Using the GaWC service value of service institutions and their frequency of occurrence in the Bloomberg database by way of comparison, Deutsche Bank shows an ongoing presence; the U.S. financial institutions Citibank and JP Morgan Chase could even extend their engagement. The other half of service providers ranked in the GaWC list show a lower rating in our inquiry. It is striking that four GaWC ranked firms (WestLB, Rabobank International, Barclays and BTM) do not appear as asset managers; British Barclays does not even maintain an office in Santiago at the time of writing. British HSBC and Dutch based Rabobank, ABN AMRO, and ING reduced their activities, selling parts of their local offshoots to other banks (Estrategia 2002). The Bank of New York serves exclusively as ADR depository and keeps no direct presence in Chile (because of that the bank was not recorded in the GaWC ranking; that also goes for Morgan Stanley Dean Witter). As in the case of Mexico, the regional dominance of the Spanish banks was not revealed by the GaWC inquiry.

How can the differences between the results of the GaWC study and our Bloomberg inquiry be interpreted? An explanation of the reduced engagement of Japanese banking and financial service firms can be found by looking at the re-structuring of the Japanese financial and banking sector that took place between 1999 and 2003. All of the GaWC-listed Japanese banks have undergone severe changes in their company structure mostly by merging with another bank or by being taken over. Although with the exception of the Sumitomo Bank they are all present with representative offices in Mexico City (the only one in Santiago is the Mitsubishi Tokyo Group), they are not active in asset management.

US-American Banks, however, have significantly extended their engagement – either by merging with another (US-American) Bank which was also active in Mexico and Chile, by benefiting from the re-privatisation and liberalisation of the banking sector or, in the case of Mexico, by taking over large equity stakes of financially troubled domestic banks. An example of the first case is Chase Manhattan who merged with JP Morgan. The banking institution has made efforts to strengthen its presence in the Latin American market especially by expanding the JP Morgan Institutional Trust Services network which delivers a broad range of services, including traditional corporate trust, structured finance, global securities clearance, and ADR services. A second example is Citigroup that expanded its activities by buying up Salomon Smith Barney in 1998. Moreover, Citigroup acquired the Mexican Grupo Financiero Banamex-Accival in 2001. The transaction is regarded as the largest ever U.S.-Mexican corporate merger.

The Spanish banks owe their expanding market shares to acquisitions, too. In 2000, Banco Bilbao Viscaya Argentaria took over a controlling share in Bancomer and merged with their already existing local branch to create Grupo Financiero BBVA Bancomer. Through the acquisition of Banco BHIF, BBVA has come to hold the sixth position in the Chilean ranking of financial institutions. Another major Spanish Bank, Banco Santander Central Hispano, bought the Mexican Grupo Financiero Serfin in 2001, and the Chilean banks Osorno in 1996 and Santiago in 2002. Since then Banco Santander has been the largest bank in Chile.

Interpretation of the Empirical Findings

Our empirical investigation yields two results. First, foreign financial institutions are predominantly engaged in stock market transactions by order of large enterprises operating in Mexico and Chile. Furthermore, the more global a company in Mexico or Chile is (according to exports or stock/bond emissions at international stock markets), the more likely it is that it decides to work with a global financial service intermediary in order to issue bonds and shares. In Mexico, foreign banks concentrate on Mexican and foreign based TNCs in the telecommunications, the retail, and the steel/petrochemical sector. In Chile, the results are similar. Foreign banks perform financial services almost exclusively for transnational and export oriented companies. Their clients are the TNCs in the telecommunications and energy sectors, a large private enterprise in the forestry sector, and the state-owned mining company Codelco. It is important to note that there is neither a Mexican nor a Chilean national finance institution active in bond or share issuing in foreign stock markets.

More striking is, however, the second result of the study. Demand for financial service intermediaries is concentrated in firms operating *both* at a global and a local scale, combining thereby a world wide network of offices and regional presence. The locational strategies of banks and other financial institutions can best summarized through the "glocalization" concept (Swyngedouw 2004) or, in the words of UBS: "We operate in two locations: Everywhere, and right next to you". The preference for glocalised financial service firms is also echoed in the advertising slogan of HSBC, which is, according to its self-portrayal, "the world's local bank".

This preference can be attributed to several factors. First, leading companies in Mexico and Chile seek out banks with sufficient global experience in order to place bond and share issues at major financial markets (in this case New York, Luxembourg, Frankfurt). Second, it is reasonable to assume that the Mexican branch of a transnational company chooses a bank already involved in stock market transactions of the headquarter in, say, the United States. The importance of a local office goes well beyond the so-called "soft" factors, such as the initiation of business deals, an in-depth analysis of the company that sets out to issue bonds or shares, preparation of the "pitch material" (information on financial position, investment strategies, profile of costumers, production description, etc.). According to the interview with the Executive Director of a (sizeable) Mexican office of a global bank (which also maintains an office in Santiago) local presence is "vital, 'importantísimo', because all deals originate in the country". Given that the big banks offer very similar quality of services, "the client chooses the one who is at hand", says the interviewee (private conversation 2007). Though it is a must that at the end every deal needs to be approved by the bank's centralised authorisation committee, the Executive Director stresses that the Mexican city office has the sole responsibility for all deals initiated and negotiated: "The approval you need not only here in Mexico, in Europe or the United States it's the same". In addition, the local office might ask the global headquarter to send an expert in order to assist a deal with specialised knowledge (e.g. on a specific industrial branch), "but not as a supervisor".

Conclusion: Towards a Geography of Governance in Global Commodity Chains

The empirical evidence presented reveals that in Mexico City and Santiago de Chile service inputs are provided that are essential for the successful operation of specific companies. Two New York banks with local offices in Latin America are particularly important: Citibank/Citigroup services four of the top ten firms in Mexico and two of the top ten in Chile, while JP Morgan/Chase Manhattan provides financial services to three of the top 10 firms in Mexico and to four of the top ten in Chile. Through the local offices of these two banks, global production networks of such diverse goods as petroleum, copper, cement or Coca-Cola are, at least partly, serviced from Latin America.

Putting this result in the context of the guiding themes of this book – geographical perspectives on governance and local development – we assert that Mexico City and Santiago de Chile are places wherefrom governance functions for globally organized production are exercised. This is because producer services are more than simply inputs that allow for the smooth functioning of production processes and hence of commodity chains. They represent the techniques necessary for the "practice of global control" (Sassen 1991, p. 325). As such, producer services are instruments for the exercise of governance in commodity chains – and places like Mexico City and Santiago, where producer services have become concentrated, assume the capacity to create the means of control of value creation and distribution as well as the power to deploy them. It is in this sense that we emphasize that the Latin American cities studied are not at all "off the map" of global city formation. Parts of each city – a limited number of firms, people, and places – have become integrated into the new geography of centrality, the world city network.

Is this now an indicator for local development? Our research suggests that the world city network is geographically more horizontal structured than commodity chains. Though inter-city flows connecting Mexico City and Santiago to other world cities are surely not even, we found no indication for a clear-cut hierarchy between the financial institution in, say, New York and its regional office in Mexico City or Santiago. This is, however, not to say that the terms 'center' and 'periphery' are not appropriate anymore to describe the geography and social hierarchy of the world. On the contrary, core and peripheral processes still produce and re-produce uneven geographies all around the world and at different scales. Core processes are not limited to the centres of the world economy; we find them, as has been shown in this chapter, also in Mexico City and Santiago (as we will find peripheral processes in New York or London). This is why both Mexico City and Santiago have core-areas, people and activities that form part of the cross-border network of cities, and that are embedded in and served locally by peripheral areas, people and activities. Though global city formation is certainly associated with some kind of economic development (both cities studied experienced, for example, a rapid growth and internationalization of its respective property market [Parnreiter 2009]), we would not relate global city formation to what is commonly understood as "local development".

Rather, we suggest a *spatialized* dependency theory perspective. According to Galtung (1971), imperialism (defined by Galtung as the exercise of power of a core-nation over a peripheral nation) inevitably requires that the "center in the center" connects to what he called the center's "bridgehead" in the periphery – the "center in the periphery". Though Galtung thought of this relationship in terms of social groups, and though we do not conceive uneven development primarily in terms of nations, we stick to the notion of bridgeheads as necessary pre-conditions for the organization and management of uneven development. In this perspective, one might call Mexico City or Santiago "relay global cities" oriented to and dominated by more powerful pole(s) and linked to other "relay cities" (compare Braudel 1986, pp. 22–33). The important point here is that cities like Mexico City or Santiago might be as *individual* cities, nonessential to the functioning of the world economy, while they are, as a group and as a category, indispensable for the governance of uneven development.

Chapter 5
The Impact of Decentralisation on Local Development: The Case of Bolivia

Gery Nijenhuis

In recent decades, decentralisation – the transfer of functions, responsibilities and financial resources to lower levels of government – has become quite a common element of public policy in developing countries. The implementation of decentralisation policies is often driven by economic motives. By transferring responsibilities to lower levels, planning in public policy can become more effective and public funds can be allocated more efficiently. Furthermore, decentralisation is believed to have a positive impact on public policy because projects implemented by lower levels of government are more responsive to local development-related demands. However, many authors also point to the limitations of the local level to generate local development: the capacity to generate external funds is often limited and the executed projects tend to focus on the social sector. This is often the case in relatively small rural municipalities.

This contribution analyses the impact of decentralisation policy on local development in six small rural municipalities in Bolivia. Bolivia introduced an ambitious decentralisation programme in 1994, combining the transfer of responsibilities and funds to the local level with far-reaching measures to increase popular participation in local decision-making. This contribution is based on Ph.D. research conducted in the period 1996–2002 in six rural municipalities in the department Chuquisaca.[1] The first section introduces the concept of local development and gives an overview of the main limitations in practice. In the second section the case of Bolivia is introduced. Then the impact of the implementation of Bolivia's decentralisation programme on local development in rural municipalities will be discussed, followed by some concluding remarks.

The Concept of Local Development Revisited

The debate about local development in developing countries, its objectives, actors and the policies to be implemented, emerged in the early 1990s. It has not yet resulted in the development of any particular paradigm. Lathrop (1997, p. 95)

---

[1]See for a detailed overview Nijenhuis 2002.

P. van Lindert and O. Verkoren (eds.), *Decentralized Development in Latin America: Experiences in Local Governance and Local Development*, GeoJournal Library 97, DOI 10.1007/978-90-481-3739-8_5, © Springer Science+Business Media B.V. 2010

states: 'so far, and probably for very good reasons, there seem to be no attempts at coming up with an integrated field of knowledge that can be called 'the theory of local development''.

Some observations can be made with respect to the efforts that have been made nonetheless to conceptualise local development. First, many authors approach local development from a predominantly economic perspective, using location theory, capital accumulation and technological change as the main theoretical frameworks (Bingham and Mier 1993; Blakely 1994; Rogerson 1995). Exponents of this view emphasise the need for developing local industrialisation by attracting external investments or by the development of small-scale enterprises. Although the first strategy might be viable in larger cities which have an established market and are well-accessible and well-organised, in large parts of rural Latin-America this strategy is not a realistic option (Rogerson 1995, p. viii).

Lathrop warns against focusing exclusively on economic conditions when considering local development (1997, p. 96), and defines local development as a strategy enlarging people's access to opportunities, be it in the form of 'income, employment, or the consumption of public goods and services'. People's access to these opportunities is determined not only by the presence of these opportunities, but also – and especially – by the way they are distributed. The increase of opportunities will mainly be an economic affair, but access to these opportunities is an essentially political question.

A second observation is that within this new approach to local development, the emphasis is not so much on external factors as on endogenous processes and actors. Blakely (1994, p. 50) points out that local economic development should emphasise 'endogenous development' policies using the potential of local human, institutional and physical resources. A major role is assigned to civil society, since 'obviously only local social forces will be able to identify objectives and instruments of intervention in relation to the actual situation in each area' (Garofolli 1990, p. 95–96; see also Wilson 1995, p. 645). The increasing attention paid to the local institutional context in explaining local development is also expressed by Shepherd in his classic work on sustainable rural development. According to Shepherd (1998, p. 1), rural development refers to 'the set of activities and actions of diverse actors – individuals, organisations and groups – which taken together leads to progress in rural areas'. In the rural local context, and in that of decentralisation, this institutional context includes both local government and the private sector. This last category is represented by the local population, their organisations, and NGOs (Nijenhuis, 2002, see also Helmsing, 2005 and Huisman, 2006).

In line with the above-mentioned changing views on local development, a revaluation of the role of local government in development can be noticed, with a focus on the role of (particularly the local) government as an 'enabler' (Helmsing 2000, p. 6 and World Bank 1993). Instead of direct intervention and the delivery of services (in the production sphere), the role of the new local government is one of facilitating and regulating this service provision. The main functions of the government in this view are to formulate strategies of public-private sector cooperation and to create the basic conditions for policy implementation, in particular with respect to the mobilisation of funds. Several important elements influence the performance of local governments to fulfil this new role in development, such as the financial and fundraising capacities, the administrative capacity and the creation of economies of scale.

A basic condition for the adequate performance of functions that have been transferred from the central to the local level and for meeting all popular demands is the availability of sufficient financial resources. For most local governments this proves to be a problem. One way to tackle this problem is to raise additional funds locally. Manor (1999) mentions two types of the 'mobilisation of local resources': firstly levying taxes, and secondly investments made in cash or in kind (e.g. labour or materials) by target groups at the local level when implementing projects.

Some authors write glowingly about the untapped fiscal potential of local government, but in practice local governments face several problems in raising funds at the local level, particularly in rural areas where resources are limited (Manor 1999, p. 111). Moreover, many central governments are reluctant to transfer tax-levying powers to sub-national authorities, but even if they would devolve these powers, it would not be easy to collect taxes at these levels given the lack of administrative capacity, especially in rural areas, and the absence of cadastral surveys. Local governments themselves are often reluctant to levy taxes because this might affect their popularity in the eyes of a reluctant population that has seen few services in return for their tax payments. Schuurman (1996, p. 17) mentions with respect to local governments in Chile that: 'many of the poor municipalities remained very dependent upon redistributed national funds. They did not succeed in developing an autonomous tax base to warrant greater financial independence from central budgets.'

A more practical way to mobilise local resources is to involve the population in the implementation of communal projects. Manor (1999) and Rendon Labadan (1996) mention this as a potentially successful strategy, provided that these contributions of the population are properly guided. Under Colombia's co-participation system, the local community provides labour and local materials, and the local government carries a certain part of the costs (Santana Rodríguez 1995). Fiszbein (1997, p. 1036) refers to this system as *minga*, which functions in Colombian municipalities, especially in the road and water sector. The system proved to provide good access to services, contributed positively to the cost-effectiveness of the projects that were undertaken, and secured the responsibility of the population with respect to continued project maintenance. However, in most cases encountered in Latin-America, local investments remain very fragmented due to insufficient access by the local governments to resources. Mexico offers an example, where due to the lack of financial resources the Municipal Funds Programme led to a multitude of small projects that had very little developmental significance (Fox and Aranda 1996).

A major limiting factor inhibiting local governments from effectively contributing to local development are the shortcomings in the administrative capacity of the new local governments. In a study on capacity development in Colombian municipalities, Fiszbein (1997, pp. 1031–1032) discerns three dimensions of administrative capacity: qualified human resources (the human dimension), financial capital (the physical dimension) and technology (the internal organisation and the management style). He found that there is a close relationship between political reforms and capacity development, since competition for political office offered more incentives for responsible and innovative leadership to rise up. He also found that capacity development in small municipalities is strongly related to the particular mayor, as these municipalities generally have only very limited staff. He notes:

> 'Small and remote *municipios* experience particular difficulties in upgrading the quality of their workforce. In the first place, scale imposes a natural or structural limit on the number of professionals working for the municipal administration. A majority of the Colombian *municipios* simply cannot afford the expenses of a cadre of adequately remunerated professionals in the different areas of government responsibility. Second the cost of hiring even a few well-qualified professionals might be too high for many small *municipios* that would have to attract them from other – sometimes distant – places.' (Fiszbein 1997, p.1034)

However, Fiszbein concludes that municipal administrative capacity is not necessarily a function of size. In Colombia, a successful effort was made to increase local capacity through competitive hiring, sharing professionals between municipalities and rotating personnel through the different departments within municipalities, increasing their experience and know-how (UNDP 1998). In Honduras, Lippman and Pranke (1998) noted the importance of prior development experience of the professionals in achieving local development, which helps to develop professional and technical expertise.

Creating economies of scale seems to be an important condition for decentralisation to contribute to development. Small municipalities are often at a disadvantage in attracting qualified staff due to the lack of career opportunities. Lippman and Pranke (1998) show that in relatively small municipalities, effective municipal governance is hindered by the poor education of the mayors and councils that govern them. Furthermore, the need to create economies of scale also becomes apparent in the implementation of development projects aimed at the provision of services. The problem is that financing institutions often prefer small and clearly delineated projects within a fixed timeframe, while the lasting impact of these projects on local development is generally small. Fiszbein (1995, p. 1039), in his study on capacity development in Colombia, notes the difference between small and larger municipalities with respect to the presence of development plans. He found that small municipalities generally do not have these plans, but work with listings of priorities, whereas larger municipalities do have municipal development plans.

Bolivia's Decentralisation Programme

During the bureaucratic-authoritarian regimes of the consecutive military governments which ruled the Bolivian State for most of the 1960s and 1970s, the Bolivian political and administrative structure was characterised by a strong centralist tradition.

Although in theory a departmental level (headed by a prefect) existed, in practice all decision-making and policy implementation occurred at the central level. Investments were mainly directed at urban development: the ten largest cities absorbed 94% of all public funds; the remainder was invested in the rural areas through Regional Development Corporations – semi-governmental entities established in the 1970s to promote economic development in Bolivia's rural provinces. These heavily bureaucratic and corrupted investment entities (Galindo, 1996) were in fact the only state agency present in rural areas.[2] This situation remained largely unaltered during the first democratic regimes of the 1980s.

In 1993, MNR[3]-presidential candidate Gonzalo Sanchez de Lozada won the national elections with his ambitious *'Plan de Todos'* campaign. In line with this plan, his government introduced several drastic reforms, such as bilingual education, privatization of state enterprises, land reforms and pension laws. The decentralisation programme in particular is seen as one of Bolivia's major steps forward on the path towards democratization, a programme now serving as 'best practice' for decentralisation in other countries. The Bolivian decentralisation model is based on two laws: the Law on Popular Participation (LPP), which took effect in July 1994, and the Law on Administrative Decentralisation (LAD),[4] which came into force in January 1996. The LPP was meant to improve the living conditions of the Bolivian population. The main objectives are a better distribution and administration of public funds and an increased participation of civil society in policy-making. The law encompasses three aspects: (1) restructuring municipalities, (2) encouraging popular participation, and (3) redistributing funds in favour of the population.

Municipal restructuring implied the creation of 314 new municipalities, whose borders are based on existing sections of provinces, each with its own juridical status. The new concept of municipality refers explicitly to rural–urban municipalities, and thus includes the rural population. The responsibility for infrastructure in the areas of health and education was transferred to the local level, as was that for transport, the promotion of rural development, agricultural infrastructure and services in the area of sports, recreation and culture.

The popular participation aspect was intended to stimulate participation of the population in local government through the registration of already existing neighbourhood committees, peasant communities and indigenous communities (*Organizaciones Territoriales de Base: OTBs*). By formal registration, OTBs obtain legal status. They are then expected to formulate their demands and present them to the municipal council. This is a form of participatory, bottom-up planning. Only territorially-based organisations are accepted for registration. Other important but not territorially-based organisations (e.g. *clubes de madres* or sectoral organisations) are excluded from participation.

---

[2]NGOs are considered far more important in rural areas.

[3]MNR: Movimiento Nacionalista Revolucionario (Nationalist Revolutionary Movement).

[4]The Law on Administrative Decentralisation, wherein the structure and responsibilities of the departmental level are defined, gives more power to departmental governments and their head, the prefect. This law will not be considered here.

A point of criticism with respect to the element of popular participation is that the LPP has been designed from above (i.e. is top-down) and that civil society was not involved in the elaboration of the law (Molina Monasterios 1997, p. 206). Originally this resulted in strong resistance on the part of the peasant communities, organised in the *sindicatos*, who considered the LPP an attempt by central government to gain control over the rural areas. In later years, however, they became strong proponents of the LPP, when they saw the benefits of the decentralisation process and the opportunities it created for them to participate in local decision-making.

Funds were redistributed in order to provide municipalities with adequate resources to meet their obligations, i.e. to finance projects in the fields of health, education and transport, and to meet the other demands of the urban and rural population. Some 20% of all national tax revenues are now distributed to the country's municipalities. The amount a municipality receives is determined by the number of persons registered in that municipality. Municipalities have to invest 85% of these funds in projects; the remainder can be used to cover administrative costs and salaries. Additional funds can be obtained by collecting municipal taxes, cooperating with NGOs, or applying for funds from other public entities. Municipalities must present an annual investment plan which, theoretically, is the outcome of a midterm planning document *(PDM: Plan de Desarrollo Municipal)* describing the projects and activities planned for the coming year.[5]

Introducing the Research Area: Six Rural Municipalities in Chuquisaca

The research for this contribution was conducted in one of the poorest departments of Bolivia, Chuquisaca. This department is situated in South-east Bolivia, and is located outside the La Paz-Cochabamba-Santa Cruz axis and is therefore not part of the country's economic core region. Within this department six municipalities were selected for an in-depth study: Yotala, Poroma, Sopachuy, Presto, Monteagudo and Huacareta (see Fig. 5.1).

The six municipalities have a number of socio-economic characteristics in common. First, they are all relatively small municipalities, except Monteagudo. Second, they are mainly rural municipalities, since the majority of the households live in peasant communities in a rural setting, and work in the agricultural sector. Third, the municipalities can be considered marginal, located outside the main commercialisation routes. The population is mainly involved in subsistence agriculture, with the exception of the municipalities of Yotala and Monteagudo, where non-agrarian activities are a more important source of income for the population. Fourth, they are poor municipalities, with scores on the Human Development Index among the lowest in Bolivia.

---

[5]To guarantee the implementation of all this, an Oversight Committee (OC: Comité de Vigilancia) has to be established in each municipality. This OC consists of representatives of the population within a municipality.

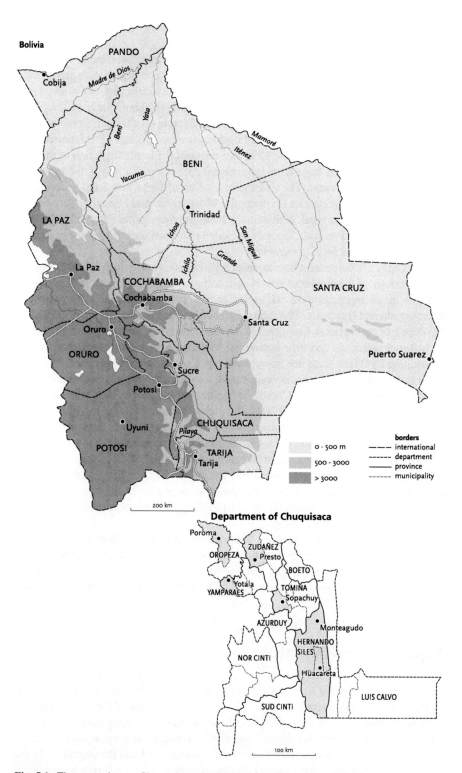

Fig. 5.1 The research area: Six rural municipalities in the department of Chuquisaca

With respect to the physical geographical context, the mountainous character of the environment, intersected by rivers, accompanied by soil degradation and erosion, makes changes in the current system of agriculture very difficult. As a result, levels of migration (both temporary and permanent) are high, particularly in the higher regions of Poroma, Presto and Sopachuy, where there is no alternative employment.

As regards the institutional context, the administrative structure of all municipalities underwent significant changes in 1994 as a result of the implementation of the LPP. Each municipality now has a local government consisting of a mayor, the municipal council and civil servants. The exact composition of these new local governments differs. In some municipalities (in particular Monteagudo and Huacareta), traditional elites, urban as well as rural, dominate the local government. In other municipalities (e.g. Sopachuy and Poroma), formerly excluded sectors of society (e.g. the peasantry) are now involved in local government.

Within the OTBs, peasant communities are most common, which is in line with the rural character of the municipalities. Neighbourhood organisations can be found in the villages in all municipalities, whilst indigenous communities are only present in Monteagudo and Huacareta. The main difference between the three types of OTBs is in the degree of organisation. Compared to the two other types, peasant communities tend to be better organised and their communal meetings have higher attendance figures. In addition to OTBs, there are many other types of community organisations. Since these organisations are not territorially-based, they do not have access to participation in formal decision-making. A Comité de Vigilancia functions in each municipality as the formal representation of the OTBs, charged with controlling the local government on the proper implementation of the Law on Popular Participation. Representatives of rural OTBs have a majority in the composition of these committees.

The existence of a private sector is limited in all municipalities except Yotala and Monteagudo, where there are quite a few enterprises. This finding corresponds with the main characteristic features of the economic structure in the research municipalities described earlier. By far the majority of the private sector consists of relatively small-scale, family-run enterprises.

Lastly, it is important to mention the presence of NGOs in these municipalities. Although NGOs are active in all municipalities, their characteristics differ greatly with respect to the relation they have with local government (expressed in the presence of an agreement between each NGO and the local government) and the intensity of the contact.

Impact on Local Development

As described above, the Bolivian decentralisation programme had rather ambitious goals, and overall expectations were high. The participation of the population was expected to increase, favouring especially women and the indigenous population, and the transfer of responsibilities and funds to the local level would stimulate the local economy, thereby improving the conditions for local development. In the following sections the main impacts of the decentralisation programme on local development will be discussed, in particular on the ability to generate funds, the character of local investments and their focus on the productive sectors of the economy, and the impact on local employment.

Generating Funds

The amount of available funds determines a local government's investment capacity and the opportunities for contracting a greater number and more qualified civil servants, hereby facilitating local development initiatives. This section analyses and explains the financial position of the six research municipalities since the implementation of the decentralisation programme and the impact it has on local investments.

During the period 1995–2000, all research municipalities experienced an increase in the total budget. This budget comprised the following sources:

(a) LPP-funds supplied by the central government, the *co-participación tributaria*, a percentage of the national tax income. As is shown in Fig. 5.2, the amount allocated to the municipalities under the LPP increased steadily every year. In 1994, each municipality received US$ 9.8 per inhabitant, an amount that increased to US$ 35.2 in 1999. In 2000, the absolute amount of LPP-funds dropped due to a reduction in national tax income.

(b) Own resources. These can be divided into the sale of goods and services, tax income (property, vehicle, patent, and other taxes) and non-tax income (fees, fines, tolls, interest and other rents).

(c) Contributions from OTBs in the form of labour and materials, which can be translated into money.

(d) Contributions from NGOs.

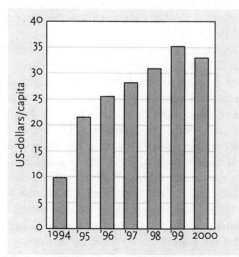

Fig. 5.2 LPP-funds transferred to all municipalities in US-dollar per capita

(e) Other governmental funds: funds supplied by the national and departmental
    government to pay the wages of public employees, especially in the local health
    and education sector.
(f) Credit and donations coming from the national funds: FIS (*Fondo de Inversión
    Social:* the Social Investment Fund), FDC (*Fondo de Desarollo del Campesinado:*
    Rural Development Fund) and the FNDR (*Fondo Nacional de Desarrollo
    Regional*: Regional Development Fund).
(g) Other funds.

Table 5.1 presents the composition of the programmed budget for the six research
municipalities in the period 1995/2000 with respect to these different sources.
A number of observations can be made with respect to the information in this table.

A first observation is that the LPP-funds coming from the *coparticipación tributaria*, which account for 28–43% of the annual budget, are not the only source of
income for the municipalities. This indicates that the research municipalities are
able to mobilise other financial resources. When considering the individual years,
a tendency towards a decreasing share of LPP-funds can be seen.

One such alternative source of income is the mobilisation of own resources.
Own resources consist mainly of taxes on production – such as on *chicha* (maize
beer: US$3 tax per gallon) and leather (US$9 tax per coat) – and on retail sales.
The introduction of taxes is not a popular measure and many producers refuse to
pay them. From a political perspective it is therefore difficult to implement.
Although preparations have been made to levy taxes on all property, taxes have
thus far been levied only on urban property such as land. However, this is only
done in Monteagudo and Yotala, since levying taxes is rather complex due to a
lack of a register of property (*catastro*). The share of own resources in the municipal
budget ranges from zero to 5%, with the highest shares in Yotala and Monteagudo.
Taking into consideration the main characteristics of both municipalities, it
appears that these more commercialised villages have more potential to generate
own funds. Nevertheless, it has been observed that the other municipalities have
also recently started to levy taxes.

In addition to LPP-funds and own resources, the contributions from OTBs
constitute another source of income for the municipalities. The contribution of
peasant communities is generally paid in kind and, translated into *bolivianos*,
incorporated into the annual budget. The contribution from the peasant communities
may comprise of work, food, offering shelter, etc. Neighbourhood organisations
generally contribute cash. Although almost all OTBs are involved in the implementation of (mainly infrastructural) projects, the share of this support in the
municipal budget is small, ranging from 2% in Huacareta to 5% in Presto.
The share of this source further decreased slightly during the period 1995/2000.
Local governments have indicated that they prefer to execute projects without this
contribution from OTBs. Reasons given against involving OTBs include the
difficulties in organising projects and the fact that *comunarios* do not stick to
the agreements. They sometimes fail to show up or work less than was agreed
upon. A last factor limiting the participation of the *comunarios* in the implementation

of projects is their lack of knowledge and experience with the technical aspects of project implementation.

This description shows that the internal funds (popular participation funds, own resources and the contribution from the OTBs) are an important component of the budgets of the municipalities. During the period 1995/2000, however, external funds accounted for more than half of the municipal budget. The two main sources of external funds are NGOs and national funds, such as the FIS, the FDC and the FNDR. With regards to the principal source of external funds, the six municipalities in our sample can be divided into two groups. In the budgets of the municipalities of Sopachuy and Presto, NGOs were the main providers of external funds. For the budgets of the other four municipalities, national funds were much more important. The main differences between the contribution of NGOs and national funds are that NGO-funding involves smaller amounts of money and that access to NGO-funds is relatively easy, since in most cases NGOs and local governments know each other quite well, and that administrative lines are relatively short. Obtaining access to the resources of national funds is more difficult due to complex application procedures. Applying for national funds is also a rather time-consuming process, since the period between sending the application and the final approval can take up to 20 months.

Political differences play a role in the access to funds, as does lack of knowledge of the procedures. The capacity of small rural municipalities to attract qualified staff is limited and it is therefore mainly the young, less experienced professionals who work in these municipalities. This was also the case in the municipality of Poroma until 1998, when it decided to contract the former *official mayor* of the city of Sucre, the provincial capital. This person had ample experience with the acquisition of funds and in exchange for a more than modest salary he was able to arrange several long-term contracts with national funds.

In sum, the availability of funds, hence investment capacity, have increased considerably since 1994, especially for the rural municipalities. The contributions of LPP funds and tax incomes to the total budget are important, but access to national funds and funds from NGOs have also increased substantially. In the next section, we will highlight the kinds of investments that are made with these budgets.

Table 5.1 Composition of the budget of the six research municipalities, 1995/2000, as % of total budget. (Financial records 1995/2000 municipalities)

	Internal funds			External funds				
	LPP	Own	OTBs	NGOs	Government[a]	Funds	Other	Total
Yotala	41	5	3	15	5	28	3	100
Poroma	42	0	3	8	8	34	5	100
Sopachuy	29	1	5	36	7	16	6	100
Presto	28	1	5	35	8	22	1	100
Monteagudo	30	5	2	14	8	39	2	100
Huacareta	43	2	2	7	10	34	2	100

[a]Departmental as well as national government

Main Characteristics of Local Investments

The implementation of the LPP in Bolivia meant an enormous increase in the investment capacity of local governments. Immediately after the LPP came into force in June 1994, bank accounts were opened for the new municipalities to receive the LPP-funds channelled to them from the central government. A substantial part of these funds had to be invested in projects realized according to the system of participatory planning. Table 5.2 shows the investments made by the local government in the six municipalities of the study area by sector in the period 1995/99.

Social sector investments dominate, with a substantial proportion of the funds invested in education, health and basic sanitation. Within the education sector, the construction and improvement of schools were the most important projects. When the LPP was launched, the state of most rural schools was deplorable: many rural communities lacked a school building and classes were often held in small, one-room adobe buildings. Equipment was often limited to wooden benches without writing desks, and school utilities such as books and pencils were absent. The situation with regard to health services was more or less the same: most communities had no health posts and only limited facilities. The sports and culture category has two main components: the construction of playing grounds and the organisation of cultural manifestations. 'Communication' refers to the provision of radio systems in rural communities.

A second important sector is the productive sector. Investments aimed at the agricultural sector – the main source of income for the rural households in the study area – are relatively low. This means that the problems of the majority of the OTBs in this field are not translated into projects. The projects implemented in this sector mainly involve improving the production infrastructure by, for example, constructing irrigation systems, storage facilities for cash crops, and dykes to protect agricultural land from flooding. Industry and tourism projects are directed at the provision of facilities (e.g. mills) and the promotion of tourism respectively.

Funds are also directed to infrastructure, for example for the construction and improvement of local rural roads. Dirt tracks make up 95% of the vital infrastructure in all the research municipalities. During the rainy season these tracks are vulnerable to washouts and consequently many of them are accessible only in the dry season. Municipalities usually start improvement activities around April each year. Another important category within the infrastructure sector is that of urban improvement. Projects in this category include improvement of the central square, construction of community buildings and the maintenance of streets within the town. 'Energy' refers to the construction of electricity systems.

The last sector 'Other' refers to projects aimed at institutional strengthening, which comprises training of local government officials, leaders of the OTBs and members of Comités de Vigilancia. It also includes the costs for local administration, such as salaries of the municipal council and equipment. The figures for the municipalities of Sopachuy and Presto, and to a lesser extent also of Huacareta, show a relatively high share of this sector 'unspecified', i.e. projects that are specified neither in the budgets nor in the balances of the implemented projects.

Table 5.2 covers the period 1995/99. An analysis of each individual year shows that investments in education and roads remain high, and that investments aimed at institutional strengthening gained importance after 1997. Investments in health and basic sanitation (e.g. the construction of sewerage systems and toilets) have decreased slightly. This indicates an investment pattern that is strongly aimed at infrastructural projects, with an emphasis on the social sector.

This pattern is confirmed by a comparison between investments in production-oriented and non-production-oriented projects. Production-oriented projects are those directed at strengthening the agricultural sector of a municipality. Examples are projects in the agricultural sector (irrigation), marketing and commercialisation, veterinary services, seed supply, forest management and non-agricultural, alternative employment (such as weaving and pottery). In this study, roads are considered non-production-oriented investments, as are investments in education, health, sports, culture or urban improvement. Most of these investments are in the social sector. Table 5.3 shows the share of production-oriented projects as of the total costs of implemented projects.

Table 5.2 Investments per sector as % of total investments, 1995/99. (Implementation reports of the municipalities, 1995/99)

	Yotala	Poroma	Sopachuy	Presto	Monteagudo	Huacareta
Social sector						
Education	30	32	21	18	26	18
Health	12	8	7	4	8	10
Sport and culture	4	4	3	1	3	1
Basic sanitation	14	12	4	5	5	2
Communication	0	1	1	0	0	0
Productive sector						
Agriculture	5	4	8	4	4	1
Industry and tourism	0	0	1	0	6	0
Roads and urban infrastructure						
Roads	9	31	10	26	16	22
Energy	1	0	0	1	1	3
Urban improvement	3	12	5	5	5	9
Other						
Institutional strengthening	2	8	12	4	6	11
Other	1	0	2	3	2	0
Local administration	19	7	11	9	12	9
Unspecified	0	6	14	18	5	12
Total investments in US $	1,033,354	1,883,933	2,150,433	1,503,396	6,017,231	1,820,552
	100	100	100	100	100	100

Table 5.3 Share of production-oriented projects in % of total investments.
(Implementation reports municipalities)

	1995	1996	1997	1998	1999	Mean
Yotala	0	0	1	8	5	4.9
Poroma	0	0	1	3	7	3.6
Sopachuy	3	11	20	3	5	6.7
Presto	7	4	9	7	2	4.6
Monteagudo	16	20	20	3	7	11.0
Huacareta	2	2	0	2	1	1.4

The share of production-oriented projects in the total overall investments over the period 1995/99 is very low (ranging from 1.4% in Huacareta to 11% in Monteagudo) compared to that of non-production-oriented projects. If the average cost per production-oriented project is compared to that of each non-production-oriented project, the costs of the former are only a quarter to one third of the latter.

Investment patterns in the six research municipalities can thus be characterised as directed mainly at infrastructural projects, with an emphasis on projects in the social sector (education, health and basic sanitation, sports and communication), both in terms of costs and absolute numbers. These findings are at odds with the problems experienced by the population, which mainly relate to the production sector. Findings of the Bolivian government (UIA 1998) show a similar divergence between demand and implementation with respect to production-oriented projects. In their study of 98 Bolivian municipalities, they found that 36% of the problems of OTBs were in the agricultural sector. However, only 3%t of investments were made in this sector.

The dominance of social sector investments can be attributed to several factors. First, especially during the first years of the LPP, most municipalities were not aware of their possibilities to promote and/or stimulate local economic development. This was mainly due to the fact that originally the Lozada government had presented the LPP as a law that would improve the social living conditions of the population, thus leading them to underestimate the opportunities the law offered for local economic development. In 1997, the Bolivian government tried to correct this by imposing various rules regulating the investments of local governments, such as the rule that 30% of all funds coming from the co-participation funds should be invested in the social sector, 6% in basic security and 25% in the production sector.

Second, the lack of consultation with the private sector, cooperatives and representatives of farmers (i.e. producers' associations) in the participatory planning process inhibited projects in the productive sector from receiving attention and funding. The lack of technical capacities among the administrative staff of the municipalities had a similar effect, as production-oriented and technical assistance projects are generally complex to implement (UIA 1998, p. 79), while the construction of a small school building or health post is much easier.

A fourth factor explaining the dominance of social sector investments is related to elections. During the run-up to elections, mayors are primarily concerned with improving their image and thus try to execute as many projects as possible.

Since projects in the social sector are the most visible, these will yield most votes and therefore receive priority.

Investments that favour the municipality as a whole have increased in the period 1995/99. This shift was accompanied by a shift towards fewer, but larger projects which could benefit from economies of scale. Related to this shift are strategies to increase access to the national funds. The acquisition of these funds demands much of local governments, and in order to limit the costs and time required to acquire these funds, many local governments decided to bundle their requests for funds into larger projects. Moreover, projects favouring the municipality as a whole are an easy way to satisfy the demands of all OTBs at the same time.

The Impact of Decentralization on Local Employment

In addition to offering favourable conditions for local economic development, the LPP is expected to have a positive impact on employment in the municipalities. Local government has an important role to play here. An example is the increase of employment in the local public sector. It is estimated that, as a result of the LPP, at least 32,000 jobs have been created in the local public sector nation-wide (SNPP 1996). However, the local public sector is not the only sector that has shown an increase in employment.

Another sector that has benefited is the hotel and restaurant industry, following the increased number of visits by public sector officials such as the *prefectura* and NGO officials. Before the implementation of the LPP, adequate lodging was lacking in all research municipalities except Monteagudo. In other municipalities visitors depended on the hospitality of NGOs, the priest or the school. Now, pensions have been established in all municipalities, in particular in Huacareta, Sopachuy and Presto.

In 1997 the local government of Sopachuy took the initiative to build the Hotel Municipal, a two-storey building on the edge of the central square. Although the guest house of the Sisters of the Congregation provided some lodging possibilities, the municipal council felt that this accommodation did not meet the requirements of today's visitors (i.e. representatives of the departmental government, NGOs and embassies). Therefore, they proposed to build a new hotel to provide adequate lodging for outside visitors. An additional attractive prospect was that this would generate extra municipal income, increasing the investment capacity of the municipality.

The hotel was constructed in 1998 by a local contractor with the help of some municipal employees. By taking the initiative to build this hotel, the local government performed a pronounced entrepreneurial role. Although such initiatives are promising, the question arises why individual entrepreneurs in Sopachuy were not interested in such an enterprise. This may have had something to do with the viability of the hotel. Although the council thought the hotel would attract enough guests to survive, no feasibility study or cost/benefit analysis was made before construction. Neither were agreements drawn up about the organisation and administration of the hotel.

In Presto, the only available accommodation was the guest house of the priest. There were no restaurants, although it was always possible to ask the woman who prepared the almuerzo (dinner) for the personnel of a local NGO to prepare an extra tray of rice and chicken. In 1998, during a second visit of the author to Presto, this woman had transformed the living room into a 12-seat restaurant. In 1999, business was good and they decided to build some extra bedrooms on the patio. This was mainly the initiative of the mother of the family, who expanded her business slowly but steadily.

Expansion of the hotel sector also took place in Huacareta. There the female owner of the local restaurant decided to expand her business and transformed a bedroom on the patio into a comfortable guest room. Her main incentive to do this, as she pointed out, was the increase of visitors since the mid-1990s and the lack of appropriate lodging in the village.

In addition to increased employment in the public sector and services, one would also expect a positive effect of the LPP on the construction industry in the form of increased employment, following from the execution of infrastructural projects such as schools, health posts and storage facilities at the local level. Although there are possibilities for the LPP to have a positive impact on the employment possibilities in the construction sector, the impact itself has so far been limited.

Figure 5.3 shows the percentage of projects that were executed by local contractors and the percentage of the project budget that was used for the project by local contractors, in the period 1996/97. Two issues become apparent from this figure. Firstly, the share of local contractors in the execution of projects is limited, ranging from 8% in Presto to 57% in Yotala. This means that external contractors are brought in to carry out at least 40% of the projects. Also, the smaller municipalities more often contract external contractors than the larger ones.

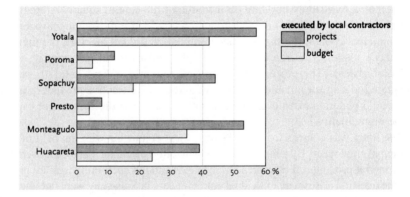

Fig. 5.3 Percentage of projects executed by local contractors and percentage of the budget used by local contractors, 1996/97 (Nijenhuis 2002)

Secondly, the overall tendency is for local contractors to be contracted only for smaller projects, which involve less money. This means not only that locals execute a limited number of projects, but also that the bulk of municipal investment flows to other regions, inhibiting the multiplier effect and a positive effect on local development.

Most of the larger projects are executed by companies from one of the three large cities: La Paz, Cochabamba and Santa Cruz. The use of external firms can be explained by the limited presence and experience of the construction sector in the predominantly rural municipalities. Although each municipality has a number of construction workers, by far the majority of them are unskilled labourers. They are perfectly able to work under supervision or build a simple construction, but lack the skills to design and implement larger projects. Besides deficient qualifications, local construction firms often also lack the legal requirements for being contracted for larger projects. In order to be considered for larger projects, entrepreneurs must show their financial viability by means of bank guarantees. They must also be registered at the departmental Chamber of Construction. Most local construction companies and workers are not able to meet these requirements.

In addition to the outflow of investments, another less favourable aspect of contracts with outsiders is the use of labour and materials by these firms. Most external firms do not use the unskilled labourers living in the municipality concerned, but bring labourers with them.

As one supervisor stated:

> Most large projects are executed by firms from outside. They come here with large trucks and bring both materials and labour. Sometimes we suggest the input of local workers, but the contractors reject this, arguing that they can better manage the input of their own people, generally workers they have worked with before.

Thus the employment generated by the LPP in the construction sector remains limited, as does the occurrence of a multiplier effect as a boost for the local economy from the use of local inputs. Although some municipalities, such as Monteagudo, have tried to curb this development by municipal regulations, such regulations are largely ignored by construction firms.

Conclusion

This chapter has discussed the impact of the Bolivian LPP on local development through the implementation of projects in the context of the LPP. With respect to the ability to generate funds, it has been shown that the municipalities depend on LPP-funds for 28–43% of their budget. The importance of locally generated resources in municipal budgets remains small, which can be explained by the fact that the base for levying tax is weak in most municipalities. Next to LPP-funds, the municipalities depend on external funds such as NGO and national funds for an important share of their income. Too much dependency on national funds however entails a risk, as the procedures necessary for obtaining these funds are complex and time-consuming. In this regard, it would be more efficient for municipalities to attract NGO funds.

An overview of the projects implemented in the period 1995/99 in the six municipalities shows that investments in the social sector dominate in all munici-palities, followed by improvements in road infrastructure and, to a lesser extent, agriculture-oriented investments. The relatively small share of such investments is remarkable considering the predominantly rural character of the municipalities, the bias towards agriculture in the problems faced by OTBs, and the relatively high share of production-oriented projects that are incorporated in the municipal development strategies as expressed in the PDMs.

Decentralisation can have an important multiplier effect by generating extra local employment through the execution of local public works by the construction industry. An analysis of the impact of the LPP on the construction industry however showed that employment increased only slightly, growth being restricted by the limited supply of local contractors (both in terms of absolute numbers and capability). This has resulted in the contracting of external construction firms for particularly the larger projects, while only the smallest projects are left for local contractors. Besides the slight increase in employment in the construction industry, LPP-related employment in the public sector has also increased, as has to some extent the income generation in the hotel and restaurant industry.

Summarising, the implementation of decentralisation in Bolivia has resulted in an increased investment capacity of the six research municipalities, an increased number of projects implemented at the local level, and a slight increase in local employment. However, these developments are strongly related to the way project planning is designed and to the opportunities to acquire other funds. Finally, it can be concluded that the Bolivian case shows many similarities to other experiences in Latin America: the local tax base is often small, the necessary administrative infrastructure is lacking, and small rural municipalities often encounter many difficulties in contracting experienced staff.

Chapter 6
Political Reforms and Local Development in the Bolivian Amazon

Martina Neuburger

Good governance has over the 1990s rapidly become one of the key terms in the international discussion on suitable development strategies for Third World countries. Because previous strategies such as the modernisation of agriculture, the promotion of industry, development of the social infrastructure, and project support to target groups did not have the desired effects, numerous development organisations have started to provide assistance to institutions involved in the planning process. However, corruption, clientelism and the inefficiency of national institutions still dramatically impact the success of such measures. This is why recently much attention has been paid to modernisation of the states themselves. Under the keyword of good governance, measures like administrative reforms and institution-building, educational and training programmes for administrative personnel, and political consulting have become an integral part of many development strategies.

The concept of good governance, however, does not only refer to the improvement of the efficiency of state institutions. It also implies the capability to formulate suitable objectives as a basis for political decisions. Central elements of good governance also include the equal participation of all population groups as well as transparency in the decision-making process (Nijenhuis 2002). In addition, good governance is determined by whether the decisions made have the desired effects in the implementation phase. This is true for all levels of political action: the global, the national, the regional and the local levels. In order to meet these demands, various development organisations have over the last years integrated the reorganisation of political decision-making processes as a central element into their development policies. In this context, decentralisation is one of the most prevalent concepts. Decentralisation entails the reallocation of power and funds to lower levels of decision-making. It is based on the assumption that the local level has a special role to play, as it is at this level that decision-makers have direct access to the citizens and thus can better tailor their policies to their specific needs.

As one of the states in which great efforts are being made to improve governance, Bolivia has received quite some international attention already (e.g. Birle 1996; Van Dijck 1998; Nohlen 2001). It is repeatedly mentioned as the typical example of successful realisation, and numerous analyses at the national level show that fundamental principles such as the participation of all social groups have been

P. van Lindert and O. Verkoren (eds.), *Decentralized Development in Latin America:*
Experiences in Local Governance and Local Development, GeoJournal Library 97,
DOI 10.1007/978-90-481-3739-8_6, © Springer Science+Business Media B.V. 2010

translated into policies and practical planning processes. However, academic studies that investigate whether and how these policies are being realized at the local and regional levels are rare, let alone that it is known what effects they have had on the socio-economic framework at these levels.

In this context, the question arises whether the institutional reforms in Bolivia, which were decreed in a top-down manner and have transferred numerous decision-making competencies to the local level, have actually contributed to good local governance. This chapter therefore seeks to analyse the institutional and social conditions present at the local level and what they mean for bringing about good governance, which will then enable us to discuss the effectiveness of the political reforms.

The analysis focuses on the Bolivian Amazon region, i.e. the departments Beni and Pando, where the realisation of reforms is rendered rather difficult due to an extremely weak presence of the state. The chapter starts with a brief overview of the historical political context, followed by an outline of the key features of the political reforms in Bolivia. The characteristics of the national political framework are especially important here, as the political context directly influences the possible successes of the implementation. Then, after a brief introduction to the Bolivian Amazon region, the analysis zooms in on the effects of the reforms in the regional and local contexts.

Political Reforms in Bolivia – Hollow Words or Drastic Change?

Historical Context

Bolivia is known for its extremely unstable political conditions and high incidence of poverty. Up to the 1990s, basic social statistics indicated that Bolivia had one of the highest poverty indices, one of the highest rates of illiteracy, and the lowest life expectancy among the Latin-American countries. Even though the figures for basic social services have now clearly improved, Bolivia, along with Honduras, still comes last in the Latin-American HDI-ranking. Compared with other world regions, only Africa averages behind Bolivia (PNUD 1998, 2000, 2002).

Moreover, the political climate in Bolivia has not been very conducive to effective reforms. Political instability has prevailed ever since the national revolution of 1952, as illustrated by the quick change of governments and presidents. From 1964 to the 1980s, military dictatorships ruled over Bolivia. Over these decades, Bolivian politics have been dominated by the interests of the political parties, the trade unions, and the indigenous organisations. Confrontations between the leftist trade unions – in particular the largest among them, the COB (*Central Obrera Boliviana*) – and the military or the respective governments were frequent.

Considering this history of political instability, the swift implementation of the various state reforms of the 1990s was a remarkable accomplishment. What allowed this to happen was the climate of political change brought about in the 1980s (Eróstegui 1996; Goedeking 2001; Jost 2003). During that time, the most influential actors in the nation's political arena were simultaneously caught up in deep crises, so that the confrontation between them – already a tradition – had become less important. Many state-owned mines had been closed due to the Structural Adjustment Policies and large masses of miners had been kicked out. As an immediate consequence, the COB lost its political vigour since it could no longer play the role of Bolivia's most powerful civil society organisation. Furthermore, the big political parties suffered a severe loss of credibility as none of them was able to offer effective programmes to fight the economic crisis and the political stagnation. At the same time that some of these key institutions in La Paz responsible for the maintenance of order in the entire nation were losing some of their power, Santa Cruz de la Sierra became more pivotal because of its economic successes, which also induced its elites to seek more political autonomy.

The Reforms

The reforms carried out since the mid-1980s can be divided into two different types. The so-called reforms of the first generation were comprised of the economic reforms of the 1980s which included economic stabilization, structural adjustment, and other neo-liberal measures. It was the reforms of the second generation that brought about the rearrangement of the political landscape in the 1990s. While president Gonzalo Sánchez de Lozada maintained the same neo-liberal economic policy he himself had developed as the Minister of Finance in the preceding government, he also implemented some major administrative reforms which were part and parcel of his ambitious 'Modernization of the State' project. These state reforms created the basic preconditions for the realization of good governance (República de Bolivia 1997).

The law on Popular Participation and on Administrative Decentralisation are especially worth mentioning in this respect.[1] The essence of these two laws lies in the decentralization of political decision-making combined with the right for citizens to participate in these decision-making processes at the municipal level. For this purpose, it was necessary for municipalities to be created as new political entities with their own administrative functions. Until then, only settlements with over 2,000 inhabitants had had their own administrations. Such administrations, however, had only had jurisdiction over their so-called 'urban' area. The vast zones of 'non-urban' territory in Bolivia had always remained under direct control of the central government (Fig. 6.1).

Starting with the promulgation of the state reform laws in the mid-1990s, numerous important competencies for local management and local development were transferred to the municipal level. The local government became responsible for the health care and education sectors and for infrastructure. The public financial system was also reformed in order to enable municipalities to cope with

---

[1]The *Ley de Participación Popular, No. 1551* (of April 20, 1994) and the *Ley de Descentralización Administrativa, No. 1654* (of July 28, 1995).

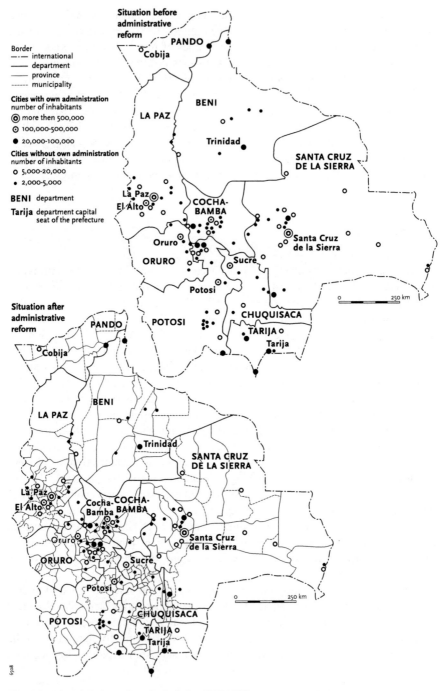

Fig. 6.1 Administrative reform in Bolivia. (INE 1999)

their new duties. A change in the allocation of funds by the central government was the most important element for the municipal governments. From 1994 onward, the municipalities received funds in proportion to their population size and not, as had been the case before, in accordance with their own tax yields. Before, the economically strongest cities La Paz/El Alto, Santa Cruz de la Sierra and Cochabamba had been assigned about 90% of the national tax revenues, while the remaining 10% was allocated to the rest of the country. The fiscal reform led to an increase in funds for the small, rural municipalities of Bolivia's periphery, which until then had been the poorest.

The offices of mayor and local council members were created in order to institutionalise the democratic decision-making process at the municipal level, where the population now directly elects all administrators. In the new situation, local administrators and municipal councils formulate objectives for the municipality and decide on the use of municipal funds after having consulted the local population. To facilitate this process, the *Ley de Participación Popular* provides for the foundation of so-called OTBs (*Organizaciones Territoriales de Base*).

Every OTB represents the population of a certain territory in the form of a civil society organisation. Their chairpersons are not necessarily elected democratically. Traditional leaders such as chiefs, eldest, or shamans can take the position of chair of such territorially defined groups. The OTBs have received the status of legal entities and can thus take part in political life. They are actively involved in the development of municipal development plans and they have a say in the annual budgeting. They have also been given the capacity to control the municipal administration during its legislative period. Each OTB of a municipality sends one representative to the so-called *Comité de Vigilancia*. These oversight committees monitor the municipal administration, especially with respect to the implementation and performance of the projects that were approved by the OTBs and included in the annual development plan of the municipality.

Overall, the new legislation was adopted and implemented at the local level rather quickly. By 1998, a *Comité de Vigilancia* had been set up in 192 of the 314 municipalities, and about 13,000 OTBs were integrated within them. Another approximately 2,000 OTBs were still waiting to be recognized as legal entities so they too would be able to bring their concerns to municipal politics (Jost 2003).

Reforms were also realized at the next administrative level. Before the implementation of the political reforms, the administrative bodies at the department level had been directly manned and controlled by the central government. After the reforms, they were subordinated to a department parliament elected by the municipal mayors. This newly created body controls the executive of the department – the *Prefecto Departamental* and administration – and passes the regional development plan for the department. The regional development authorities, which had previously fulfilled this function, were dissolved and have been partially integrated into the administrative machinery of the departments.

Conditions for Successful Implementation

The *Ley de Participación Popular* and the *Ley de Descentralización* brought on progress in good governance by realising participation of the people in the decision-making process in Bolivia. The shift of political decision-making powers to the lower administrative levels is essential for the realisation of planning practices adapted to their particular regional and local contexts. These political reforms therefore constitute the necessary formal basis for reshaping the economy and society. However, political reforms at the institutional level alone are not sufficient. The success of these reforms is largely determined by their implementation in the every-day reality of the population. For this to go smoothly, the state of Bolivia required considerable funds, for example for the reorganisation of administrative operations, to create new jobs and to provide training. The high level of debt seriously challenged the success of the reforms. Thanks to its participatory approaches to poverty reduction, however, Bolivia was among the first countries to receive debt cancellation in 1999 (Klauda 2001). Several governments including the USA, Germany, and the Netherlands have also increased aid to Bolivia as part of their respective development policies, so that the necessary financial conditions for the implementation of the reforms were also met.

Civil society also had to be prepared for political participation to be able to deal with its newly obtained power in a conscious and sensible way. Also in this respect positive developments could be observed in Bolivia. Increasing NGO activity by international and local NGOs demonstrated the high level of commitment within Bolivia's civil society.

Despite the overall positive developments, many factors that will determine success in the coming years remain unknown. Although the implementation of the institutional reforms has already progressed considerably, completion will certainly take many more years, if not decades. The political turmoil and intensive popular protests in recent years against the government's neo-liberal measures show in what unstable context these new democratic institutions still operate. This situation hasn't changed decisively with the presidency of Evo Morales, the first indigenous president of Latin America. To assess the effects of the reforms on the local and regional level, in the next sections we will focus on the current development in the Amazon departments and provinces.

The Amazon Region of Bolivia: Effects of Institutional Reforms in a Peripheral Region

The Bolivian Amazon region is characterised by extremely low population density and lack of presence of the state, so that the implementation of the political reforms for good governance has proven very difficult. The reasons for the problems of implementation of the reforms will be elaborated, as well as the effects of these reforms for local development.

Geographical Conditions

The Amazon region of Bolivia, referring to the departments Beni and Pando as well as the province of Iturralde of the department La Paz, are characterised by their extremely peripheral location. Road connections with the political and economic centres of the country have only existed for a few years and these roads are only navigable during the dry season. Air traffic between the various cities of the region – Trinidad, Cobija, Riberalta, and Guayaramerin – and other department capitals is also limited, as flights are often cancelled due to heavy rainfall during the wet season making it impossible to land on the grass airstrips. Some airports are not even equipped with radar systems.

Internal communication between the widely scattered settlements is also difficult in this vast and scarcely populated rural region. As the rivers were traditionally used as the main traffic routes, the downstream cities of Riberalta and Guayaramerin used to be of great importance for the local population up until just a few decades ago. Mainly due to the crisis of the economy, however, these two cities have lost most of their central functions. Although these functions have been taken over by the departmental capital cities Cobija and Trinidad, these cities are barely accessible for the population living along the rivers. Families from remote settlements only sporadically visit the nearest urban centres to buy goods or to settle administrative matters. The capital city of the department is visited very rarely. Only in the last 10 years, the situation has slowly improved thanks to state-aided road construction programmes.

For participatory political decision-making processes as introduced by the reforms, a constant and abundant flow of information between the local administration and the population, between the different population groups, and between the individual families is of great importance. Participatory democracy can only work if each citizen has the same access to information relevant for decision-making. The existing communication obstacles are often taken advantage of by the more powerful groups in Amazonia in order to exclude families living in the periphery from particular decision-making processes. There is an especially high risk for this to happen if social disparities prevail and an asymmetry of power exists. In this respect, the historical inheritance of patronage-relations in the Bolivian Amazon region is very disadvantageous for participatory decision-making.

Economic Conditions

In the past, the Bolivian Amazon region was of great importance. At the end of the nineteenth and at the beginning of the twentieth century it was among the most dynamic regions of the country along with the bordering Brazilian forestlands (Stoian 2000; Roux 2000). The extraction of rubber was the basis of this dynamic activity, sustained by approximately 80,000 rubber tappers and controlled by three big 'rubber barons'. Riberalta and Guayaramerin were the urban market centres. However, due to growing competition from the rubber plantations of Southeast

Asia, the rubber production was thrown into a deep crisis already during the first half of the twentieth century. While the 'rubber barons' left the region, the rubber tappers migrated to the cities or kept the pot boiling under very poor conditions in the forest. There, they carried on with the extraction as collectives in so-called *comunidades libres*, or they kept working in so-called *barracas patronales* for starvation wages after the area had been taken over by one of the former proprietors.

The regional economy has experienced some new and modest growth as well as diversification since the 1980s (Henkemans 2001; Stoian 2000; Assies 1997). Besides rubber, products such as Brazil nut, palm heart, and exportable tropical woods (especially mahogany) have become ever more important in the region. Moreover, extensive bovine pasture farming has been continuing to expand in the direct surroundings of the cities. These developments have brought about a shift in the regional structure.

The former economic centre of the region, which comprised of the areas of rubber production and the markets of Riberalta and Guayaramerin, is becoming less important. Areas gaining more and more influence on politics in the Bolivian Amazon are the southern part of the department Beni, because of its spatial vicinity to the booming department Santa Cruz de la Sierra, and the cities of Cobija and Trinidad, because of their functions as departmental capitals. Moreover, the borderlands are evolving into the economically most dynamic areas of the region. Cities such as Cobija and Guayaramerin located at the border are becoming more important in cross-border, especially informal, commerce. At the same time, Brazilian settlers have invaded Bolivian territories along the border with Brazil over the past few years to occupy and cultivate land virtually inaccessible from the Bolivian side and unnoticed by the state.

The shift in the regional economic structures has prompted new streams of migration. The migration to the cities is steadily increasing and the dynamic cities in particular keep growing. Cobija for example, the capital of the department Pando, grew from 8,000 inhabitants in 1986 to approximately 25,000 today. The majority of the urban population lives in absolute poverty on the outskirts of the city under sub-human living conditions (Henkemans 2001). Only during the harvest of the Brazil nut, from November till March, a part of the population finds employment. Other than that, these marginalized groups cultivate parcels of land for subsistence production close to their urban neighbourhoods. Except for informal commerce, even the urban economy offers few job opportunities that are accessible to the former rural population.

Civil Society Activity

When the reforms were implemented, civil society in the Bolivian Amazon region was not prepared for its new participation opportunities. As several decades before, the poor rubber tappers were not able to organise themselves to build up a powerful organisation. The rubber barons were replaced by stockbreeders and the so-called *barraqueros*, who still keep the poor groups of the region in dependency and marginality.

In contrast, indigenous groups today are showing some organisational activity. Until the 1980s, the indigenous population of the Bolivian Oriente had barely been

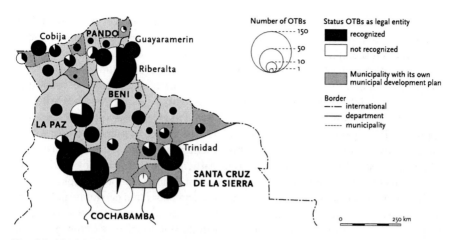

Fig. 6.2 Municipal development plans and OTBs in the Bolivian Amazon region. (Ministerio de Hacienda (1998): Primer censo de gobiernos municipales)

organised (Gros 2005). Neither had such strong, well-structured and hierarchically organised trade unions come into existence as had happened in Bolivia's uplands. In 1986, however, various indigenous groups, some of which had even been enemies before, came together and founded the Confederación Indígena del Oriente Boliviana (CIDOB). This grassroots organisation brought forward the needs and demands of the *indígenas* before the government in the uplands for the first time, and eventually succeeded, among other things, in integrating the collective land title – the so-called *Territorios Comunitarios de Orígen (TCO)* – into the land reform act of 1996.

At the time the political reforms were introduced, these still weak organisational structures of civil society in the Bolivian Amazon proved an insufficient basis for active participation. The population would have to join forces in the *Organizaciones Territoriales de Base* (OTB) mentioned above to take full advantage of their potential influence in the municipal planning process. However, with a population density of about four inhabitants per square kilometre, the great distances between the different settlements made the foundation of organisations of civil society and OTBs (see Fig. 6.2) very difficult. Moreover, indigenous settlement areas often stretch across municipality borders, so in many cases OTBs are unsuitable for the representation of the political interests of indigenous groups.

Problems and Effects of the Reforms: Participation

Due to the weak organisation of civil society and the uneven social structures, the political reforms had some unexpected and unwanted effects. It was, for example, not sufficiently clarified whether the representatives of the OTBs would be picked up for the important sessions of the community boards or whether they would have to organise the trip for themselves. As effect in many cases the OTBs didn't have the conditions to realize their participation. This situation was a result of little interest of the political decision-makers to guarantee the participation of the civil society. Such seemingly small issues in the starting phase of the political reforms made it easy for the 'old' political elite to misuse the institutions for their own purposes, especially in Amazonia, where the distances between individual settlements and the main settlement of the community could well amount to several hours or even days by foot or boat. This is why the local elites often secured their influence by standing up as founders of OTBs themselves and recruiting their clientele by guaranteeing representation of their interests without restrictions. The inadequacy of the new mechanisms of participation is revealed by the fact that today numerous communities of the department of Pando vote for the exploitation of their own natural resources (especially in the wood extraction economy and pasture farming) based on decisions of the *Comités de Vigilancia*, although traditional rubber tappers and indigenous groups, which constitute important population groups in this area, suffer from this exploitation (Pacheco 2004).

In recent years, however, it has become evident to all that the *Comités de Vigilancia* are of great significance in the political decision-making process at the local level by their important position in municipal planning. As a result, the awareness as well as the will of the population to make use of this opportunity of participation has increased. Against this background, the foundation of OTBs has been increasingly supported by regional, national, and international NGOs operating in the region. However, an uneven spatial distribution of OTBs that do not centre their activities around the department capitals has thus been created. This is due to the preference of the NGOs to be located in regions attracting national or international attention, such as municipalities that own parts of national parks.

When considering the important functions of the NGOs in the democratisation process and the shaping of political ideas, it is important to note that half of the NGOs are under non-Bolivian control. Moreover, the vast majority of the NGOs are not based in one of the Amazon departments (see Fig. 6.3). The cities Santa Cruz de la

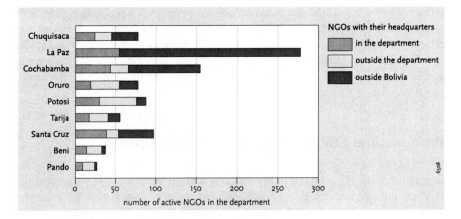

Fig. 6.3 Non-governmental organisations (NGOs) with activities in the Amazon region of Bolivia. (Ministerio de Hacienda 2000)

Sierra and La Paz in many cases serve as hubs of international activities. Even as non-place-based-actors, they are able to significantly influence local events. In this case, like with all NGOs worldwide, the democratic legitimacy is questionable (Wils 1998).

In spite of the relatively great number of OTBs in the Bolivian Amazon region, popular participation is still not warranted in many municipalities. For one, many OTBs could not receive the status of legal entities which would grant them access to the *Comités de Vigilancia*. Considering the high number of unacknowledged OTBs, one possible explanation is that their acknowledgement was delayed because they were politically not wanted. On top of that, *Comités de Vigilancia*, the actual bodies of control, have so far been founded in only 13 out of 36 municipalities. Even in these 13 municipalities, however, there are problems due to the fact that the local civil society has no experience with democratic practice, lacking strategies for solving conflicts of interests. As a result, there are frequent blockades during the process of decision-making, which renders consensus virtually impossible (Jost 2003). An institutionalised equal participation of all population groups in Amazonia has thus far proved very difficult if not impossible.

The slowly developing civil society is also confronted by the deficient and rigid structures of administration. These partly neutralise the positive effects of the political reforms. The departments' regional development corporations, which formerly had been appointed by the government, were dissolved, but their personnel was integrated into the new department administrations of the *Prefecturas*. The continuity in personnel has resulted in a reluctance on behalf of the new administration employees to accept the control function of the department parliaments. Moreover, the employees often show greater loyalty to the central government than to regional and local decision-makers (Urenda Díaz 1998).

Problems and Effects of the Reforms: Decentralisation

Despite the problems with participation, the decentralisation measures have brought about important changes in the political everyday life at the local level. Prior to the *Participación Popular* law, there were only 12 cities with their own administrations in the Bolivian Amazon region. The remaining areas were controlled by the central government. It is likely that only a few of its members had ever been to the Amazon region, let alone to areas beyond the cities. Thanks to the administrative reforms, 36 municipalities came into existence in this region practically overnight. They received political autonomy and thus the right to administer their own territory and manage municipal finances. In most cases, however, the new administrations were not prepared for these extensive responsibilities. Especially the small rural municipalities have to this day difficulties to fulfil their functions.

A major impediment is the lack of capable human resources – both in numbers and in qualifications. In some municipalities of the department Pando, public administration has only one employee – presumably the mayor himself. With the exception of the municipalities of the department capitals, the administrative apparatus hardly ever consists of more than ten employees.

The lack of professional qualification is also a common and almost insurmountable problem. The educational infrastructure in these settlements with only several hundred families at most is unstable and just good enough to teach the children how to read and write. At the same time, it is virtually impossible to recruit qualified personnel from other municipalities or departments. Skilled professionals from the big cities only rarely agree to move to such rural areas. Moreover, due to former political practice, few municipal administrations have experience in the fields of management and planning. The central government does offer training programmes to local administration employees in the hope of alleviating this problem, but as of yet has had meagre results.

The lack of qualified human resources is especially acute now that the decentralization and participation measures have taken effect and central importance is given to the municipal administration. Equipped with considerably higher budgets, the main responsibility of the municipalities is now to set up and implement a so-called *Plan de Desarrollo Municipal*. These municipal development plans are meant to codify the targets of development for the municipality for 5-year periods, but only few municipalities can properly perform this task. After our discussion of the fragile personnel conditions in the local municipalities it will come as no surprise that the majority of the Amazon municipalities do not set up such a *Plan de Desarrollo Municipal*, let alone develop detailed *Planos Directores, Planos de Manejo de Áreas Forestales*, or any other strategic and action plans (see Fig. 6.2).

Conclusion

The example of the Bolivian Amazon region shows how difficult it is to achieve good governance. Over the past decade, far-reaching reforms have undoubtedly been made in Bolivia, attracting great international attention. As they are implemented on the regional and local level, however, they quickly encounter their limits. Although national policy aims such as democratisation, decentralization, and privatisation include numerous elements which could offer a suitable basis for good governance, they meet with socio-political structures that counter their underlying ideas.

Unlike on the national level, the traditional social 'rules of the game' still prevail in the Bolivian Amazon region at the regional and local levels. There is a risk that influential actors inside and outside the region will abuse the evolving political vacuum resulting from a lack of neutral control for their own purposes. In most cases, this causes a participation deficit for the marginalized population. Thus, taking into account the weakness of the state and the still weakly established civil society, institutional reforms with participatory approaches may in part have contrary effects.

Despite all this, the state reform laws offer great potential. First of all, they have created the indispensable framework which allows for participation of even the marginalized groups. Additionally, the level of political decision-making has shifted to the level of implementation. Conceptual design and planning of local development programs now lie in the hands of regional and local decision-makers who can set up adapted strategies based on their knowledge of the regional problems and needs. Furthermore, the local administrative structures and funds are certainly secured by the political reforms.

Whether the reforms will actually achieve their goals depends last but not least on the support of the democratisation process from national and international actors such as NGOs and public institutions in Bolivia as well as internationally acting NGOs, governmental institutions of industrialized countries and international development agencies. The local power structures and the dynamics within civil society in this particular region are critical to the success of the reforms. Especially if political ideas are shaped and the population is empowered, there are good chances that good governance will promote local development in the region.

Chapter 7
The Changing Role of Farmers' Organisations in Rural Development and Decentralisation in Bolivia

Dicky de Morrée

In the Bolivian rural areas peasant households participate in different organisational forms. In this chapter these different forms, their functions in the agricultural production systems and the household economy, and how development organisations relate to them will be analysed. Research was carried out in villages in the north of the departments of Chuquisaca and Potosí, considered one of the poorest and most backward areas of Bolivia. The main organisational forms encountered in the research area are informal networks for the exchange of resources such as land, labour and capital; village-level organisations and village authorities; and economic farmers' organisations like producers' associations and cooperatives.

Special attention will be paid to the implications of the introduction in 1994 of a decentralisation policy in Bolivia for the above-mentioned forms of organisation. Under this policy, 314 municipalities were created, of which 280 are predominantly rural. In the rural areas, the population could present its priorities to the municipal council through the existing peasant and indigenous communities (the 'territorially based organisations'). Municipal planning exercises were carried out annually, using participatory planning techniques. The so-called 'vigilance committees', composed of representatives of the population, were formed to control local government actions.

Views on how decentralisation policies impact peasant organisation differ widely (Booth et al. 1997; Urioste 2001). In the optimistic view, decentralisation would lead to a strengthening of the organisational forms inherited from the past, popular organisations would present their own candidates for positions in the municipal council and gain power in the municipal decision-making structures, and the participatory planning model would generate a process of sustainable development in the villages. In the pessimistic view, however, traditional organisations would weaken as a result of competition with new municipal structures, the power and sphere of operation of the traditional political parties (which do not represent the peasants, but the *mestizos*) would be strengthened, and the new municipal planning procedures would produce 'shopping-lists' of desired projects rather than a coherent long-term development strategy.

P. van Lindert and O. Verkoren (eds.), *Decentralized Development in Latin America:*
Experiences in Local Governance and Local Development, GeoJournal Library 97,
DOI 10.1007/978-90-481-3739-8_7, © Springer Science+Business Media B.V. 2010

This chapter is based on research carried out by the PIED-Andino project[1] (Research Project on Livelihood Strategies), that was aimed at facilitating the implementation of appropriate rural development policies in the Andes region, taking into account the dynamics and diversity of livelihood strategies at household and community levels. In the research area seventeen representative[2] communities were selected. In each of these communities research was focused on eight households, totalling 136 households. During an agricultural cycle (1 year) the weekly time utilisation of all members of these households over the age of five was registered. Furthermore, in-depth research was carried out as to their sources of income, land use, sale and barter of products, types of organisational involvement and participation in development projects.

The Research Area

The research area consisted of the provinces of Oropeza, Zudáñez and Yamparáez in the north of Chuquisaca, and the adjacent province of Chayanta in northern Potosí (Fig. 7.1). This is one of the poorest regions of Bolivia. The landscape in the research area shows great ecological diversity. Seven different agro-ecological

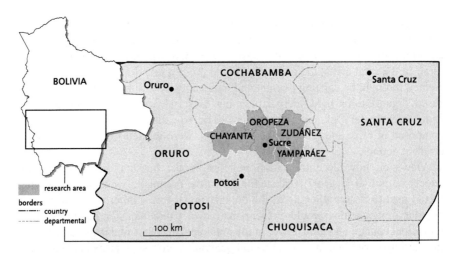

Fig. 7.1 The northern provinces of Chuquisaca and Potosí: the research area

[1]The project was implemented by a multidisciplinary team of Bolivian and Dutch researchers from January 1995 to April 1997. The research was funded by the Dutch ministry of development cooperation and carried out by the Royal Tropical Institute (KIT) and the consultancy firm SUR. The project resulted in two books (Zoomers (comp.) 1998, and Zoomers 1999).

[2]In terms of agroecological circumstances, market access, farming systems and the presence of development organisations.

zones can be distinguished. The area goes from valleys at 1,500 m to mountain ridges with a height of more than 4,500 m. Going from the west towards the east, it traverses the high *puna* of Chayanta with a cold and harsh climate and arid and rocky lands till it arrives at the low and temperate valleys of Zudáñez, with a pleasant climate and relatively abundant vegetation.

Landholdings are generally small and farming is household-based. At high altitudes the population is mainly dependent on livestock (lama raising), supplemented by small crops of *tarwi*, oats, *oca* and *papalisa*. In the intermediate zones, the main crops are potatoes, wheat, maize and barley. Here agriculture is subsistence-oriented. In the lowest zone the conditions are relatively favourable for the irrigated cultivation of fruit and horticultural crops for the market. Many households do not succeed in living on their agricultural income alone and try to get an additional income from other sources such as weaving and other handicrafts, or seasonal migration. The population belongs to different *quechua*-speaking ethnic groups (*llameros, jalqa's, tarabucos* and *pampeños*, among others).

In the last decades, since the 1960s and 1970s, processes of profound change have taken place, such as the introduction of agrochemical agricultural inputs and new means of transport, the massive migration to cities and colonisation of areas in the eastern lowlands of Bolivia, the emergence of new organisational models such as the *junta escolar* and community committees, and finally the introduction of vaccinations and other elements of modern health care. An important factor that contributed to these changes was the presence of development institutions and projects in the region since the beginning of the 1980s. These include both governmental/semi-governmental and non-governmental development organisations, which have implemented a large number of projects; both productive projects and projects focused on basic services (health care and education for example). The geographical distribution of these projects is quite uneven, with a high concentration of projects in easily accessible villages with a relatively large population.

Different Forms of Economic-Productive Organisation in the Research Area

In the researched villages, peasant households participate in various networks and forms of economic-productive organisation simultaneously. Many farm households have had contact with development organisations as well. For each of the different forms of organisation an analysis was made of the functions it performs in the peasant economy.

First, there are informal networks for the non-monetary exchange of such resources as land, labour and capital. Households engage in different relationships for the exchange of resources. These networks of peasants can be classified according to three variables: the types of activities the exchanges involve (content), the modalities of exchange (organisation), and the socio-economic status of the participants (stratification). In this study five categories were distinguished: cooperation based on kinship ties, *ayni* groups, *mink'a* groups, patron-client relationships, and inter-ecological exchange.

A second layer of peasant organisation comprises the village organisations (and authorities in the villages) that play an important role in the agricultural production systems. In this category the most important organisations are the *sindicatos*. In addition to the *sindicatos*, ancient, pre-Incan forms of organisation – such as the *ayllu* – also still exist in many villages. Since the 1980s many new organisations have been formed such as *clubes de madres* (mothers' clubs) and irrigation committees, many of which were founded to facilitate the implementation of a development project[3] and are linked to the *sindicato*.

The most important function of the *sindicato* is to defend the interests of the villagers and to represent them externally. The *sindicato* and other village organisations also play a role in the agricultural production systems. They create the necessary conditions for the functioning of the production systems by making rules and controlling their observance. The village organisation guarantees land tenure and solves conflicts over land, creates the conditions for rain-fed agriculture (by, for example, ruling that cattle should be tethered during the growing season), arranges the distribution of water in irrigated agriculture, organises the construction and maintenance of roads and other large pieces of infrastructure, and manages the collective natural resources such as forests and pastures.

In theory the organisational structure at the village level is flexible and can thus be adapted to changes in the production systems following the introduction of technological innovations. The introduction of irrigation technologies, for example, requires the executive committee of the *sindicatos* to take on new responsibilities for water distribution and the maintenance of the irrigation infrastructure. In practice it is not always easy to change the structure and functions of a village organisation. Processes of change can be slow and troublesome, and can cause conflicts between groups within a village or between villages.

Finally, there are economic farmers' organisations such as producers' associations and cooperatives, which have been established in order to support their members in their productive activities and the selling of agricultural products. Most cooperatives were founded in the 1960s, while producers' associations were founded more recently. Although there are only three regional economic farmers' organisations in the 17 researched villages, their importance should not be underestimated. They have many members and their activities are also important for non-members. Two of the economic farmers' organisations in the research area are involved mainly in trading agricultural products, selling agricultural inputs, hiring out tractors and providing other services. These two organisations are managed as a business. The main function of the third organisation is to channel funds for the

---

[3]Within villages benefits of projects are unevenly distributed. The most favoured persons are relatively well-to-do middle-aged males, with a relatively high level of education and experience as a board member (in the village organisation).

implementation of projects in support of small-scale dairy farmers. This producers' association operates as a development organisation, but is managed by farmers.

The way these organisations function produces a tension between the requirements of commercial management and the democratic character of the organisation. Mechanisms for rapid decision-making often do not tally with a process of consultation of the membership. As a result, the economic farmers' organisations hardly have any possibilities to offer a better price than traders. Despite these difficulties, the three investigated organisations have had a significant impact on the peasant economy in the region. They have, for example, brought about the regulation of the prices of agricultural products, fertiliser, pesticides and foodstuffs, as well as the regulation of transport rates and rates for tractor hire, and the provision of services that previously did not exist. Indirectly these organisations have also contributed to the strengthening of the position of agricultural producers vis-à-vis other regional actors (traders and transporters), and have influenced municipal policies.

Comparison of the Different Organisational Forms at the Village Level

How do these different layers of economic-productive organisation relate to each other? In Table 7.1 the three general types of economic-productive organisation of farmers as well as development organisations are compared based on nine variables.

The networks for the exchange of resources do not have a formalised organisational structure: they have a flexible design as regards content and how they function (rules of the game). The *sindicatos*, on the other hand, have a formalised, vertical structure. Through the frequent rotation of board members (a striking characteristic of this type of organisation) power is broadly spread. In the economic farmers' organisations the board is composed, either completely or partially, of representatives from the villages, but decisions are often top-down and the members (villagers) have less influence than members of *sindicatos*. The development organisations generally have a hierarchic and bureaucratic organisational structure, without farmers' representatives.

In general, the functions these networks and organisations perform in the peasant economy and agricultural production systems are complementary, which is why farm households usually participate simultaneously in different organisations and organisation types. The exchange networks facilitate access to labour and other resources a household may lack. The *sindicatos* (and other village organisations) promote the collective interests of the villagers and determine norms and rules for the optimal functioning of agricultural production systems. The economic farmers' organisations render services to support the production process (e.g. commercialisation, the provision of agricultural inputs and transport) and/or implement development projects. As is the case with many economic farmers' organisations, development organisations influence production systems by implementing projects. These projects are not always complementary to the functions performed by the

Table 7.1 Comparison of the different types of economic-productive organisation in the villages (De Morrée 2002, p. 148)

Scope	Exchange networks	Sindicatos and village authorities	Economic farmers' organisations	Development organisations
	Group of households	Village level	Several villages or a region	Several villages or a region
Role of the villager in the organisation	Participant	Member or member of the board	Member or member of the board	Target group
Organisational characteristics	Flexible and interwoven informal networks	Vertical, with a frequent rotation of board members	Vertical, with a board consisting of farmers and paid staff	Hierarchic
Physical infrastructure	None	Meeting hall	- Store/shop - Office	- Office - Training centre
Main function	Exchange of labour and other resources	Promotion of the interests of the members	- Services towards the agricultural production- Implementation of development projects	Implementation of development projects
Role in the agricultural production systems	Facilitates access to resources	Regulates the functioning of the agricultural production systems	- Services in support of production - Intervenes in elements of the production system (through projects)	Intervenes in elements of the production system (through projects)
Relationship with similar organisations	Interwoven exchange networks	Several *sindicatos* constitute a '*sub-central*'/a centralised organisation up to the national confederation	Can be part of a regional or national federation	Weak coordination mechanisms and competition (for funds and target groups)
Relationship with development organisations	None	Organises the village contribution (labour etc.) to a productive project	- Is given advice and support - Is given funds to carry out projects	(Not applicable)
Duration	Permanent, with a long-term perspective	Permanent, with a long-term perspective	Unlimited duration, in principle self-supporting (financially)	Emphasis on concrete and measurable short term results
Relationship with municipality	None	Mediation for projects	Weak ties	Advice to municipality, implementation of projects

exchange networks and farmers' organisations; in fact, some compete with or are harmful to the functioning of this type of organisation.

Another variable in Table 7.1 is the relationship with similar organisations. This study demonstrates that the village level organisation is part of higher level organisations, just as economic farmers' organisations often are part of umbrella organisations at the regional and/or national level. Development organisations, however, are characterised by a nearly complete lack of effective coordination mechanisms amongst themselves. They sometimes even compete for funds or target groups.

The exchange networks are permanent structures with a long-term perspective. Although the villages are becoming more and more integrated into the market economy, farmers continue to make non-monetary exchanges. An explanation for this is that participation in the networks gives households access to resources they lack in exchange for resources of which they have plenty, without having to pay cash. Furthermore, this kind of exchange gives them the opportunity to share risks with other households. As is the case with the networks, the *sindicatos* and other village organisations are also permanent structures with a long-term perspective. The economic farmers' organisations are in principle permanent as well. However, because they usually depend at least partially on donor funds, their survival can be quite uncertain. The activities of a development organisation in a certain village usually have a limited time-span. The development organisations aim at achieving specific, concrete and measurable results in the short term (in order to guarantee the continuation of funding).

In the villages of the research area there are different layers of peasant organisation. These layers constitute an intricate complex that performs numerous functions in the agricultural production systems. The characteristics of these organisational types differ from each other and from the characteristics of development organisations. For development organisations it is important to have a good knowledge of the different types of economic-productive organisation in the villages and their characteristics. When designing a productive project, development organisations should take into account the functions performed by informal exchange networks, *sindicatos* and economic farmers' organisations in the agricultural production systems, and the effects that the proposed project might have on these organisation types.

Roles of Peasant Organisations and Other Institutions in Rural Areas

How do these different forms of peasant organisation and development organisations compare to other types of organisation in the rural areas? Table 7.2 presents an overview of the different types of organisation in rural areas. In the table three dimensions are distinguished: the orientation of the organisation, the roles of individuals in relation to the organisation, and the mode of operation (Uphoff 1993).

Table 7.2 Characterisation of organisation types in rural areas (De Morrée 2002, p. 149 based on Uphoff (1993, pp. 613 and 610))

Orientation of the organisation	Roles of individuals in relation to the organisation	Mode of operation
Public sector:		
* Local government/municipality	* Political	* Voters and constituents	Bureaucratic/top-down
* Local administration	* Bureaucratic	* Citizens	
* Governmental development organisation	* Bureaucratic	* Beneficiaries	
Private sector:		
* Non-governmental organisations*Private businesses	* Charitable/non profit	* Clients or beneficiaries	Market processes/individualistic
	* Profit-making	* Customers/employees	
Civic sector:		
* Economic farmers' organisations	* Membership organisation (common economic interests)	* Members	Voluntary associations/bottom-up
* Village organisations	* Membership organisation (common political interests)	* Members	
* Informal networks for the exchange of resources	* Non-formalised organisation (common socio-economic interests)	* Participants	

The New Role of the State: Implications for Forms of Organisation in Rural Areas

In 1994 Bolivia introduced its decentralisation policy, with the passing of the Law on Popular Participation (LPP) followed by the Law on Administrative Decentralisation (LDA). Bolivia's political-administrative structure used to be top-down, with hardly any presence of the state at the local level and the exclusion of the rural population from local decision-making. In the framework of the new laws, a number of functions and competencies were delegated to the municipal government. The local government received some funds from the central government, but it could obtain additional resources mainly from national funds and international donors or through non-governmental organisations. The Bolivian government of that time had high expectations: the new mechanisms for the participation of the population in the planning of projects at municipal level would strengthen the role of village organisations in development processes.[4] Initially, the rural population was quite distrustful of the new laws. The so-called OTBs,[5] territorially based organisations of the local population were thought to be introduced as new and parallel structures competing with the existing *sindicatos* and other village organisations, with the intention to make them disappear. Furthermore, people feared that the municipal offices were primarily strengthened in order to initiate tax collection in rural areas (Booth et al. 1997; Torres 1998).

Next we will analyse how the changes brought about by the Law on Popular Participation have interfered with the different types of organisation in the villages, that is, whether the extension of competencies of the local government has strengthened or weakened the farmers' organisations. We will look at how decentralisation worked in rural areas.

The initial resistance towards the Law on Popular Participation and especially the OTBs was overcome quite soon. Many *sindicatos, ayllus,* and other territorial organisations in rural areas had themselves officially registered as an OTB in order to present their plans to the municipality and have access to municipal funds. Furthermore, quite surprisingly, during the first municipal elections of 1995, a peasant or indigenous mayor was elected in more than 100 of the 280 predominantly rural municipalities in Bolivia, and in 210 more than half of the councillors had a peasant or indigenous background (Urioste 2001).

As to the investments realised within the framework of decentralisation, the emphasis has been on small projects in the social sector, especially in education and health care. This dispersion has to do with the annual planning cycle. The municipality tries to allocate funds to all OTBs[6] every year, in stead of approving larger

---

[4]The implications for the exchange networks and the economic farmers' organisations were less clear.

[5]OTBs: *Organizaciones Territoriales de Base*

[6]Although the easily accessible OTBs benefit relatively more than the less accessible OTBs (Nijenhuis 2002; Torres 1998).

projects once every few years. It is also noteworthy that even in rural settings relatively small amounts of money have been invested in projects oriented towards agricultural production. These projects are more complex and difficult to execute, they are less visible, and their results materialise only in the long term. Especially in election times, this is not attractive at all for the mayor and councillors. Neither was it very helpful that functional organisations such as producers' organisations were excluded from the municipal planning procedures because they were not a territorially based organisation. Finally, the Law on Popular Participation was explicitly presented as a way of improving general living conditions and not as a rural development policy. As a result, municipal councils did not feel responsible for rural development.

As to accountability and transparency of the new local governance system, the main instrument was the forming of vigilance committees formed by representatives of the population in all municipalities. In practice, the functioning of these committees was weak. They did not receive sufficient information from the municipal council on the allocation of funds and they were not well informed of the demands of the OTBs as they did not participate in the municipal planning sessions. The model of vigilance committees is also said to conflict with the political culture in the Andes and it sometimes competes with existing organisations (Booth et al. 1997).

Final Reflections

Looking into the effects of decentralisation for the existing forms of peasant organi-sation, a number of problems stand out. Firstly, the administrative division of the country does not always coincide with areas that constitute a unity according to ecological, socio-cultural or economic criteria. In some cases the existing indigenous territories and traditional organisations are not recognised or respected because their boundaries do not coincide with administrative boundaries. This weakens existing organisations. Secondly, in municipalities where traditional organisations are still strong and where the new social structure clashes with the old one, the existing organisations are weakened. In contrast, in municipalities where the mayor and/or a large proportion of the council members are of farm extraction (often with experience as a farmers' leader in the *sindicato* structure), village organisations experience less problems. But in all cases, a political logic of re-election tends to dominate the functioning of the municipal government, and not the broader and more long-term development perspective propagated by many village organisations (Urioste 2001). Thirdly, it should be remarked that the economic farmers' organisa-tions do not have a clear role in the municipal structures and planning procedures because they are not territorially based organisations in spite of the fact that these organisations might have a bearing on production-oriented investments. A positive effect of decentralisation is that the position of village organisations vis-à-vis non-governmental organisations is perceived as having become more equal (Nijenhuis 2002, p. 169). This can be explained by the fact that these organisations can only gain access to national funds if they form a partnership with local government. This means they have to respect the municipal planning priorities. Therefore it is the community and the municipality that decide on which projects are to be implemented in a certain village, not the non-governmental organisation.

To sum it up, the Law on Popular Participation has created a new context with new conditions for the performance of the peasant organisations. However, the first results of research concerning the operation of these organisations are not unambiguous. Shaping the process of people's participation in the rural areas in such a way that the different types of farmers' organisation are valued and respected remains a big challenge.

Chapter 8
Constructing Regional Integration from Below: Cross-border Partnerships and Local Development in Southwest Amazonia

Cora van Oosten

Southwest Amazonia, a region which consists of Peru's Madre de Dios, Brazil's Acre and Bolivia's Pando (Fig. 8.1), may be perceived as a promising example of a cross-border alliance. Here, in the very heart of the tropical rainforest were Peruvian, Brazilian and Bolivian borderlands meet, local stakeholders have taken the initiative to build regional cross-border partnerships in order to combat their common problems and design and shape their joint development in a sustainable way. Since this process only started a few years ago, it is still too early to determine its larger impact. Nevertheless, the example is interesting enough to see how cross-border partnerships are being constructed and to speculate how they could form a platform for regional integration. The so-called MAP initiative provides an example of how regions could be shaped from below.

The Major Processes of Socio-economic Change in Southwest Amazonia

During the last century, Southwest Amazonia has undergone considerable change. In the socio-economic sense, the region changed from a typical provider of raw materials to a more diversified and more dynamic economy. Consequently, the region became more attractive for new investments and human settlement, which in turn triggered a process of socio-economic development. At first, new settlements were mainly concentrated in the rural areas (agricultural colonisation), but later on migration was more and more directed towards the urban areas, causing a rapid growth of cities and towns.

From a Borderless Indigenous Territory to a Provider of Raw Materials

Before the arrival of the first rubber tappers, Southwest Amazonia was usually seen as an endless, almost uninhabited 'no man's land'. In reality however, the area was home to a considerable number of indigenous peoples, living a (semi-) nomadic life

P. van Lindert and O. Verkoren (eds.), *Decentralized Development in Latin America: Experiences in Local Governance and Local Development*, GeoJournal Library 97, DOI 10.1007/978-90-481-3739-8_8, © Springer Science+Business Media B.V. 2010

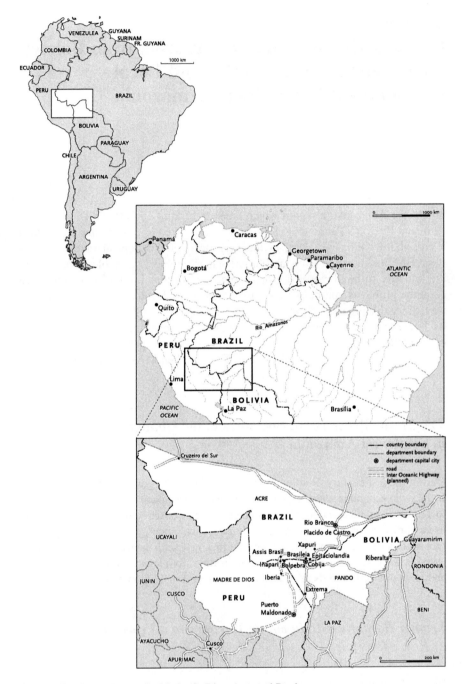

Fig. 8.1 Southwest Amazonia: Madre de Dios, Acre and Pando

built on hunting and gathering of forest products. In those early days, official boundaries were poorly demarcated and the 'Alto Acre' was considered to be part of both Peruvian and Bolivian territory.

With the increasing importance of rubber, a major resource for the rapidly expanding automobile industry in Europe and the US, the region gained importance. The area was increasingly occupied by pioneering rubber tappers coming from the Northeast of Brazil, from the area of Santa Cruz in Bolivia, or from the Peruvian Andes. Between 1910 and 1913 however, the rubber economy collapsed as a result of competition from Asian countries. With the rapidly declining prices, the rubber barons left the area, leaving their estates behind. In Acre and Madre de Dios the rubber estates were rented or abandoned, and the population established agricultural colonies or moved towards towns like Rio Branco and Puerto Maldonado. Production of rubber continued on a much smaller scale, heavily subsidised in the Brazilian case by the government. In Bolivia, the former administrators of the estates continued the production, although to a far lesser extent, leaving feudal production systems intact. In all three regions a start was made with the collection and exportation of Brazil nuts and the production of timber. The growth of Rio Branco, Riberalta and Puerto Maldonado opened up local markets for timber and agricultural products.

When the rubber economy temporarily revived during the Second World War, a beginning was made with new infrastructural disclosure. New roads not only facilitated a more rapid transportation of products, but also induced a new flow of migrants. When after the War however rubber prices dropped for a second time, these new migrants were left to their own devices. With the final bankrupt and disappearance of feudal landlords, peasant communities were established all over the area and a new class of autonomous rubber tappers and peasant farmers emerged (Assies 1997). People who did not find themselves a place in the changing rural economy migrated to cities like Rio Branco, Puerto Maldonado and Riberalta, where the first urban slums appeared.

During the 1970s, oil, gold, and other minerals were discovered in some places in Acre and Madre de Dios. This led to a sudden flow of migrants attracted by occasional profits. Concessions were given out to companies from outside the area and even foreign companies, underlining the original function of the region as a mere provider of raw materials and leaving little or no profits within the region itself.

The Emergence of an Agricultural Front

During the 1960s, more impacting colonisation projects were implemented by the Brazilian government and to some extent by the Peruvian government. In Brazil, the military regimes from 1964 onwards tried to populate their remotest border regions by means of settlement projects. Successive governments regarded the Amazon as unoccupied land where landless peasants from the overpopulated North could be settled, and where lucrative investment opportunities for the expansive economy of the South could be found (Godfrey 1996). In the same decade, Peru underwent a period of agrarian reform. The lowlands became earmarked as potential settlement area for landless farmers, with the hidden aim to avoid sensitive land redistribution in the highlands. Meanwhile, in Bolivia, similar programmes were carried out in and around the Santa Cruz department, where rapid colonisation and both government and private investments allowed for the economic take-off of Bolivia's Eastern region. The northern part of the country however remained largely untouched and maintained its image of remoteness.

The colonisation has had a devastating effect on the environment. Aerial photographs show that considerable deforestation has taken place around major towns and roads, especially in Acre, and increasingly in Madre de Dios and Pando. Around the Brazilian stretch of the new Inter-oceanic Highway hardly any virgin forest is left. Deforestation and its relation with agricultural colonisation have been studied by Naughthon-Treves (2004), who shows that deforestation in Madre de Dios was most rapid during the 1980s, when credit and guaranteed markets for agricultural and livestock products were available for colonists. Later, when these measures were removed, deforestation slowed down.

The Emergence of a Cattle Front

Raising cattle was highly promoted during the 1960s and 1970s, particularly in Acre, but to a lesser extent also in Madre de Dios and Pando. Further extension of the road network caused a spectacular increase in speculative land purchases and the establishment of ranches. The conversion of rubber estates into ranches and the expulsion of rubber tappers led to a renewed migration to the towns. More recently, the planning of the Inter-oceanic Highway through Madre de Dios has initiated a trend of land speculation along the Puerto Maldonado-Iñapari stretch, where forestland is now rapidly being converted into pastures.

Animal husbandry in Pando is a fairly recent phenomenon. It expanded during the 1980s, when a small and temporal credit line of the Inter American Development Bank became available to land owners (Bojanic 2001). Although in those days many producers managed to convert forestland into pastures, only a few were able to set up profitable businesses. Besides the advantage of credit facilities however, cattle ranching did not demand considerable capital, and offered one of the few investment opportunity for those with some financial reserves. When during the 1990s increased investment (both public and private) led to an increased inflow of financial resources, commercial ranches were established following the Brazilian model.

Deforestation started during the agricultural expansion, and rapidly increased with the expansion of the cattle front. While farmlands can still be restored to a certain extent after only a few years of exploitation, the damage done by the creation of pasture land is irreversible. The devastating effect of land conversion into pastures can most clearly be observed in Acre, particularly along the road between Rio Branco and Brasileia.

The Emergence of an Urban Front

The first Amazonian towns were established during the rubber era as centres of collection and commercialisation of forest products. As in those days the rubber business was highly profitable, these towns were exorbitantly wealthy, with architectonic masterpieces not to be expected in the middle of the jungle. The various periods of economic decline however resulted in the deterioration of these cities, and their glamour faded. Some towns found themselves a new destination as administrative centres, particularly important during the expansion of the agricultural front, where they played an important role in the commercialisation of products and public administration. These towns became attractive because of their employment opportunities, which brought about a process of urban–urban migration. Various authors like Godfrey (1996) for example describe this process for the Brazilian context. He states that, despite massive investment in land development by the government, the agrarian frontier had become an urban frontier.

Immigration from the highlands in Bolivia and Peru has had a changing influence on the cultural environment. Towns like Puerto Maldonado and Cobija underwent a process of cultural change: in Puerto Maldonado nowadays, almost 70% of the urban population is formed by highland settlers, dominating the commercial and industrial sectors. On the one hand, this cultural change leads to closer social and cultural ties with the national centres, something strongly desired by central governments who have 'nation building' high on their political agendas. On the other hand, it has brought about an increased debate between autochthonous and migrant groups, both of which strengthened their respective cultural identities, which has led to series of ethnically centred disputes and conflicts.

Urbanisation has had a positive influence on trade and primary processing of forest products. The combination of a consumer market and the availability of a labour force stimulated the production of agro-pastoral products and small-scale local processing activities. Particularly around Rio Branco, many small-scale vegetable, dairy and fish farms and production units of sweets, jellies and soft drinks can be found. Traditional processing industry such as the Brazil nut cracking factories were established decades ago, as they were financed with capital once accumulated in the rubber business. More modern oriented industries have also emerged during the last decades. Some of these were established with strong government support, while others were established purely through private initiative by companies that were attracted by the availability of raw materials, like the timber companies in Pando, Puerto Maldonado, and along the Brazilian side of the Peruvian and Bolivian border. Favourable fiscal conditions like Cobija's Free Trade Zone certainly stimulated the establishment of forest product processing plants.

Processes of Political Change

Besides the socio-economic changes, Southwest Amazonia has also undergone a number of political changes during the last few decades. On the one hand, processes of national incorporation have brought the region closer to the national political systems. But on the other hand, political decentralisation, together with a process of democratisation and social organisation, has made the region more independent from its respective political centres, and has left the region more than ever able to choose its own partners in development.

Increasing Incorporation in National Development Processes

The twentieth century was for most Latin American countries a century of nation-building. Countries like Brazil, Peru and Bolivia with arbitrary boundaries disrespecting cultural lines have always had problems with internal diversity and low national coherence, particularly in their border regions. The creation of a national identity has therefore been high on the political agendas. Acre, Madre de Dios and Pando are typical examples of such border regions, where national sentiments have always been overshadowed by a feeling of being 'different'. Migration policies were and still are being used by national governments to stimulate cultural assimilation and incorporation of remote areas into mainstream national cultures. Most of the time however, governments' attention was drawn towards more urgent problems of economic decline and social unrest in the densely populated central regions which had higher political priority, hence remote border regions were rather left alone.

Southwest Amazonia however has several attractions for national governments. First of all, Acre, Madre de Dios and Pando have always had large reserves of natural resources which temporarily enjoyed favourable market conditions such as rubber, Brazil nuts, timber, gold and oil. Declining economic growth during the past decades has renewed national interest in exploitation of the region's forest reserves. Secondly, in contrast with the densely populated central regions, the forested borderlands were far less populated and seemed to offer great opportunities for colonisation. Especially from the 1960s onwards, when population grew and land distribution politics stayed behind, migration offered a possibility for governments to relieve land pressure by stimulating colonisation of new lands within their borders.

Social Organisation and Political Awareness

The region's internal socio-economic transformation as described above has also brought about socio-political change. During the rubber era the region was dominated by a class of foreign pioneers, adventurers and entrepreneurs.

After the collapse of the rubber boom the majority of this dominating class simply left the region in search for other places where quick fortunes could be made. Their dominant role was handed over to their administrators and high rank employees, who took over the rubber estates and tried to maintain an image of powerful, however impoverished, elite.

In Pando, this group maintained its position almost up to the present day. Besides small-scale production of rubber (indirectly subsidised by the Brazilian government), the new landlords invested their meagre profits in Brazil nut processing plants, and maintained the feudal system of land ownership. Only very recently a beginning was made with a process of land reforms.

In Madre de Dios, land reform already took place during the 1950s, and the collection of Brazil nuts was organised in concessions, comparable to the exploitation of timber and gold. From the 1950s onward, Madre de Dios has been subject to immigration from highland farmers in search for land or, from the 1980s onward, escaping the violent highlands then dominated by the leftist movement 'Shining Path'. The land reform of the 1950s did provide access to land ownership for immigrant farmers, but hardly any social organisation took place since the major part of the country was ruled by 'Shining Path', destabilising the country and preventing any form of social organisation or political formation at either local or regional level.

The political transformation in Acre has been very different. Here, when the rubber barons left, the estates were abandoned or taken over by labourers. Migrants bringing along their own styles of production and social organisation soon started to dominate the social structure of Acre. A large number of the original workers of the rubber estates migrated to the towns, where a remarkable process of emancipation of the working class took place. Rural Workers' Unions were formed and soon gained considerable political influence, first by the organisation of resistance and land occupations, and later through the preparation of clear proposals for agrarian reform adapted to the needs of the populations living from the extraction of forest products. Their leader, Chico Mendes, gained international fame, not so much as the frontline fighter for land rights he actually was, but as a promoter of environmental protection, putting him in the frontline of the international environmental movement. He was killed in 1988, supposedly by assassins hired by influential land owners.

State Decentralisation

The strong state centralism of the 1970s was replaced by the transfer of political power and administrative management to lower levels of governance during the 1980s. The failure of states to help their countries out of the financial crises of the early 1980s and a strongly growing call for democratisation finally resulted in this process of decentralisation and administrative reform. The actual nature of the specific decentralisation processes within the three countries has differed according to their particular historical and political contexts.

In general, Brazil can be said to be the most decentralised of the three states. As a federal republic, the country is composed of a number of relatively autonomous federal states. This implies that de facto political power is decentralised to the state level, and that the state government of Acre has had relative freedom to design and implement regionally focused policies for a long time.

Bolivia and Peru have a unitary form of state organisation, meaning that the highest state authority is at the central level. Nevertheless, a process of decentralisation that started in the 1980s has brought about fundamental change in society. In Bolivia, special efforts were made in the field of participatory planning. Although the correct implementation of this law leaves much to be desired, Bolivia has managed to involve the entire population in a legally based system of popular participation.

In Peru, a democratic transition took place during the 1980s, following the general decentralisation trend in which the whole of Latin America was involved. In contrast to Brazil and Bolivia however, it didn't change the centralist character of the State's organisation. Decentralisation was a rather cosmetic operation, since the Fujimori regime of those days did not allow a serious process of democratisation to develop. Moreover, the country's political functioning was seriously hampered by 'Shining Path', which dominated large parts of the country throughout the 1980s and 1990s. Its doctrine claimed that open political participation and democratic reform would lessen the revolutionary fervour, and did everything it could to stop the electoral process as part of its revolutionary campaign. It is has only been since the defeat of 'Shining Path' that a real process of democratisation and decentralisation could take off in the more remote regions like Madre de Dios.

Increasing Influence of Regional Politics

While Acre, Madre de Dios and Pando were gradually incorporated into national economic and political systems, social organisation led to an increasing political awareness at the regional level. Decentralisation processes brought forth a new class of regional and local politicians responsible for the elaboration of regional development strategies, emphasizing the region's own particular identity. This has stimulated regional and local debates on the direction that regional development should take, a debate that regularly draws attention to the fact that different actors have different and often conflicting interests. More than once these debates have resulted in conflicts, sometimes even leading to violent eruptions such as in 2002, when in Puerto Maldonado the offices of NGOs and government agencies were burned down by local timber producers.

Although the region has to cope with regular conflicts of interests, these are in sharp contrast with the conflicts taking place at the national level, particularly in Peru and Bolivia. Economic decline and social unrest cast a shadow over the central regions of these two nations, and reduce the urgency of the relatively minor problems faced by Madre de Dios and Pando. This has contributed to a greater awareness of the region's peripheral location, which has given rise to regionalist feelings.

Especially in Pando, where relations with the national centre are least developed, expressions like *'let the highlanders resolve their own problems, we are half Brazilians anyhow'* can be regularly heard in the streets of Cobija.

Turning away from national issues and looking for regionally inspired models for development, Pando and to a lesser extent Madre de Dios tend to look more and more towards their neighbour Brazil, where in recent years the economic situation seems to have improved, and Acre's government ('Goberno da Floresta') is actively searching for appropriate strategies for sustainable development. There is an increased realization that Brazil is indeed one step ahead, and is therefore facing opportunities, but also problems far bigger than those in Madre de Dios and Pando (such as deforestation and urban poverty). In these days of weakening nation-states and threatening national disintegration the feeling is growing that a strong regional alliance might have more to offer in terms of economic growth.

Towards Increased Regional Integration

In the previous parts the major socio-economic and political changes taking place in Southwest Amazonia were described and translated into two major trends: one of gradual incorporation of Acre, Madre de Dios and Pando into their respective national economies, and one of growing regional autonomy of the three borderlands and their mutual integration. At present, the process of regional integration seems to be prevailing, influenced by the external trend of globalising markets and the internal trend of political changes. Moreover, regional integration has received a strong impulse by the promotion of cross-border partnerships through the so-called MAP initiative, which will be described later on.

Increasing Cross-border Activities

Economic ties between Madre de Dios, Pando and Acre have always been strong. Border town clusters like Assis Brazil-Iñapari-Bolpebra, Brasileia-Cobija-Epitaciolandia, Placido de Castro-Montevideo, and Guayaramarin-Guayaramirim strongly depend on their cross-border trade, which is to a large extent illegal because of the long and poorly controlled borders. The trade in timber is a good example of such illegal trade. Since Bolivia owns large and relatively untouched forest reserves, Peruvian and Brazilian timber processing plants are mainly concentrated along the Bolivian border. Another good example is the illegal trade of drugs. It is commonly known that Madre de Dios and probably also Pando contain a number of illegal laboratories which provide the cocaine demanded in the Brazilian coastal metropolises and abroad, and that Southwest Amazonia is a natural passageway.

The completion of the Inter-oceanic Highway has a huge impact on the region's integration and the incorporation of the region into the overall Latin American economy.

This 'Inter-Oceanico' is about to connect the Atlantic Ocean with the Pacific Ocean, crossing Brazil and Peru and touching on Bolivian borders (Fig. 8.1). The road has become part of the IIRSA-initiative ('Integración de la Infraestructura Regional en América del Sur'), a multi-national agreement between all Latin American presidents which aims at promoting regional integration through investments in infrastructure. It is largely paid for by Brazil's Federal Government in the framework of 'Avança Brasil', a huge investment programme which aims to boost the Brazilian economy and to integrate the region in national and international markets. The publicity around this road drew the cluster of Southwest Amazonian boomtowns into the (inter)national spotlights. Furthermore, the availability of natural resources, a growing labour force and a progressive political climate make for an attractive environment for investors. Several studies have attempted to predict the negative environmental impact, which will definitely be considerable. But so far, local and regional governments have been more interested in the expected positive effects it will have on the regional economy in the form of an increase in trade, investment and employment (Brown 2003).

Another indicator of increasing regional integration is the recent growth of cross-border investments. The Peruvian stretch of the Inter-oceanic Highway is actually co-financed by the Brazilian federal government, and constructed by a Peruvian-Brazilian consortium. It is said that Asian capital is also involved because of the estimated gas, oil and gold reserves yet to be exploited. All along the planned and already completed stretches a flurry of activities (hotels, restaurants, and fuel stations) is being undertaken by border-crossing Brazilian, Peruvian and Bolivian entrepreneurs. The new bridges connecting Brasileia-Cobija and Iñapari-Assis Brazil were paid for by the Brazilian government, while the construction of the Cobija International Airport and the new cold store facility in Cobija's Free Trade Area are joint Brazilian-Bolivian efforts. Alliances were established between Bolivian, Brazilian and Peruvian Brazil nut companies and timber companies, and a consortium of Peruvian-Bolivian-Brazilian timber firms is exploring new processing techniques and common commercialisation routes. A waste processing plant to be constructed in Epitaciolandia will serve the processing of both Brasileia's and Cobija's waste. Negotiations for a common energy supply are underway in Bolpebra-Assis Brazil. Along with the increased cross-border movements, the custom services of the three countries have recently created a task force to assess the possibilities for the creation of a regional Free Trade Zone and free movement of people and services.

These economic manifestations of increased integration are reinforced by the political changes which have taken place during the last decades. Social organisation and increased political awareness have formed the basis for the development of a regional identity, which became important in the light of political decentralisation. Although not yet perfect, all three areas are experimenting with new forms of democratic governance and participatory planning. A new class of regional politicians has emerged and taken up the responsibility for the elaboration and implementation of regional strategies. Regional and local politicians realize more and more that internal alliances might be advantageous and even necessary given the deplorable overall status of the Peruvian and Bolivian economies.

The 'MAP' Initiative as a Catalyst for Regional Integration

In 1999 a workshop was organised by the University of Rio Branco, and attended by a variety of institutions from Madre de Dios, Acre and Pando. The participants of this workshop shared the opinion that the region's environmental sustainability should be safeguarded within the changing regional context, and that this could only be done through joint action. Participants were convinced that the academic world could and should play a critical role in the development of such a regional approach, and a multilateral agreement ('Declaración de Rio Branco') was signed, giving birth to 'MAP', which stands for Madre de Dios, Acre and Pando. The intention of MAP was to create a regional approach towards sustainable regional development through the regular exchange of experiences between the three participating departments/states. A first regional 'MAP' meeting was organised in December 2000 in Rio Branco, focused on the theme of land use and land conversion, and its consequences. A second MAP meeting followed in 2001. The central theme of this meeting was the construction of internationally connecting infrastructure and the positive and negative impacts it would have on the region. A third meeting was organised in Puerto Maldonado in 2001, paying particular attention to the environmental effects of the construction of the Inter-oceanic Highway. In the declaration that resulted from this meeting it was stated that since the Inter-oceanic Highway would cut across the common borderland, joint efforts were indispensable in order to avoid negative environmental effects while optimising the economic and social benefits. This meeting was not only visited by academics and university-related institutions, but also by a number of NGOs and private entrepreneurs.

A fourth meeting was organised in 2002, around the topic of sustainable development of the Assis Brazil-Iñapari-Bolpebra cluster of municipalities. In the same year, a group of MAP participants developed a new concept of environmental education, based on regional realities. Moreover, a forum for timber producing companies on the potential of sustainable exploitation of the region's timber reserves took place. All these meetings were attended by local governments, civil society groups, and private entrepreneurs. By the end of 2002, the Monument of Trinational Integration was erected at the tri-national border, celebrating the occasion of the opening of the next-to-last stretch of the Inter-oceanic Highway. This ceremony was attended by the presidents of Brazil and Peru and high political representatives of Bolivia.

Subsequent meetings took place on a yearly basis. In 2002, in Cobija, a conference was organised around the theme 'sustainable development of the MAP region', which was attended by over 200 people representing universities, NGOs, national and regional governments, entrepreneurs, and a wide range of civil society groups. At the end of 3 days of debate an action programme was drafted to streamline activities for 2002/03, the results of which were to be presented at the next meeting in 2003.

In 2003, a meeting in Brazileia-Epitaciolandia carried the ambitious title of 'construindo uma historia de cooperação para desenvolvimento da região MAP', and was attended by more than 600 people representing almost all sectors of society. The programme was made up of the results of the many smaller meetings held during the year before. The general spirit of the meeting was defined as 'the growth of a cross-border social movement with the aim to promote cooperation and integration of the various segments of the local, regional, national and international society for a sustainable development of Southwest Amazonia' (Carta de Brazileia-Epitaciolandia 2003).

In 2004, a meeting in Puerto Maldonado was attended by over 1,200 participants. This meeting was characterized by a strong representation of national and international organisations and national government representatives. Central theme meeting was 'Education without borders'. For the first time, national governments and international institutions showed their interest and 'descended' to the region to listen to local ideas and initiatives. The plans and projects proposed by the IIRSA initiative were formally presented and seriously discussed with representatives from civil society and the private sector. After this, a multitude of general and sector-specific meetings (e.g. health, education, timber, Brazil nuts, customs) took place, shaping and guiding the trinational debate. In 2005, the three national governments officially acknowledged the importance of the MAP initiative, and the Federal Government of Acre decided to financially support the annual meetings.

In 2006, again in Cobija, a meeting was organised on 'Strenghtening the roots for a joint future of the MAP region'. During this meeting, the initial results of the first two joint projects on environmental education (*"Bosque de los Niños"*) and the trinational management of the Rio Acre river basin were presented. This was motivating indeed, since the preceding year was marked by a number of conflicts over some internal organisational aspects within MAP. There was a tendency to formerly institutionalise the process, allowing foreign donors to support the process, which rather led to internal division and competition. However, the meeting was well attended, and functioned as a necessary step-back to allow for further growth.

The 2007 meeting, in Brasileia-Epitaciolandia, showed that the MAP process had survived the organisational crisis of the previous year. The meeting carried the ambitious title of *"Cambios globales, soluciones regionales – sociedades locales diseñando soluciones regionales"*. A title which perfectly expresses the intention of the MAP initiative: local people taking their development in their own hands, and together searching for ways to cope with the impacts of global change, regardless the national boundaries cutting through their shared territory. Much time was reserved for discussions on global warming, and the importance of controlling further deforestation and environmental degradation. Hence, the seeds were sawn for a subsequent meeting, which is yet to take place in Puerto Maldonado, and which will have a strong focus on climate change, payment for environmental services, and reduced emission through avoided deforestation, which is totally in line with the international debate on climate-change.

All the MAP meetings have had a strong result-oriented character. Sector-specific meetings throughout the year all resulted in tangible recommendations, which were presented at annual MAP plenary meetings. Examples of sector-specific meetings include: MAP Indigena organised and attended by indigenous people, MAP Campesino organised and attended by farmers' associations, a MAP on education, on health, on municipal management and governance, on phytosanitary issues, agro-forestry, female municipal councillors, public security, customs, culture (including a film festival), etc. Moreover, several projects were born out of the MAP meetings, such as a project for environmental education, and the trinational management of the Rio Acre river basin. During the last MAP meeting (2007), a parallel academic conference was organised by the three regional universities, to present and exchange the results of research related to regional development and regional integration. This conference triggered the interest of local scientists to take the issue of regional integration in all its forms as a subject for academic studies and intellectual debate. So far, all outcomes of meetings, conferences and research, have been published on the MAP website and diffused through an electronic e-group.[1]

Is the MAP Initiative Considered a Political Threat or a Political Opportunity?

Brazil, Peru and Bolivia have all three experienced the threat of state fragmentation and the emergence of regional independence movements. Particularly Peru and Bolivia are actually passing through a difficult phase in their political history, threatened by strong manifestations of often regionally-based social unrest. In a way it can even be said that Peru and Bolivia presently find themselves in a process of disintegration, to the extent that many fear that regional differences might lead to a breakdown of the actual nation-states. Promoting regional integration movements in border areas therefore does not sound very attractive to the ears of national politicians, searching for unification of their national territories. This fear has been fed by local populist politicians who have been using the MAP initiative to their own advantage, to turn away from national political problems and gain personal popularity. Expressions like '*el futuro está aconteciendo*' and '*MAP, o nosso centro do Universo*', sometimes euphorically used in MAP documents, do not help in this regard.

Brazilian politicians do not suffer from this fear as much as Peruvian and Bolivian politicians do. In contrast, following the higher ambitions of President Lula, Brazil has taken up regional integration as a major aim. '*No entanto, os Acreanos estavam de costas para a Bolivia e o Peru e agora estarão de frente, tendo que conhecer um mundo diferente*', says Jorge Viana, governor of Acre, in a recent speech. Brazil, which is economically by far the strongest of the three countries, has always been marked by its desire for 'Grandeza' and domination on the Latin American continent. Regional integration forms a sophisticated way to actually do so.

Although neither regional independence nor expansionism are the intentions of the MAP initiative, and thus should not be misinterpreted as such, MAP is clearly more than just a manifestation of 'happy togetherness'. Without taking into account the Brazilian political attitude which may influence the outcome of the ongoing process, MAP should primarily be regarded as a positive attempt to 'construct a

---

[1] See for the MAP website: *http://www.map-amazonia.net;* for the e-group: *http://groups.yahoo. com/group/mapv*

region from below' through the development of a common identity, offering a platform for exchanging experiences and ideas, and forming concrete partnerships with tangible results. It has the potential to grow into a regional lobby mechanism compelling concrete actions from higher political levels, seen as the interest of the international development lobby has been raised.

It is difficult to assess the sustainability of the MAP initiative. Latin America has known many examples of positive initiatives which, after a period of rapid growth, lack tangible impact and die a silent death. But in this case, it is possible that the MAP initiative will realistically offer an opportunity for local cross-border partnerships to be formed and sustained. Partnerships which are able to trigger development processes beyond the level of the state, taking into account regional realities and economic linkages crossing national boundaries. It could be that in this way, MAP might provide a politically neutral ground for stakeholders with conflicting interests to interact and form coalitions. The platform function of MAP might thus offer an excellent opportunity to raise development planning to a larger political scale, and form a basis for regional and transnational governance processes to be constructed from the bottom up.

Conclusion

In the previous paragraphs an assessment was made of the socio-economic and political transformations in Acre, Madre de Dios and Pando, which together form Southwest Amazonia. Despite fundamental differences in the socio-economic and political contexts, the region is presently marked by the formation of cross-border partnerships, providing the basis for regional integration from the bottom up. Although the positive influence of this fast-growing network of cross-border partnerships on regional development is starting to be recognized by the three national governments involved, it cannot be denied that the three political entities of Peru, Brazil and Bolivia are also subjected to centralist state policies, characterised by strong incorporative drives, negatively impacting on the emerging cross-border partnerships.

From the 1990s onwards, Latin America has become gradually more incorporated into the global economy through increased international capital flows in the form of transnational investment and international loans, infrastructural development, and cross-border migration. Neo-liberal economic policies are increasingly focusing on the elimination of border tariffs and harmonisation of price policies, cutting down government spending, and privatising the public sector by opening up state companies to foreign capital bidding. This economic liberalisation has generated the need for an internal integration of the continent, in order to increase regional competitiveness on the global market. The formation of MERCOSUR and the Andean Community were first attempts to strengthen regional economies, but will soon be overshadowed by the Free Trade Area of the Americas (FTAA). Once this free-trade zone is opened up to participation of the Southern states, regional integration of South American states becomes less relevant. The formation of the FTAA however, has triggered large-scale protest throughout the continent, showing strong resistance against present global neo-liberal change.

Regional reactions to global changes however vary greatly. In Southwest Amazonia social resistance seems to be weaker than in other regions of the three countries, most likely because Southwest Amazonia consists of a shared borderland, built upon already existing cross-border social networks, with a strong external orientation. Instead of relying on national politics, the population of Southwest Amazonia seems to be involved in a pro-active search for alternative development models, which are externally oriented, and based on cross-border partnerships. The enthusiasm with which the MAP initiative was embraced, and the dynamic process of cross-border exchange it has triggered, are signs that local stakeholders do believe that regional integration offers realistic alternatives for economic development. Tangible cross-border investments confirm this belief.

The success of such regional integration from the bottom up however not only depends on local stakeholders' commitment, but also on the way in which national governments stimulate the process. Promotion of regional integration by stimulating cross-border activities, harmonising government measures, reducing obstacles in the field of trade barriers such as complicated custom formalities and tariffs on trade, would have a very positive impact indeed. But the willingness of national governments to do so is not guaranteed. It is quite imaginable that national governments, especially the Peruvian and Bolivian ones, would rather tend to frustrate the process because they view it as another regional divergence threatening their political mission of nation building. Furthermore, the Brazilian 'expansionist' attitude might also have a negative impact on national perceptions of cross-border integration processes.

No national democratic government is likely to be opposed to an attractive process of sustainable growth and democracy based on broad popular support. It does become complicated, however, if an emerging regional identity and regional economic interests do not correspond with political boundaries and interests. New regional alliances could result in a gradual fading away of national boundaries, giving way to other, more suitable forms of regional and transnational governance. Yet they might also provide arguments for nationalist political leaders to suppress regional processes which might feed separatist aspirations and claims for regional autonomy, with the argument of national sovereignty.

The future of Southwest Amazonia's process of regional integration from the bottom up is highly unpredictable. Unpredictable because of its internal dynamics, but more importantly, because of the nationalist reactions it might provoke. Given its importance in the light of globalisation, it is an important subject for further research, especially for development geographers, interested in local-global relations and translocal development. Lessons learnt from this particular process of bottom up regional integration might provide a useful example for other regions on the continent and beyond.

Chapter 9
Government, Governance and Governmentality in Pará, Northern Brazil

Dörte Segebart

Participatory planning approaches have become almost standard in rural development projects promoted by international cooperation agencies. In Brazilian governmental politics, an increase in participatory budget planning processes (*orçamento participativo*) on the municipal level can also be observed – until now mostly in urban areas.[1] Over the past few years attempts have also been made to introduce participatory planning in rural development, integrated into an official state programme to promote small-scale agriculture.

Despite such positive tendencies in planning, when it comes to the implementation of those plans formulated in a participatory way, local authorities – especially in rural areas – often fail to accomplish the plan due to a lack of personal commitment by political decision-makers and insufficient institutional capacity. Adequate participatory monitoring tools could contribute to facilitate public administration, serve as a management instrument, control governmental action, and improve the accountability of local governments, thereby strengthening good governance.[2] Successful (and unsuccessful) participatory planning processes and the implementation of participatory development plans may depend on the actions of the actors involved as well as on the specific political, institutional, economic, ecological, and socio-cultural structures.

Based on an action-research study in two municipalities in the Northeast of the Brazilian Amazon federal state of Pará, this chapter analyses the experiences of the implementation of participatory monitoring processes on the municipal level to identify some conditions for good governance and relevant factors influencing them. In the conclusion, some policy recommendations will be given for the implementation of effective participatory (monitoring) instruments and the strengthening of local governance capacity.

---

[1] The most popular case is the City of Porto Alegre in the Southern federal state of Rio Grande do Sul (Abers 1998, 2000; Genro and de Souza 1997; Lindert and Nijenhuis 2004).

[2] Examples of Participatory Monitoring processes in Brazil can be found in: Abbot and Guijt 1999; Sidersky and Guijt 2000; Franco et al. 2000; Segebart 2007.

P. van Lindert and O. Verkoren (eds.), *Decentralized Development in Latin America:*   129
Experiences in Local Governance and Local Development, GeoJournal Library 97,
DOI 10.1007/978-90-481-3739-8_9, © Springer Science+Business Media B.V. 2010

Assessing Governance

Good governance is not only hard to implement but also difficult to assess empirically. The concept of *governance* and especially *good governance* became famous from the 1980s onwards. Initially it was used by international (financial) institutions (World Bank, IMF, UN) to denote a set of criteria (such as participation, rule of law, transparency, responsiveness, consensus orientation, equity and inclusiveness, effectiveness and efficiency, accountability) (UNDP n.d.) that constituted the conditions for providing official development aid and conducting loans negotiations.

Governance means 'the process of decision-making and the process by which decisions are implemented (or not implemented)' (UNESCAP 2004). The term governance does not define specific actors, but operates under the assumption that in society there are various actors participating in or influencing decision-making and the implementation of decisions. The official state government is considered to be only one actor in governance; in rural areas, others may include small farmers, cooperatives, trade unions, landlords, religious leaders, political parties, finance institutions, NGOs, military etc. In order to further assess the complex concept of governance, it would be useful to elaborate first upon two other concepts which – when analysed complementarily – help us to formulate a framework for the assessment of governance: government and governmentality.

Government and Governmentality

The term government is usually more associated with state actors than governance. This can still include a huge number of different actors and interests, as the following definition states:
Government can be understood as

> '(...) any more or less calculated and rational activity, undertaken by a multiplicity of authorities and agencies, employing a variety of techniques and forms of knowledge, that seeks to shape conduct by working through our desires, aspirations, interests and beliefs, for definite but shifting ends and with a diverse set of relatively unpredictable consequences, effects and outcomes.' (Dean 1999, p.11)

The term *governmentality* was first used by Foucault (1991)[3] and was recently rediscovered in sociology, political science, public administration and development studies (e.g. Dean 1999; Murdoch 1995; Watts 2003; Ziai 2003). This concept is

---

[3]Foucault delivered a lecture about 'governmentality' in 1978 at the Collège de France, which was first published in *Ideology and Consciousness* in 1979 and republished in 1991 in Burchell et al. (1991).

even more complex to assess than the concept of government, as it refers to what we think about governing, governing others and governing ourselves:

> 'Thinking [about governing] here is a collective activity. It is a matter not of the representations of an individual mind or consciousness, but of bodies of knowledge, belief and opinion in which we are immersed.' (Dean 1999, p.16)

The concept of governmentality proved to be helpful in analysing political culture in a planning process or project and provides crucial information needed to determine the design of participatory monitoring instruments.

Government, understood in a conventional way as an official, legitimate institutional structure designed and acting in accordance with its legal mandate, and *governmentality* as the expression (or origin) of individual action could lead to a dualistic structure-action model of *governance*. *Governance* could then (in a simplistic way) be understood as being influenced by the specific local institutional *structure* and setting as well as by the *agency* of the individual actors and especially by their governmentalities (Fig. 9.1).

Returning to the initial, more complex definitions of government and governmentality, it becomes obvious that those institutional structures (government) and the governmentality and agency of an individual actor are located in a complex field of interrelations (Fig. 9.2). This makes the analytical dualism of action and structure obsolete and calls for analytical tools which consider that complexity.

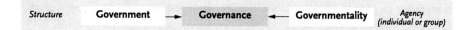

Fig. 9.1 Governance, government and governmentality in a dualistic structure-agency model

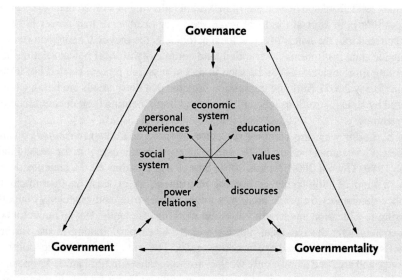

Fig. 9.2 Governance, government and governmentality contextualized

For promoting *good governance,* at least two strategies are discussed today, which depend quite heavily on each other and to some extent reflect the action-structure model: (a) to create positive external and internal (economic, juridical, political, institutional, cultural, social, etc.) conditions for the development, implementation and consolidation of good governance, and (b) to invest in capacity development, on both the individual and institutional level (GTZ 2003).

Local Context of the Study

Ever since the 'political opening' (*abertura*) in Brazil, the transition period between military dictatorship and democracy in the 1980s, attempts have been made to accompany and fortify the democratisation process with measures of political decentralisation. Finally, the new constitution of 1988 laid the foundations for the political decentralisation project (Soares and Gondim 2002). Although political and social scientists are aware that decentralisation is not by definition positive or negative, but that it depends on the design (Rauch 2001), this conclusion is not yet widely accepted in politics, also not in Brazil. Here the idea often prevails that decentralisation equals democratisation: it is considered the panacea to create *cidadania* (citizenship), participation, self-governance, empowerment and ownership, and also good governance. Moreover, decentralisation is often seen as a measure to propagate *new public management*, which aims at improving the efficiency of public administration.

In the light of the Amazon reality, and particularly its political culture (Emmi 1988; Hoefle 2006; Simmons et al. 2007), the decentralisation process at the municipal level is being judged quite sceptically by some scientists (Carvalho 2001; Dagnino 2002; Toni and Souza 2003). Instead of believing in a broad democratisation process that is to start at the local level, they fear or observe that power is being concentrated into the hands of a few local actors, e.g. the mayor. Clientelism (within or outside state institutions), corruption, and complexity of local power relations are becoming more evident as can be seen in recent research reports carried out in the region (Leroy 2003). Still, the impression remains that these trends are being widely ignored by state institutions when planning and implementing their decentralisation programmes.

In a similar way, the creation of sector-oriented councils (*conselhos*) on the municipal level since the late 1980s, and to an even greater extent in the second half of the 1990s (Jacobi 2000; Santos 2001; Soares and Gondim 2002), are considered to be a kind of monitoring or control instrument, or at least an instrument to enhance democracy. In urban areas this might remain true, and especially councils referring to education and health issues are working efficiently. But so far, actors of civil society who discuss local politics broadly when participating in the various councils have only had advisory competence. The councils have little political authority and are, as it stands, only weakly institutionalised in rural areas. Even so, in rural development programmes, the councils are allowed to participate in operational planning processes of the local administration, as well as in the definition of municipal development plans for sustainable rural development (*Planos Municipais de desenvolvimento rural sustentável - PMDRS*).

However, capacity in the field of public management is not automatically generated by the creation of new institutions or programmes. Political and administrative staff in municipal administrations in rural areas of the states of northern Brazil have generally had poor formal education, no specific training in public administration, and are characterised by a high fluctuation rate, which hinders the accumulation of administrative experience and skills in individuals and even more so in public departments as a whole.

The situation among actors in civil society is quite similar. The national programme for the support of small-scale agriculture (*Programa Nacional de Fortalecimento da Agricultura Familiar – PRONAF*) has carried out some training sessions and issued didactic publications for the council members, but these training sessions have not been offered in all municipalities served by this programme, and where they were offered, they were not established as permanent institutions. This means that adequate training for new councillors is still not part of a regular institutional routine. Besides, PRONAF only cooperates with the councils for rural development, and it does so only in some selected municipalities. In rural areas, the trade unions for rural workers may also play an important role in political education, but in general, the self-steering capabilities of the municipalities in rural areas in Pará continue to be relatively deficient.

Participatory Monitoring in Two Municipalities in Northeast Pará

The two municipalities analysed in this study are located in the northeast of the federal state of Pará (see Fig. 9.3). Ourém has a size of 562 km² and 15,000 inhabitants. Its economy is strongly based on agriculture (black pepper, manioc, beans, maize and some permanent crops such as coconut and orange). The majority of the population are small-scale farmers. Already in 1986, 73% of the original tropical rainforest vegetation had been altered. São Domingos do Capim has a size of 1,691 km² and 28,000 inhabitants. It is an important producer of manioc for Pará; other crops include banana, maize, black pepper and açaí. Only 20% of the population lives in the town. Eighty percent of the land cover is still forest.

On the one hand the research area is characterised by an economy based on exploitation of natural resources, strong social disparities, corrupt governors, insufficient and inefficient public administration, and clientelistic social structures. On the other hand, there is an active civil society. Moreover, a federal decentralisation policy is being carried out including a policy of poverty relief and the promotion of sustainable development.

In the early 1990s, the social movements in Brazil fought for more active government support for small-scale agriculture and finally achieved their goal:

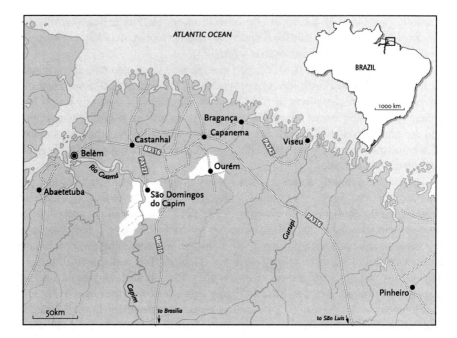

Fig. 9.3 The location of Ourém and São Domingos do Capim (NE Pará)

in 1996 the above mentioned National Programme for the support of small-scale agriculture (PRONAF) was created, which transfers federal financial resources directly to the municipalities each year. To be eligible for this kind of support, the municipality needs to meet certain conditions indicating poverty,[4] create a Municipal Council on Sustainable Rural Development (CMDRS), and draw up a Municipal Plan for sustainable rural development (*Plano Municipal de Desenvolvimento Rural Sustentável* – PMDRS). Today, PRONAF represents a central element in the Brazilian decentralisation process with regard to the development of rural areas. PRORENDA, a Brazilian-German Technical Cooperation Project under the supervision of the State Ministry of Agriculture of Pará (SAGRI), cooperates with PRONAF and supports the participatory setup of municipal development plans in Northeast Pará based on a Participatory Rural Appraisal (PRA).

In the federal state of Pará only a small number of municipalities carried out a participatory planning process. An evaluation showed that in most of those municipalities that did realise participatory planning processes, PRONAF's money was in fact used for activities and infrastructure projects supporting small-scale agriculture, but the strengthening of the council structures could rarely be observed (PRONAF/IBAM 2000). Unfortunately, in all of the cases only a few of the envisioned activities of the plans were actually put into practice. Therefore PRORENDA decided to support the implementation of the plans by testing a participatory monitoring system in two municipalities.

---

[4] They applied the International Human Development Index (HDI).

Participatory Action Research on Participatory Monitoring

The implementation of the participatory monitoring system was embedded in a participatory action research process (2001–2004) (Segebart 2007) in which the researcher analysed the process as well as serving as a mentor to the group involved in the participatory monitoring process. The monitoring methodology was constantly adapted according to local demands and conditions. At the same time, interviews with stakeholders in the monitoring process and decentralised regional planning processes were carried out.

Each of the selected municipalities had developed, with participation of the population and the support of PRORENDA, a municipal plan for sustainable rural development (PMDRS) in 1999 and 2001 respectively. The municipal council for sustainable rural development (*Conselho Municipal de Desenvolvimento Rural Sustentável* - CMDRS) was responsible for drawing up and implementing the plan. At the end of 2001 a preliminary evaluation was carried out to assess the implementation of the PMDRS as it had been carried out thus far. However, the results showed high deficiencies in the plan implementation. On this occasion the participatory monitoring system was presented, discussed and approved of by the Council.

At the beginning of 2002, 15 council members of each municipality were instructed in participatory monitoring in 2-day training courses. About nine of them – mostly small-scale farmers – afterwards formed the local monitoring committee. From then on the committee met once a month to discuss the implementation of the measures agreed upon in the plan. They tried to collect missing information where necessary, and all results were communicated to the Municipal Board of Agriculture and the Municipal Council for Sustainable Rural Development.

Some Empirical Observations

The performance of the monitoring systems differed considerably between the two municipalities during the first year of their implementation (2002). The monitoring process in São Domingos do Capim was accompanied by the author through monthly meetings with the monitoring committee from Jan–Dec 2002 and less frequently (every 2 months) in the first half of 2003.

In São Domingos do Capim the participants of the training course decided that the criteria for participating in the monitoring committee should be availability and commitment, meaning that the person should always be able to be present at the meetings. They decided that those individuals who had not yet held a leadership position in other civil society organisations should be given priority. It thus seems that they thought it would have the effect of decentralising power and capacitating new leaders at the same time, or at least strengthening their basis. The committee consisted mainly of small-scale farmers who had had a very low level of formal education. Even though everybody participated in the municipal council, not even half of the members can be considered active participants in civil society, participating in activities offered by a trade union, agricultural cooperative, church, or neighbourhood association. Different levels of participation in the committee could also be observed: people who participated more actively in the monitoring committee were also active members of civil society, displayed a highly political motivation and shared the same governmentality and vice versa. During the interviews it became clear that reasons for different levels of participation (more or less active) can be found in intellectual capacity (mostly based on informal education) and governmentality of the individual, and that there is a strong interrelation between the two. Brazilian civil society organisations mostly combine literacy education and any further capacity building measures with political education inspired by the work of Paulo Freire (Freire 1970).

While during its implementation the participatory monitoring process in São Domingos yielded many positive results and many direct positive impacts, the institutional sustainability of the local monitoring group could not be achieved. In 2002 the monitoring group in São Domingos had strong institutional support and was integrated into the administrative routine (Fig. 9.4). One possible explanation for this initial success was the presence of the Municipal Secretary of Agriculture during the years 2001/03, who was linked to social movements and civil society. The Municipal Board of Agriculture took shape, increased its resources and improved its internal organisation due to the work of the Municipal Secretary. At the end of 2003, however, the Municipal Secretary of Agriculture resigned, and the activities of the monitoring committee were not continued when the new Secretary assumed office. The development in 2004 showed that the monitoring committee had no institutional sustainability and highly depended on the Municipal Secretary of Agriculture – his person and his commitment.

In Ourém, the committee was formed during the training course, but the proper and continuous operation of the committee could not be established due to several political conflicts within the council. Therefore, some of the official members of the committee, who were actively involved in civil society activities in Ourém, had high intellectual capacities and shared the same governmentality, founded

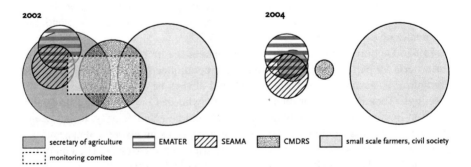

Fig. 9.4 Institutional setting of the monitoring committee of São Domingos do Capim in 2002 and 2004

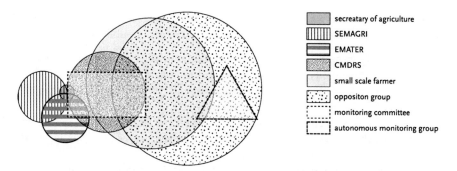

Fig. 9.5 Institutional setting of the monitoring committee in Ourém in 2002

at the end of 2002 an autonomous monitoring group to assess the whole public financing and spending of the municipality. This group is neither democratically legitimised nor does it have a legal regulation or a fixed internal organisational structure. Its influence and visibility in municipal politics is still quite limited; nevertheless, the group does still exist and monitors the actions of the municipal government (Fig. 9.5).

Civil society and its social capital were already quite well developed and politicised in Ourém, which allowed for better self-organisation. The civil society has a high capacity for governance, gained through experience in various organisational processes, proved by, for example, their building up and managing of a cooperative and a factory, the coordination of development programmes, and the administration of trade unions and farmer associations.

Conclusion

This comparative study has shown that

1. Institutional structures of municipalities in rural areas in Pará are still little developed. Therefore they are strongly influenced by persons holding office in a certain administrative department. The person's action inside the administrative structure, political position or general political commitment is determined by his or her 'personal' governmentality.
2. Even though government structures are similar in both municipalities, the governmentality of the actors differs even within a municipality and within the monitoring committee. The governmentalities of the actors determine their capacity of self-governance and therefore the effectiveness and institutional sustainability of the monitoring committee.
3. People actively participating in civil society possess a higher level of self-organisation and self-governance.

This analysis leads to following *policy recommendations* for a successful implementation of participatory monitoring instruments in public administration:

1. Participatory monitoring instruments should be flexible so they can be adapted to the governmentality patterns of the involved individuals.
2. Capacity development for good governance should consider local governmentality patterns.
3. Capacity development should be implemented on all levels, i.e. institutional structures should be addressed as well as the development of capacities on the individual level.
4. Governmentality patterns should be addressed in training courses: existing governmentalities should be made visible and possibly a common governmentality of the monitoring committee should be developed or agreed upon.
5. If institutional sustainability of a participatory monitoring instrument for community development planning is desired, the implementation should be accompanied by a rigid formal institutionalisation of the instrument and integration in existing administrative routines.

In summary, the consideration of governmentalities and governmental structures provides interesting insights and enriches the analysis of governance. The participatory monitoring instrument analysed here can only be as effective as its range of action permits. Its effectiveness is influenced by political and institutional structures, governmentalities, power relations and capacities. Even when conditions for implementation and institutional sustainability of the instrument are not very favourable, at least it provokes discussions about good governance and reinforces the official commitment.

The two case studies have shown similar as well as different conditions and results. Nevertheless, the analytical results listed above can at least be transferred and applied in other cases which present some of the following conditions: lack of access to information for the population, poor formal education of the involved actors, limited steering capacity of the governors, a lack of functioning administrative routines, high social disparities, and unequal power-relations.

Chapter 10
Changing Prospects for Sustainable Forestry in Brazilian Amazonia: Exploring New Trends

Mirjam A.F. Ros-Tonen

Over the past decade, issues related to territory, local governance and globalisation have changed tropical forest management in Brazilian Amazonia. Firstly, there is a trend towards decentralised forest management, the devolution of land rights to local communities (in the form of indigenous and extractive reserves), and a more significant role for civil society organisations (CSOs) in forest management. Secondly, globalisation is bringing about trade liberalisation, expansion of external markets for timber and soybeans, and the spread of a worldwide concern for the fate of forests. While trade liberalisation and expanding world markets may spur increased deforestation, globalising concern about the loss of the forest's ecological and livelihood services is creating new market-driven incentives for sustainable forest management and donor support to community-based forest management. The expectations regarding the outcome of these changes point to different directions. Many fear that the recent expansion of soybean cultivation and associated investments in road paving and improved waterways will further encourage deforestation and predatory logging (Carvalho 1999; Fearnside 2001). On the other hand, shifts in forest governance and market-driven incentives for sustainable forest management may signal a trend towards more sustainable practices.

Focusing on the Amazonian timber industry, this chapter explores the aforementioned trends and their implications for the prospects of developing more sustainable forestry.

Timber Extraction and the Agricultural Frontier in the Early 1990s

In the early 1990s, we carried out a study of the features and consequences of the timber industry in the state of Pará in Brazilian Amazonia (Ros-Tonen 1993). We applied a semi-structured questionnaire with the owners, managers or other staff of 71 sawmills and timber companies in the Santarém region (Fig. 10.1) and the city of Belém. Additionally, we conducted nine open interviews with autonomous lumbermen working in the Santarém region. These lumbermen, locally

P. van Lindert and O. Verkoren (eds.), *Decentralized Development in Latin America: Experiences in Local Governance and Local Development*, GeoJournal Library 97, DOI 10.1007/978-90-481-3739-8_10, © Springer Science+Business Media B.V. 2010

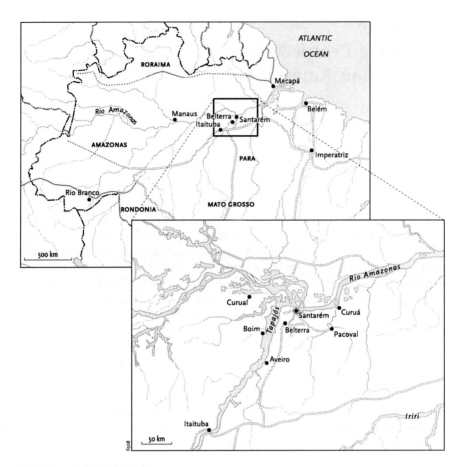

Fig. 10.1 The Santarém region

referred to as *madeireiros* or *toreiros*, earned their living by felling, transporting and/or selling logs.

Traditionally, in times when forests were hardly accessible over land, almost all roundwood came from seasonally flooded *várzea* forests which were only accessible by river. This changed with the opening up of the Amazon region and the road building programmes initiated in the 1960s. Since then, logging in the Amazon region is intimately related with the advancement of the agricultural frontier. By the early 1990s, we estimated that 85% of all roundwood originated from upland forests in recently opened and occupied areas (Ros-Tonen 1993, p. 74). As a result, much roundwood came from tracts of forests that were being converted into farming land and pasture. We estimated that 71% of all roundwood inputs of the sawmills in the Santarém region and 49% of the total log consumption of the surveyed companies in Belém came from clearings for agricultural land uses (Ros-Tonen 1993, p. 75).

The autonomously working lumbermen played an important role in the relationship between agriculture and the timber industry. The typical lumberman of the upland forest was the owner of a logging truck and often a small piece of land, who combined logging with farming. In the early 1990s, an estimated 60–70 lumbermen were active in the Santarém region. At the time, most of them lived in or near the city of Santarém. They were engaged in both logging and transportation, usually with help of three men: a chainsaw operator and two labourers to clear the logging road and load the truck that was driven from tree to tree. Equipment was simple and consisted of a logging truck equipped with a winch and steel cables to tow the logs, a chainsaw and a machete. The tracts of forest that were logged belonged either to the lumberman himself or to small farmers who had settled along the roads and had planned to clear the forest to plant their crops. Large landholders (*fazendeiros*) usually hired labourers to do the felling, often in combination with an investment in a mobile sawmill to saw the logs. Other large landholders made a deal directly with a sawmill or timber company to log their area, without interference of a lumberman. Deals between lumbermen and large landholders were therefore not common, in contrast with deals between small landholders and lumbermen.

In 1989, lumbermen provided 80% of all logs used by the sawmills in our survey, and 42% of the sawmills depended entirely on lumbermen for their roundwood supplies (Ros-Tonen 1993, pp. 75 and 85). At that time, the organisation and high costs involved in logging operations meant that even the larger sawmills preferred to buy logs from third parties. Another explanation for the important role of lumbermen must be sought in the traditional labour relations prevailing in the Amazonian extractive economy known as the *aviamento* system. Under this system, the extractor (rubber tapper or logger) receives an advance in the form of merchandise, tools and/or money in exchange for the physical product at the end of the expedition. Many features of this system still prevail in the extraction of forest products, including timber. These labour relations are still widespread, albeit sometimes in an adapted form.

The relation between timber exploitation and agriculture in settlement areas was also reflected in the technology employed. Of the sawmills that employed their own logging crew (58% of the total number surveyed) only 14% used specialised forestry equipment, such as front-end loaders, bulldozers and skidders. Forty-four percent used the so-called *catraca* system that was also used by autonomous lumbermen. In this system a simple logging truck is driven from tree to tree and the logs are directly togged onto the truck, using the winch and steel cables with which the truck is equipped. The rest of the sawmills that had their own logging operations, 42%, used one extra machine in addition to the logging truck and chainsaw. This was usually a modified farm tractor which was also used in agriculture, equipped with hooks and steel cables to haul the logs.

Another characteristic that reflected the connection between timber exploitation and the agricultural frontier in Brazilian Amazonia was the source of roundwood: 61% of the surveyed sawmills regularly made a deal with agricultural colonists who exchanged trees for money, sawnwood, the construction of a secondary road or a small bridge, or machine loans. Selling trees or logging rights thus provided both peasants and cattle raisers with the financial or technical means for the conversion of forests into farm land or pasture.

The conditions under which roundwood was provided to the sawmills did not make a sound basis for the sustainable management of forest resources. Most sawmills had no direct links to the roundwood source, and where they did, they tended to convert their forest into farmland. Most sawmill owners were agricultural colonists, for whom operating a sawmill was mostly a temporary and collateral activity to benefit from valuable timbers that became available from clearings. Only a small minority of saw-mills engaged directly in logging with the primary purpose of timber exploitation. Although they were the only potential actors to invest in sustainable forest manage-ment, competition from cheap tropical hardwood supplies from clearings by colonists and cattle ranchers discouraged them to do so. In sum, the close association between the timber industry and the expansion of agricultural frontiers in Brazilian Amazonia seriously hindered the development of sustainable forestry, which was hardly able to compete with cheap timber from unsustainably managed sources.

The Situation Today

More recent diagnostic studies of the timber industry in Pará (Veríssimo et al. 2003) and the Brazilian Amazon region as a whole (Macqueen et al. 2003; Lentini et al. 2003, 2005) largely confirm the patterns described above (Table 10.1). There is still a strong relationship between colonisation and timber exploitation, as shown by the emergence of new timber-processing centres (*polos madeireiros*) in recently opened up frontier areas such as Novo Progresso in Western Pará and the declining production in the old frontier areas of Southern and Eastern Pará, where forest resources are being depleted. Smeraldi (2003) estimated that 75% of all extracted

Table 10.1 Main features of roundwood supply in the state of Pará in the early and late 1990s

Feature	Source:	Ros-Tonen (1993)	Veríssimo et al. (2003)
Roundwood source			
	• Owned by the sawmill	49%*	36%**
	• Third parties	61%*	55%**
	• Publicly owned areas	17%*	9%**
Proportion of wood provided to sawmills by lumbermen		80%	44%
Proportion of sawmills depending solely on lumbermen		42%	45%
Proportion of roundwood originating from clearings		71%	n.a.
Proportion of sawmills logging at low technological level (*catraca* system)		39%	12%

* Proportion of sawmills; more options are possible so that total is larger than 100%.
** Proportion of roundwood.

roundwood currently comes from legally approved clearings in the settlement areas, where farmers are allowed to clear 3 ha of their 100 ha plot per year up to a maximum of 20% of their property.

Moreover, little seems to have changed with respect to the tenure of the roundwood source: Veríssimo et al. found that 36% of the roundwood used in Pará in 1998 came from forest land owned by the sawmill, 55% from third parties including independent lumbermen and timber merchants, and 9% from publicly owned areas (Table 10.1).

Autonomous lumbermen still play an important role in the provision of roundwood, although the various sources indicate different trends. Data presented in Veríssimo et al. (2003, p. 35) suggests a declining role for lumbermen in the Santarém region: the authors estimate that 44% of all roundwood extracted in this region in 1998 was provided by autonomous lumbermen, whereas this proportion was 80% in our 1989 survey (Ros-Tonen 1993). In the new timber-processing centres in Western Pará, the proportion of sawmills that depend on third parties for timber extraction is even lower: here only 22% of the roundwood is provided by autonomous lumbermen, while 78% comes from the sawmills' own explorations (Veríssimo et al. 2003, p. 34). However, according to Lima and Merry (2003, p. 85) the proportion of sawmills that depend on third parties for 80–100% is still substantial: 80% of the small sawmills, 50% of the medium-sized sawmills and 25% of the large enterprises. The proportion of large enterprises depending for the most part on third parties is remarkably low compared to the 89% we found after interviewing large enterprises in Belém 10 years earlier.

For the state as a whole, an up-scaling of the machinery used in timber exploration seems to have occurred. According to the inventory by Veríssimo et al. (2003) 12% of the extracted wood in Pará is exploited using the capital extensive *catraca* system in which a logging truck is used for hauling the logs. This is low compared to what we found in our 1993 study (39% of the sawmills with own operations and all operations by lumbermen). In the Santarém region, however, 65% of the logging operations are still undertaken using the *catraca* system (Veríssimo et al. 2003, p. 35), which is high compared to the other timber zones identified in their study (ranging from 0–4% in Southern and Eastern Pará to 25% in Western Pará and 31% in the Islands region).

Smeraldi (2003, pp. 50–51) notes that two government measures in the early 1990s facilitated the import of high-quality technology. First, the Brazilian government abolished the tariffs on equipment produced outside of Brazil. Second, it adopted the Kandir Act in September 1996, which included an exemption from payment of the ICMS (*Imposto sobre a Circulação de Bens e Serviços* – a value added tax or goods and services tax) for the export of primary and semi-processed goods, the acquisition of capital goods, the use of energy, and company consumption of goods. These measures enabled the Amazonian timber industry to import skidders, trucks and other equipment previously beyond the reach of most enterprises. Although this does not seem to have changed the industry's technological level as a whole, it has had a tremendous effect on the productivity and efficiency of timber companies and the quantities they exported. With regard to the efficiency of the timber industry, Lentini et al. (2005, p. 62) confirm that the average wood-processing efficiency increased from 38% to 42% between 1998 and 2004.

Expansion of Soybean Cultivation as a Catalyst for Predatory Logging

The relationship between logging and agricultural development at the agricultural frontier received a new impulse in the last decade following the expansion of soybean cultivation. Soybean cultivation in Brazil nearly doubled in the past decade from 11.7 million hectares in 1994 to 22.9 million hectares in 2005, of which 30% (7 million hectares) is being cultivated in the Legal Amazon[1] (USDA/FAS 2004, 2005). It was driven by a booming world demand, which rose by 52% between 1994 and 2004 (USDA/FAS 2004). The demand comes from Europe where soy meal is used to feed poultry and pigs, and from Asia where soy is consumed as oil (Fearnside 2001). Fearnside notes that the demand for Brazilian soybeans received an impulse in particular after the collapse of the Peruvian anchovy fisheries in the 1970s and the concomitant decline in fishmeal supplies. Declining soy yields in the US were another catalyst to the demand for Brazilian soybeans. Finally, the introduction in the 1990s of high-yielding tropical soybean varieties adapted to the growing conditions in the Brazilian Amazon "let the Genie out of the bottle" (USDA/FAS 2004).

In order to get the soybeans to the external markets, heavy investments have been made in the improvement of waterways and road paving (Carvalho 1999). The government's *Avança Brasil* ('Forward Brazil') programme of 1999 envisaged a US$ 43.6 billion investment in infrastructure, of which an estimated US$ 20.1 billion is destined for road building and paving, the construction of ports, airports, railways and cargo facilities, the canalisation and dredging of waterways and other projects that are likely to affect forests (Laurance et al., 2001). It is expected that the 6,245 km of paved highways planned under this programme will nearly double the forest area available to loggers, opening up hitherto inaccessible areas (Carvalho et al. 2002). Studies by Nepstad et al. (2002a,b) and Carvalho et al. (2002) indicate that the expansion and paving of the road network will further stimulate logging activities because of lower transportation costs, which will make the exploitation of a greater number of species profitable. The newly paved roads will also allow for larger volumes to be transported. These effects taken together make the above-mentioned authors believe that an intensification of logging is likely to occur in the zones within 50 km adjacent to the improved roads (Nepstad et al., 2002a,b; Carvalho et al. 2002). In Novo Progresso along the Santarém-Cuiabá (BR-163), for example, the number of sawmills had already increased from 10 in 1997 to 60 in 2000 in anticipation of road paving and potential savings in transportation costs (Carvalho et al. 2002).

Several authors fear that the improved waterways and roads will stimulate illegal logging. Fearnside (1997, 2001), for example, claims that the areas around the

---

[1] The Legal Amazon comprises the entire states of Acre, Amapá, Amazonas, Mato Grosso, Pará, Rondônia, Roraima and Tocantins and part of the state of Maranhão (east of the 44° W meridian).

Santarém-Cuiabá Highway are already a major source of illegally cut mahogany and that its paving would give a new impulse to illegal logging. Carvalho (1999) expects that the improvement of waterways will stimulate illegal logging as well, by providing an outlet for wood felled without proper licenses.

It should be noted that in tropical rain forest areas, in contrast to the savannah areas, the relationship between the expansion of soybean cultivation and deforestation is mostly an indirect one. The preferred location for soybean plantations is on degraded soils – usually former pastures – and other already deforested areas, because these require less intense fertilisation with lime than the more acid forest soils. Consequently, many small landholders have been expelled from their lands because of advancing soybean plantations (Carvalho 1999). These displaced farmers face the choice of migrating to nearby cities or moving deeper into the forest where they clear new land. If they choose for the latter, the model of colonisation-related logging and sawmilling described above is reproduced in the new frontier areas.

Recent Changes that May Curb the Predatory Trends

The above suggests that little has changed in roundwood supply patterns and that the infrastructural changes following the expansion of soybean cultivation will only perpetuate and strengthen predatory exploitation forms. There are, however, several trends with potentially positive effects on the prospects for sustainable forest management: (i) increasing scarcity of timber in the most accessible areas, (ii) new market and donor-driven incentives for sustainable industrial and community-based forest management, and (iii) decentralisation of forest management and devolution of forest land to local communities and forest users.

Increasing Scarcity of Roundwood Resources

It has been argued that increasing wood scarcity could serve as an incentive to increase investments in sustainable forest management, at least for large timber companies (Stone 1997, 1998). For smaller sawmills this is unlikely to occur. Sawmilling in the Amazon is a highly mobile activity, following the dynamics of the agricultural frontier as long as roundwood is supplied from clearings of virgin forest for agriculture. In recently opened up settlement areas, the sawmills are run until the roundwood supplies in the direct vicinity are depleted (Scholz 2001). The machines are then sold and their former owners focus on farming again. This process is illustrated by the recent establishment of most sawmills: in 1989 about half of the surveyed sawmills were less than 5 years old (Ros-Tonen 1993). Also data collected by Veríssimo et al. in 1998 revealed that half of the enterprises in Pará had started their activities in the 1990s (ranging from 24% in the Islands region, to 53% in the older frontier areas and 100% in the new frontier areas in Western Pará).

The sawmills are more mobile than their owners: our survey in 1989 indicated that 71% of the sawmills along the Transamazônica were bought second-hand after having been in service for one or more previous owners at different locations for many years.

Studies carried out by Stone (1997, 1998) reveal the economic dynamics of this relocation process in situations of increasing timber scarcity. He used an adapted version of the eighteenth century Von Thünen location model to analyse the dynamics of the timber industry along an ageing frontier. He found that the distance to markets, level of transportation costs, net timber prices and degree of certainty about property rights affected the spread and development of the timber industry and the willingness to invest in sustainable forest management and advanced technologies. Initially, firms cope with increasing scarcity of forest land by investing in larger trucks (to bridge larger distances and reduce transportation costs) and advanced technologies (to reap the benefits of economies of scale). When scarcity increases further, the sawmills are confronted with the choice either to re-invest in forest management (an option for larger sawmills and wood-processing industries), closing (the best option for small sawmills), or relocating to more remote areas and starting the cycle anew (Stone 1998).

Scholz (2001) found that most entrepreneurs respond defensively to timber scarcity, calling for subsidies and changes to the forest statute. She expects little investment in sustainable forest management, because the limited number of marketable species makes exploitation forms other than selective logging unprofitable. She therefore considers the option of creating plantations more plausible than investing in the sustainable management of highly heterogeneous natural forests. Since this option is only feasible for large companies, the expectation is that most sawmills will close and be re-opened elsewhere when exploitable timber in a particular location becomes scarce.

Market and Donor-driven Incentives for Sustainable Forest Management

It has often been feared that economic globalisation would pose a threat to tropical forests. It would do so by opening up markets and boosting international demand for legally and illegally logged hardwood and other tropical forest products. In light of recent developments in soybean cultivation, the opponents of globalisation appear to be in the right. There is, however, another side to the matter, as the same process of globalisation is spreading worldwide concern about the loss and degradation of tropical forests and their global ecological services such as maintaining biodiversity, carbon sequestration and watershed protection. An increasing number of international forest-related conventions and agreements have emerged to protect both these global values and those at the local livelihood level such as the supply of food, medicines, timber and fuelwood, and recreational, religious and spiritual functions (Bass 2002).

Although Brazil has always stressed that the development and conservation of its forests is a matter of national jurisdiction, it has nonetheless linked up with the trend towards global forest governance (referred to as the International Forest Policy Dialogue). It has developed its National Forest Programme with the aim of promoting sustainable forest development (Ministry of the Environment 2002) and implementing both the (non-binding) Forest Principles and Chapter 11 on Combating Deforestation of Agenda 21, both adopted at the United Nations Conference on the Environment and Development (UNCED or Rio-92). It was also one of the eight countries taking the initiative to develop the United Nations Forum on Forests (UNFF) which was created to provide a more permanent home for the International Forest Policy Dialogue and a platform for exchanging experiences among governments and other stakeholders in sustainable forest management. However, most international agreements and processes have probably had little impact on how the Amazon forest is being managed in practice. Greater influence seems to come from three other initiatives and processes that emerged or gained ground in the 1990s:

- The Group of Seven[2] most industrialised countries' initiative to set up the Pilot Programme to Conserve the Brazilian Rain Forests (PPG-7);
- The creation of niche markets for environmental services like biodiversity conservation, carbon sequestration and watershed protection and for sustainably produced timber and non-timber forest products, particularly from certified operations;
- The emergence of global-local partnerships for forest conservation and sustainable forest use.

The Pilot Programme to Conserve the Brazilian Rain Forests (PPG-7)

The PPG-7 was set up in 1992 as a partnership between the Brazilian Government, Brazil's civil society, the international community and the World Bank to promote the conservation and sustainable use of tropical rain forest resources and to reduce deforestation and CO_2 emission rates. Apart from the G-7 countries, funding comes from the European Union, the Netherlands, and Brazil itself, totalling about US$ 340 million. The World Bank administers the multi-donor Rain Forest Trust Fund and coordinates the programme together with the Brazilian government. The PPG-7 has been instrumental in particular in strengthening civil society organisations dealing with the Amazon region and in stimulating new forms of cooperation with and participation of these organisations in Brazilian public administration (Scholz 2005). Among other activities, the PPG-7 has provided institutional support to the *Grupo de Trabalho Amazônico* (GTA), a network of 602 environmental, community-based

---

[2] The G-7 comprises of Canada, France, Germany, Italy, Japan, the United Kingdom and the United States.

and other civil society organisations in the Amazon region, which now plays a decisive role in policy and decision-making with regard to the region's development. Moreover, community-based forest management schemes have received an impulse from a part of the PPG-7 programme known as 'Demonstration Projects'. Between 1995 and 2004, the Demonstration Projects under PPG-7 have supported 194 community-based projects (147 in the Amazon region and 47 in the Atlantic Forest region), with an average grant of US$ 113,607 each.[3]

Market-based Instruments

Another globalisation-related trend that might change forest management practices is the creation of market-based instruments for sustainable forest management. Part of these incentives, such as the trade in environmental services, are aimed at maintaining ecological values such as biodiversity and habitat (see Pagiola et al. 2002 for a review of market-based approaches to forest conservation). Others, such as the certification of timber or non-timber forest products from sustainably managed sources, are aimed at improving forest management practices so that forest products are produced in an ecologically sustainable, economically viable and socially equitable manner.

Consumer pressure has created a demand for sustainably produced timber and certificates testifying that forest products come from sustainably managed sources. With support from the German agency for international cooperation, GTZ, and the World Wide Fund for Nature, WWF-Brazil, 18 leading social and environmental organisations in Brazil formed a Forest Stewardship Council (FSC) Working Group in 1997 to define nationally appropriate criteria and indicators for sustainable forest and plantation management (May 2002; Freitas 2003). In 2001, FSC officially recognised the working group as an FSC National Initiative, and standards for Amazon upland forest management became official in 2002. Since then, the area of native forest has rapidly expanded. According to Lentini et al. (2005, p. 86) there were 22 certified forestry operations in the Amazon region in May 2005. Twelve of these were run by private enterprises, seven were community-based management schemes and three were private plantations of teak (*Tectona grandis*) and eucalypt (*Eucalyptus* sp.). Together, these projects cover an area of about 1,200,000 ha of native forest and 444,000 ha of plantations. In 2003, the certified projects were responsible for approximately 1.5% of the wood produced in the Brazilian Amazon (Freitas 2003). Although these developments signal a positive trend towards responsible forest management, several factors hinder more widespread certified wood production in the Brazilian Amazon. These factors include a lack of clear tenure arrangements, a lack of qualified personnel, poor access to information, an unclear and unstable regulatory framework, lack of credit facilities and, last but not least, unfair competition with cheap roundwood from clearings and illegal sources (May 2002; Freitas 2003).

---

[3] See htpp://www.worldbank.org/rfpp and htpp://www.mma.gov.br for background documents and further information about PPG-7.

Global–Local and Corporate–Community Partnerships

The third outcome of the globalisation of environmental concerns is that local actors in forest management are increasingly becoming connected with international actors such as environmental NGOs and research organisations lending support to sustainable forest use. This has resulted in new forums for stakeholder negotiations, partnerships, alliances and joint actions for the conservation and sustainable management of forests. At the local level, partnerships for the protection and co-management of forest resources are emerging between international donors, government agencies, national and international NGOs, private sector actors, research organisations and local communities (Ros-Tonen 2007).

In Pará, such multi-scale and multi-stakeholder partnerships for sustainable forest management include the GTZ ProManejo programme for sustainable forest management and the Large-Scale Biosphere-Atmosphere Experiment in Amazonia (LBA) in the National Tapajós Forest, community forestry programmes under the PPG-7, and MAFLOPS (*Manejo Florestal e Prestação de Serviços*; Forest Management and Services). MAFLOPS is a company-community partnership between a small logging company and smallholders along the Santarém-Cuiabá road (BR-163) aimed at sustainable timber extraction at smallholder level (Lima et al. 2003; Nepstad et al. 2005). The project aims to achieve this by supporting the smallholders in regularising property rights over community and 'family forests' (i.e. the 50–80% of the property that according to the Brazilian Forestry Code is to remain under forest cover) and drawing up management plans for these forest areas. There are also close links between national and international research organisations, which are strongly influencing Brazilian forest and development policies for the Amazon region. Examples are the Man and Environment Institute for the Amazon (IMAZON), which has historical links with Pennsylvania State University and the Institute for Environmental Research (IPAM), with substantial involvement of researchers from the Woods Hole Research Centre. Moreover, the Centre for International Forestry Research (CIFOR), a Consultative Group on International Agricultural Research (CGIAR) institution with headquarters in Bogor, Indonesia, has set up a regional office for forestry research in the Amazon jointly with the Brazilian Federal Agency for Agricultural Research (EMBRAPA). All these initiatives taken together provide a scientific basis for ecologically sustainable, economically viable and socially responsible forestry.

Decentralisation and Devolution

There is a discernible trend worldwide towards decentralised forest management and the devolution of land rights to local communities, which is changing the type of actors involved in forest management. First, there is a trend towards decentralisation of forest management from the central (federal) government to state and municipal level. In a comparative study on municipal forest management in Latin America, Ferroukhi (2003) notes that Brazil's municipal governments have gained considerable autonomy in education and health since the Constitution of 1988 – to an extent that compares favourably with the situation in five other Latin American countries – but that their powers in natural resource management are lagging behind. Forest management in Brazil is still mainly the responsibility of the federal government, through the Brazilian Institute for the Environment and Renewable Resources (IBAMA). Compared to the situation in the early 1990s, however, government bodies at lower government levels have gained more competencies to delimitate protected areas and production forests and to impose regulations on forest use and management. This trend towards decentralisation is also reflected in the new Law on Public Forest Management (Law No. 11,284 of 2 March 2006), in which the establishment of regulations for the decentralisation of forest management is one of the four central elements.

A second trend towards decentralised forest management, laid down in the new Public Forest Management Law of March 2006, is the creation of National, State and Municipal forests for the sustainable production of timber and non-timber forest products and maintenance of ecological services. Currently, National Forests (*Florestais Nacionais* or 'Flonas') comprise less than 2% of the Brazilian Amazon (83,000 km^2), but the Brazilian government intends to expand the area of National, State and Municipal forests in the Amazon region to a total of 50 million ha by 2010 (Ministry of the Environment 2002). In this way, the government hopes to stimulate the sustainable use of natural and plantation forests and to curb the current boom-and-bust cycle of illegal and predatory logging operations and forest burnings. Thus far, experiences with sustainable logging operations in National Forests are limited to some public–private partnership experiments in the National Tapajós Forest in the Santarém region. As long as sustainably produced timber has to compete with supplies of cheap hardwood from nearby settlement areas, it is to be expected that timber production in National Forests will be limited, but their demarcation can complement other protected areas (Veríssimo et al. 2002) and act as a buffer against further expansion of farm land and predatory logging.

Third there is the trend towards devolution of forest land to local communities and forest users. White and Martin (2002) calculated that 22% of the forest land in the 18 countries with the largest forest cover falls under either private or public community or indigenous ownership. This means that the share of community ownership has doubled in 15 years. Scherr et al. (2003) expect this share to increase in the near future, since communities are increasingly reclaiming their rights to forest land and an increasing number of countries are implementing laws recognising these rights. Although the portion of forest land under community ownership in Brazil is lower than the proportion indicated above (i.e. 13%), in the Amazon region 21% of the land is indigenous territory (Lentini et al. 2005, p.33) and 0.7% is covered by extractive reserves.[4] Extractive reserves are tracts of land reserved for

---

[4] Calculation based on data on the website of the Brazilian Ministry of the Environment (URL: http://www.mma.gov.br).

forest-dwelling communities to sustainably exploit the forests for rubber, Brazil nuts and other forest products, while being protected from encroachment by farmers and loggers. The possibility to demarcate extractive reserves was created in federal law in 1990 (Decree No. 98,897). Until 2006, 12 extractive reserves had been created in the Amazon region, covering 3.3 million hectare and involving 22,362 people.[5]

Discussion: Prospects for Forest Management

Based on the above findings, we expect that only large and/or specialised companies which have the means to invest in advanced technologies, natural forest management and plantations, and which are capable of meeting the quality standards of European and American consumers, will be able to serve the international market with certified timber. With increasing timber scarcity near urban centres and the most accessible areas and growing consumer pressure to produce in ecologically sound and socially acceptable ways, an increasing number of large firms will seek ways to benefit from the premium paid for timber from sustainably managed sources.

For small and medium-sized producers this option is less realistic. These sawmills operate with obsolete machinery, have low profit margins and produce sawnwood that mostly does not meet the quality standards of the export market. They are set up, are operational for a few years and close or relocate following the dynamics of the agricultural frontiers and infrastructural investments. A crucial factor for the prospects for sustainable forestry in Brazilian Amazonia is whether these small-scale producers will be able to play a role in the sustainable production of timber.

It has been suggested that the devolution of land to communities and smallholders, combined with increasing timber scarcity, could stimulate company-community partnerships for the sustainable production of roundwood (Scherr et al. 2003). The first examples of such partnerships in the Brazilian Amazon already exist, such as MAFLOPS described by Lima et al. (2003). The authors point to the mutual benefits of deals between sawmills and colonists: sawmills have access to cheap and legal timber supplies from areas already opened up by roads, while colonists get help with the legally required forest management plan and receive money and/or other benefits such as transportation by logging trucks. However, the ones who usually benefit most from conventional timber deals are the sawmills (Lima et al. 2003, p. 84). The prices paid to the colonists are up to ten times below market value, the payments are often delayed, and other benefits such as transport with logging trucks are mostly of a temporary nature (as long as their area is being logged). Furthermore, the colonists have little say in which species and what volumes are exploited and what kind of techniques are used (Lima et al. 2003, p. 85). Lima et al. therefore propose the 'family forests' concept, based on the MAFLOPS experience as a more equitable company-community partnership for the sustainable production of timber.

---

[5] URL: http://www.ibama.gov.br

This would also fit the aim of the National Forest Programme to have an area of 20 million hectares in private properties in the Amazon under sustainable forest management through 'enterprising partnerships' (*parcerias empreendedoras*) by 2010 (Ministry of the Environment 2002, p. 65). It would be worthwhile investigating the feasibility of this concept and the receptivity towards it among sawmills and colonists.

It should be taken into account that smallholders in settlement areas are not only suppliers of hardwood, but may also be sawmill owners themselves. These generally small sawmills lack the means and profit margins to invest in sustainable forest management. Often their owners have no intention of doing so either, because they operate the sawmill on a temporary basis. The challenge is to find incentives for these family-based sawmills to operate on more sustainable terms. This will be no easy task. Small and medium-sized sawmills would only be able to benefit from a premium on sustainably produced hardwood if they operated on the market for certified timber, but they generally lack the technology and financial means to meet the standards for certified timber. Furthermore, this market is limited compared to the immense domestic market for non-certified timber. Only with donor support or through partnerships with larger firms and owners of 'family forests' would small and medium-sized sawmills be able to upgrade their production to more sustainable levels.

Further research should attempt at finding out under which conditions small producers are able and willing to engage in such partnerships and whether small-scale logging on smallholders' properties can create a basis for sustainable family-based exploration schemes. This requires further insight into (i) the role of timber exploitation in the livelihood strategies of smallholders in settlement areas; (ii) their perception of logging and sustainable forest management of their own and others' forest reserves; (iii) larger sawmill owners' perceptions of company-community partnerships aimed at sustainable family-based forest management in settlement areas; and (iv) the economic viability of such partnerships.

Conclusions

The intimate relationship between timber exploitation and the advancement of the agricultural frontier in Brazilian Amazonia seriously impedes sustainable forestry. Enterprises able and willing to manage the forests in a sustainable manner can hardly compete with those supplying cheap timber from agricultural frontier areas. Additionally, the expansion of soybean cultivation and the concomitant investments in road and waterway infrastructure are giving a further impulse to new frontier-related logging cycles in hitherto inaccessible forest areas.

Several processes initiated in the past decade may be capable of curbing this trend, albeit on a limited scale in the short term. Firstly, the spread of worldwide concern about the loss and degradation of tropical forests is generating global support for forest conservation and sustainable management. This worldwide concern generates funds as well as market-driven incentives for sustainable forest management at both enterprise and community level, leads to multilevel and multi-actor partnerships for forest conservation and sustainable forest use, and helps strengthen local institutions and civil society organisations engaged in the quest for sustainable forest management.

Decentralisation of forest management and devolution of forest land to local communities and forest users may also lay the foundations for more sustainable forms of forest exploitation. Examples are the greater autonomy for state and municipal governments to demarcate protected areas and National, State and Municipal Forests for the sustainable production of timber at enterprise and community level. Extractive reserves for forest-dwelling communities engaged in the extraction of non-timber forest products and low-impact logging constitute another example.

The greatest challenge is to find ways to make family-based logging and sawmilling operations in settlement areas more sustainable. This could be done through innovative company-community partnerships for the sustainable management of forest reserves that, according to legal requirements, should cover 50–80% of the smallholders' plots. We suggest that further research investigate whether such partnerships fit in with the livelihood strategies of smallholders in settlement areas, and with the aspirations of private forest and sawmill owners.

Chapter 11
Looking Back on NAFTA's Promises and Realities from a Local Perspective. The State of Coahuila, Mexico

Leendert de Bell

Since the early 1980s, free market policies promoting liberalisation, deregulation, and privatisation have rapidly gained terrain throughout most of Latin America, and they became part of the mainstream political discourse in the 1990s. The so-called 'Washington Consensus' prescribed, in a highly economistic way, the same structural adjustment recipes for all nations, regardless of their level of development, regime type, or cultural context. Many governments of developing countries now widely consider export-oriented industrialisation, driven by foreign investments, to be the most viable means of capturing the potential benefits of globalisation and a 'fast-track' out of poverty.

In this context, the effectuation of the North American Free Trade Agreement (NAFTA) in 1994 between Mexico, the United States, and Canada, can be considered one of the most radical trade experiments in history. The agreement created the world's largest free-trade area in terms of total gross domestic product (GDP) and the second largest in terms of total trade volume, after the European Union. Perhaps the most significant aspect of NAFTA, however, was the fact that it was the first agreement of its kind between advanced and developing economies. According to the initiator of the negotiations with the United States and Canada, president Carlos Salinas (1988–1994), the vast power of free trade would (finally) secure Mexico's entry ticket to the 'First World' after a decade of economic crisis and restructuring.

Not surprisingly, the number of reports and studies dedicated to the expected and actual effects of NAFTA on Mexico's economy is immense. While celebrating its fifteenth anniversary, policymakers insist that Mexico has made progress in many areas. Indeed, Mexico's growth, in terms of exports and foreign investments, has been remarkable during the past one-and-a-half decade. Still, the World Bank (Lederman et al. 2003), the International Monetary Fund (IMF) (Kose et al. 2004), and for example the Carnegie Endowment for International Peace (Audley et al. 2003) have published reports which strike rather critical notes when it comes to Mexico's socio-economic development. Although it is particularly difficult to isolate the actual effects of the agreement from significant other shocks that have affected Mexico since its effectuation, NAFTA has turned out to be, to say the least, a mixed blessing for Mexico's development.

P. van Lindert and O. Verkoren (eds.), *Decentralized Development in Latin America:* 155
Experiences in Local Governance and Local Development, GeoJournal Library 97,
DOI 10.1007/978-90-481-3739-8_11, © Springer Science+Business Media B.V. 2010

This chapter will analyse some of the socio-economic effects NAFTA has had on the state of Coahuila, Mexico's third largest state, situated in the north-east of the country and bordering on Texas over a length of 500 km. Since Mexico's economic deregulation policies gained momentum in the 1980s, but particularly since NAFTA has come into operation, Coahuila appears to be one of Mexico's most successful examples of the new strategy of export industrialisation. Within its state limits, however, the impact of Mexico's economic liberalisation policies has been highly uneven.

Coahuila has historically offered a broad socio-economic diversity of sub-regions (Fig. 11.1) which have all experienced a strong, cumulative and self-reinforcing development of one specific economic sector.[1] As several analysts have already pointed out, the transition from protected markets and subsidies under the strategy of import substituting industrialisation (1940–1980) towards (international) market competition under the strategy of export industrialisation tends to polarize existing inequalities between and within regions, economic sectors, and social groups (see for example Dicken 2003; Cypher 2001; Vellinga 1999). Some companies or industrial sectors manage to overcome the challenges imposed by changes in economic outlook by shifting production (processes), organisation and markets, while others are unable to adapt to these changes because they strongly depend on specific experience and routines from the past.

The present chapter focuses in particular on the role of local governance and the local private sector in the success or failure to change local economic development from one trajectory to another. The first section of this chapter shortly addresses the 'promises' of NAFTA, its principal terms and aims, and the way in which the government of Coahuila anticipated the effectuation of the agreement. The second section concentrates on the 'realities' of NAFTA, in particular the way in which Coahuila's internal differences in local experience have influenced the socio-economic outcomes since the agreement took effect in 1994. The third section reflects on the effects of more recent cyclical economic developments, whereas the fourth section critically addresses more structural problems of this specific development model.

NAFTA's Promises

The final agreement, ratified and effectuated before the end of Salinas' term, was broad in scope, eliminating the majority of tariffs and other trade barriers in 10 years and phasing out most remaining tariffs by the end of 2008. Starting in 1994, with each passing year the integration of the three economic partners would become greater. Various provisions were included covering investment flows, financial services, government purchases, and protection of intellectual property rights. NAFTA also represented a watershed in global trade policy with regard to its comprehensiveness.

---

[1] Given the marginal economic and demographic importance of the Desert-region, most statistics and analyses commonly consider this sub-region to be part of Coahuila's Centre-region.

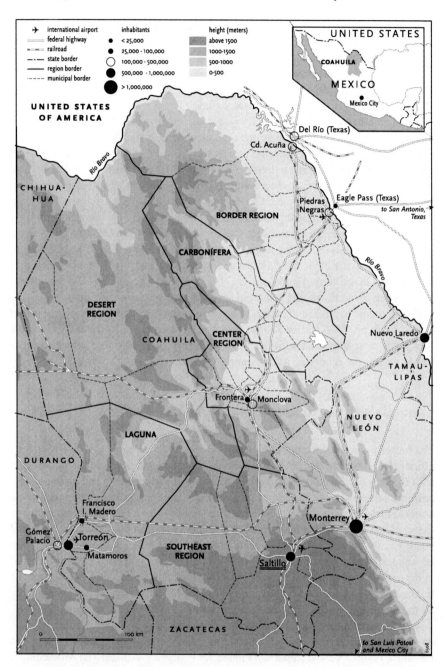

Fig. 11.1 Coahuila, Mexico: subregions

The agreement established a variety of unique mechanisms for resolution of disputes, supplementing those already existing within the World Trade Organisation (WTO), and also included side agreements on labour and environmental issues.

Since the disparities between the economic partners were huge, both economically and technically, president Salinas had put a tremendous effort into spreading publicity about the benefits of such an agreement, assuring that it would raise the standards of living of all Mexican citizens. NAFTA would not only increase the amount of foreign investments in Mexico, but at the same time secure access for Mexico's exports to the North American markets. Nevertheless, as the prospect of heightened competition grew imminent, an increasing division within the Mexican business sector became manifest. Being well prepared to compete internationally, Mexico's large business groups welcomed the government's intent to negotiate NAFTA from the very start. These groups were strongly represented in the new and influential co-ordinating body of *Organizaciones Empresariales de Comercio Exterior* (COECE) that advised the government officials during the negotiations (1990–1993). Many small and medium-sized firms, on the other hand, became increasingly aware of the obstacles they would face in becoming competitive in a liberalised economy. Their principal concern was about the timing and rapid speed of the negotiations, without yet having sufficient access to credit and capital to improve technology and quality of production (Alba, 1996, pp. 55–57). For Salinas however, the ratification of NAFTA along the 'fast-track' was important in order to make it unlikely that future administrations would reverse the economic reforms made in the previous years.

Coahuila's Opportunities Under NAFTA

The recently elected governor of Coahuila, Rogelio Montemayor (1993–1999), took office only 1 month before NAFTA was implemented. Ideologically Montemayor, with a Ph.D. degree in Economics from the University of Pennsylvania and an impressive political career within the federal government, belonged to the close inner-circle around president Salinas.[2] Like Salinas, Montemayor was a typical representative of the so-called *técnicos* that have come to dominate Mexican politics since 1982, and consequently he was a strong advocate of free market policies and NAFTA. While he was senator for Coahuila (1991–1993), Montemayor had been closely involved in the negotiations and ratification of NAFTA. Once elected governor of Coahuila, he became one of Mexico's first governors to focus his development plan completely on the opportunities the free trade agreement had to offer (Montemayor 1994).

Montemayor's carefully detailed economic program was aimed at establishing a more structured regional development, in which export manufacturing was to become Coahuila's most important engine for economic growth. The Montemayor

---

[2] Montemayor has occupied several prominent positions under the administration of President De la Madrid (e.g. Sub-secretary of Planning and Development (1982–1985), where he became closely acquainted with future president Salinas.

administration took up the task of promoting more efficiently and aggressively the establishment of national and international export manufacturing operations within Coahuila's state limits. The industrial infrastructure was improved, bureaucratic procedures were eliminated as much as possible, and an internal affairs officer was nominated to make sure that the remaining rules were clear and abided by. Typical of the Montemayor government was its close collaboration with the local business sector, which would come to play an important role in the economic promotion of the state.[3]

The basic objective of Montemayor's development plan was to create industrial agglomerations or clusters in each of its sub-regions.[4] Via specialisation in activities for which they already had the most favourable point of departure, the existing sub-regional diversity within Coahuila was to be turned into an international competitive advantage. Ideally, entrepreneurs producing similar goods would establish themselves nearby one or two pioneer firms or anchor companies, which would make a certain production site grow and perform even better. Local small and medium-sized companies were to attempt to improve their international competitiveness in order to become integrated into global value chains as subcontractors, and thus obtain benefits that previously were exclusively for large companies. In those sub-regions with high unemployment figures, such as the Carbonífera, the Centre region, and the Laguna, Montemayor focused on establishing labour-intensive *maquiladora*-operations with the principal goal of vastly increasing employment opportunity (Montemayor 1994, p. 4).[5]

When NAFTA was implemented, Coahuila already had an industrial tradition in two out of the three productive chains that clearly had good prospects of entering the U.S. market, namely the automotive and the garment sectors. The Montemayor administration decided not to actively promote the third sector (electronics), since cities like Ciudad Juárez, Tijuana, and Guadalajara already had built up

---

[3] One important conviction of the Montemayor administration was that (foreign) companies were often more easily convinced by fellow entrepreneurs. During his electoral campaign, Montemayor had already invited a large number of successful entrepreneurs from different sub-regions of Coahuila to establish contacts with potential foreign investors. Once in office, Montemayor invited several prominent local entrepreneurs into his cabinet, and encouraged the creation of private sector organisations for economic promotion in their respective sub-regions.

[4] According to cluster-theory, the value of geographic concentration of interconnected companies and associated institutions in one particular field, competing as well as co-operating, is greater than the sum of its parts (Porter 1998).

[5] *Maquiladora* is derived from the Spanish word 'maquilar', which historically referred to the milling of wheat into flour, for which the farmer would compensate the miller with a portion of the wheat. The modern meaning of the word evolved from its use to describe any partial activity in a manufacturing process, such as assembly or packaging carried out by someone other than the original manufacturer. Today, a *maquiladora* refers to a Mexican company operating under a special customs regime, established in the mid-1960s in the border areas of Mexico to absorb excess labour in the border areas and to encourage Mexican exports. Under the *maquiladora*-regime, (mostly foreign-owned) companies were allowed to temporarily import into Mexico on a duty free basis, machinery, equipment, materials, parts and components and other items needed for the assembly or manufacture of finished goods for subsequent export.

competitive advantages in that sector. Moreover, the electronics sector offered relatively few opportunities for local producers to add value. The Secretary of Economic Promotion during the Montemayor administration stated that "whenever companies producing televisions, household equipment, and so on, wanted to establish operations in Coahuila, we of course provided all the facilities, but these companies did not have our primary interest".[6]

NAFTA's Realities

Initially, NAFTA seemed to get off to a bad start. On the very day the agreement took effect, the first of January 1994, the Salinas administration was unpleasantly surprised by an armed uprising of the so-called Ejército Zapatista de Liberación Nacional (EZLN), whose objective was to improve the marginal status of the indigenous population in Chiapas. Later that (election) year, the expected inflow of foreign investments was further tempered by a couple of unsolved political homicides, including the presidential candidate of Mexico's ruling party PRI. In addition, Mexico suffered from serious economic instability. According to some critics of the Salinas administration, a hidden crisis had emerged within Mexico's financial sector since the early 1990s, fuelled by a foreign credit boom and a wave of 'misty' privatisation procedures (Cypher 2001, p. 13). Salinas counted on new foreign investments to be sufficient to reverse the growing current account deficit, and continued his expansive monetary policy throughout 1994, thereby leaving the unpopular but necessary monetary measures to his successor. In December 1994, only 3 weeks after the new president Ernesto Zedillo (1994–2000) had taken office, his administration was forced to effectuate a devaluation of the peso. This devaluation, however, was carried out rather clumsily by the inexperienced government: too late and not accompanied by supporting measures to cut down public and private expenditure, thereby leading Mexico into another serious economic emergency, the effects of which were felt throughout the rest of Latin America, the so-called 'tequila-effect'.

With substantial financial help from the IMF and Mexico's new economic partner, the U.S. government, the Zedillo administration managed to stay on course in terms of its economic reform agenda, and overcome the macro-economic effects of the economic shock in a surprisingly short period of time. By 1996, inflation, interest-, and exchange rates seemed to have stabilised. More importantly, NAFTA gained significant momentum thanks to Mexico's severe financial crisis. The devaluation of December 1994 had dramatically lowered the costs of Mexican exports and labour, which 'turbo-charged' the agreement (Cooney 2001). As a direct result of the devaluation, real wages fell by a quarter between 1995 and 1996 (Johnson 1998, p. 142). The period between 1996 and 2000 was characterised by strong growth in trade and exports, which provided a key engine of economic growth in the process of

---

[6]Interview with José Antonio Murra Giacomán, Entrepreneur and former Secretary of Economic Promotion of Coahuila (1993–1999), Torreón, 5 June 2003.

recovering from the crisis. Mexico experienced an exponential increase of foreign direct investment, most significantly from its NAFTA-partners, but also from European and (East) Asian firms attempting to gain favoured access to the U.S. market from a location with relatively low labour costs. The boost of international investments in Mexico led everyone to believe that the Mexican economy had finally overcome its difficulties for the first time since the debt crisis of 1982.

Coahuila's Realities Under NAFTA

The macro-economic effects of NAFTA, in combination with the effects of Mexico's financial crisis, have been spectacular for the state of Coahuila in terms of exports, foreign investments, and subsequent employment. The number of (predominantly foreign) investments in Coahuila increased exponentially over the period 1994–1999, while manufactured exports boomed as never before. During this period, the state registered a 5.3% annual growth of GDP, in comparison to 3.9% nationally (Rojas 2002, p. 4). The strong macro-economic growth of Coahuila turned the Montemayor administration into a model for Mexico's export-led growth.

However, when looking beyond these impressive macro-economic figures, it becomes clear that the gains have not been evenly divided across the different sub-regions of Coahuila. The free trade agreement and the effects of the devaluation above all favoured those companies, sectors, and sub-regions that were already strongly oriented towards export markets. The sub-regional distribution of investments, as presented in Fig. 11.2, is based on data distributed by the Montemayor administration itself. Consequently, the totals may be somewhat boosted, as some investments are made in two or three stages and are sometimes counted more than once, and also include the expansion of already existing operations. Nevertheless, the figure gives a fair representation of the general economic development of Coahuila's different sub-regions and their respective relationships to one another.

The Automotive Cluster in Coahuila's Southeast Region

In terms of exports, volume of investments, and employment generated, the Southeast region of Coahuila, where the capital Saltillo is situated, is undoubtedly the state's most important sub-region (see Fig. 11.2). The strong economic performance of this sub-region is based on its heavy orientation towards export manufacturing, predominantly in the automotive sector, Mexico's fastest growing industrial sector in terms of GDP and exports (Dussel 2000, p. 125). Since NAFTA, the automotive industry has been responsible for about three quarters of the total exports of Coahuila (Dávila 2001, p. 54; 1998, p. 40).

The actual urban-industrial boom in the Southeast region gained momentum in the early 1980s, after the establishment of major assembly operations by two

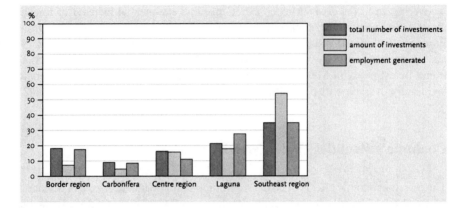

Fig. 11.2 Coahuila, Mexico: Total number of new investments, total volume of new investments, and employment generated by new investments per sub-region, 1994–1999 (%). (Based on Montemayor (1999), pp. 108–110); Secretaría de Fomento Económico (1999)

North American automobile producers in the metropolitan area of the capital Saltillo. During the 1970s, General Motors (GM) and Chrysler had both been looking for cheaper alternative production locations in their attempts to overcome stagnated U.S. demand and increased foreign competition. Unlike the manufacturing operations both companies had established earlier in and around Mexico City during the 1950s and 1960s, which were directed to obtain a share of the domestic market, the principal objective of these new plants was export manufacturing, primarily for the U.S. home market. Apart from its strategic geographic location, additional advantages of this 'greenfield' location were its minimum wage, which was considerably lower than those commonly paid in their plants in Central Mexico, and the absence of strong national unions (Micheli 1994; Shaiken and Herzenberg 1989). This type of investment and the volume of employment it created had never been seen before in the state of Coahuila, and would change local society almost overnight. The GM and Chrysler plants generated a rapidly growing agglomeration of national and foreign sub-contracting firms in the automotive sector, supplying parts and services to these anchor-companies.

The negative economic effects of the debt crisis of 1982 and the subsequent process of rigid economic restructuring were hardly felt in the Southeast region. In fact, the Southeast region was one of the few regions that experienced economic growth during the 'lost decade', since its largest companies were already operating on competitive international markets. Even the most important local industrial conglomerate, the *Grupo Industrial Saltillo* (GIS),[7] which initially suffered under

---

[7] The industrial empire of the López del Bosque-family had started out in the late 1920s as a small commercial family business producing rudimentary aluminium and laminated articles for domestic use. Under the supportive environment of import substitution (1940–1980) (e.g. market protection, import tariffs, and low priced inputs), their operations expanded and diversified rapidly, employing more than 10,000 people in the late 1970s.

the higher salaries and provisions offered by GM and Chrysler, would become one of the principal local beneficiaries of these new economic developments. With the creation of GIS in 1975, the organisational structure, production processes, and technology of its different subsidiaries were radically modernised in order to reduce costs and become more internationally competitive (Yáñez 1994). Production was limited to three main divisions: automotive (engine blocks), building materials (bathroom ceramics), and kitchen- and tableware, while the principal focus of sales shifted from the domestic market towards export markets. During the 1980s GIS supplied to the most prominent companies in the global automotive value chain, in particular its high-standard engine-blocks (e.g. to GM, Chrysler, Ford, Volkswagen, Renault).

The (gradual) elimination of tariffs and controls as provided by NAFTA, was warmly welcomed by most important companies situated in the Southeast region (Ruiz et al. 1997). One of the most important impulses that attracted many new internationally renowned companies to invest in the automotive sector in Coahuila was the opening of a second large state-of-the-art assembly plant of Chrysler in Saltillo. Relatively autonomous from specific local governance policies, the Southeast region of Coahuila, frequently referred to as 'Detroit in the Desert', was thereby turned into one of Mexico's most successful examples of industrial clustering (Mendoza 1999; 2001). Because of the abundance of employment, the population of the Southeast region has increased at a spectacular rate. Saltillo in particular has become one of the fastest growing municipalities of Mexico since the 1990s. Nowadays almost 80% of the total population of the Southeast region lives in the capital, which has created increasing problems of urban infrastructure, social conflicts, and perhaps the biggest problem with respect to future urban-industrial development: water shortage.

The Garment Cluster in the Laguna

During the 1990s, the Laguna, located in the south-western corner of Coahuila, became another successful example of industrial clustering in Coahuila. The Laguna had been Coahuila's first sub-region to experience important economic and demographic growth in the late nineteenth century, thanks to the large-scale culti-vation of cotton and related industries in its main urban centre Torreón. Since the 1980s however, the economy of the rural areas in particular had suffered greatly once the subsidies for cotton production were cancelled and protective economic measures were discontinued. In the late 1980s, *maquiladoras*, in particular those for the assembly of garments (denim), started to present themselves as alternative sources of employment to alleviate the large-scale unemployment in the sub-region. Although the in- and output of these garment producers originated from, and was directed towards the United States, most *maquiladoras* in the Laguna were in fact operated by local entrepreneurs (Van Dooren 2003, p. 136).

Whereas the developments in the Southeast region evolved according to the free market principle, in the Laguna, the Montemayor administration, in close collaboration with the local private sector, actively directed the installation of a garment sector. Although already relatively successful in the late 1980s, prior to NAFTA the garment export cluster in the Laguna primarily consisted of assembly operations (needlework), while the more value-added operations generally took place in the main U.S. distribution centre of denim, El Paso. Under NAFTA regulations, however, quotas were eliminated and cloth-making, cutting, washing, ironing, packaging and distribution were no longer restricted to the United States. Through aggressive economic promotion and providing infrastructure such as electricity, gas, and water exclusively for the garment industry, outside existing industrial parks, the Montemayor administration managed to establish two important anchor-companies producing cloth, the basis of the garment production chain, within the sub-region (*Grupo Lajat* in Torreón and *Parras Cone* in Parras). Within a short period of time, a boom of other national and international companies followed, involved in cutting, assembling, washing, ironing and distributing denim. The more capital-intensive operations (e.g. cloth-making, ironing) were promoted in the urban area of Torreón, the new 'Jeans Capital of the World', whereas more labour-intensive *maquiladora*-operations (e.g. assembly, washing) were preferably directed towards the rural communities that offered a large amount of cheap labour.

Upgrading maquiladora-Operations in Coahuila's Border Region

In terms of investments and employment generated during the 1990s, the Border region of Coahuila can also be considered relatively successful, although there are important differences between its principal cities Piedras Negras and Ciudad Acuña. Unlike border cities in neighbouring states, most notably Ciudad Juárez and Tijuana, Coahuila's border cities, remote from important economic centres in Mexico and the United States and with a relatively low population density in their hinterlands, initially proved to be too peripheral for many foreign investors participating in the *maquiladora* program. Since the 1980s, however, when *maquiladoras* became increasingly important for generating foreign currency, the number of export assembly operations in the Border region of Coahuila strongly increased, in particular in Ciudad Acuña, the smaller of the two and without any industrial tradition. The number of *maquiladoras* in Piedras Negras on the other hand, a city with a long industrial tradition, remained limited, most importantly because of its history of strong unionism that had increased local wage levels substantially, and had created a reputation of labour unrest in the process (Quintero 2003).

For the Border region, the development plan of the Montemayor administration consisted of supporting the continuation of export-oriented *maquiladora*-activities, although attempts were to be made to upgrade production where possible. In practice, this involved a shift from predominantly garment- and electronics-assembly operations towards the production of automotive-parts. An additional advantage was that assembly operations in the automotive sector generally were more sizeable, thus generating more employment. Montemayor also granted the local private sector of the Border region a significant role, which would become one of the most influential groups of Coahuila. Unlike the Laguna, however, most local entrepreneurs were not directly engaged in manufacturing operations but were predominantly active in (international) trade or services (e.g. industrial real estate) (De Bell 2005, p. 69).

Whereas Piedras Negras has experienced since NAFTA a moderate, diversified economic growth primarily of trade, Ciudad Acuña would become one of Coahuila's economic and demographic growth poles during the 1990s as a result of its spectacular increase of export manufacturing. This exponential growth was not directly the result of an increase in the total number of *maquiladora* plants, but essentially had to do with a shift towards the production of automotive-parts. Between 1990 and 2000, Ciudad Acuña has seen its population double. With a little over 110,000 inhabitants, Acuña is still relatively small in comparison with other border cities, but nowadays it has some of the highest industrial concentrations per inhabitant of the whole northern border of Mexico.

Limited Investments in Coahuila's Centre Region and Carbonífera

Not all of Coahuila's sub-regions were as successful in changing from one development trajectory to another. Two of the most affected sub-regions that were forced to restructure after the debt crisis were the Centre region and the Carbonífera, both of which strongly depended on a single company, *Altos Hornos de México* (AHMSA), Mexico's largest integrated steel foundry that was established in Monclova (Centre region) in the early 1940s. AHMSA, originating from a joint effort of the Mexican government and private capital, had been an important building block in the success of Mexico's strategy of import substituting industrialisation (Toledo and Zapata 1999; Minello and Barranco 1995). One of AHMSA's most essential and quantitatively large inputs was coal, which was extracted from mines in the Carbonífera. Located just north of the Centre region, the coal reserves in the Carbonífera represented more than 90% of Mexico's total coal reserves. In the late nineteenth century, bustling mining communities emerged here after the construction of Mexico's railroad network gained momentum, but since the early twentieth century the economic outlook of this sub-region has increasingly been linked to the metallurgic industry, and since the 1940s almost exclusively to AHMSA.

During the economic slowdown of the 1970s, federal involvement in AHMSA increased considerably, but at the cost of efficiency and profitability, which decreased dramatically as a result of the centralisation policies. Productivity at AHMSA was further negatively affected by a spectacular increase in radical unionism and widespread corruption. The deficiencies of AHMSA, and the Mexican steel sector in general, were painfully laid bare after the debt crisis of 1982 when the national demand for steel suddenly collapsed. Initial attempts to direct AHMSA's production towards export markets failed because the quality of its steel and the costs and efficiency of its production processes were not internationally competitive. Protected and isolated from the world market, international trends in steel production and consumption patterns had been disregarded. During the second half of the 1980s, in particular with the prospect of Mexico's entry to the General Agreement on Tariffs and Trade (GATT) in 1986, the Mexican steel sector was radically restructured. Some of the oldest steel foundries were closed down because they were no longer considered strategic or cost-effective. Others, like AHMSA, were eventually privatised in the early 1990s (Rogozinski 1993, pp. 62–68). The number of workers at AHMSA and its subsidiaries, including its coal mining activities in the Carbonífera, were radically downsized in the process. Having few alternative employment opportunities, the unemployment rates of the Centre region and the Carbonífera have continuously ranked among the highest nationally since the late 1980s (Cárdenas and Redonnet 1998).

The difficult economic situation and high unemployment figures of both sub-regions were matters of high priority within the economic strategy of the Montemayor administration. Preferably, an agglomeration of industries in the machinery and automotive sector were to be created around AHMSA. With the help of foreign capital and expertise, the new owners of AHMSA had managed to modernise AHMSA spectacularly within 3 years time (1991–1994), expanding and diversifying its product lines and obtaining a respectable position in the world market. Unfortunately, this did not attract many new investors to the sub-region, let alone the formation of a local cluster. Even though the local government offered numerous extraordinary incentives, new investors generally preferred other (sub-) regions above the Centre region and Carbonífera. Consequently, the majority of the investments made in the Centre region between 1994 and 1999 (see Fig. 11.2) represents investments made to modernise AHMSA. The Centre region and Carbonífera continued to suffer from the negative effects of their path-dependent development, most importantly from their relatively expensive labour force and bad reputation of labour conflicts that have lingered on since the 1970s. Significantly, the few companies that actually did invest in either of these two sub-regions, mostly *maquiladoras* in the garment sector, maintained little or no direct relationship with the local economy, except for labour. Consequently, the local economic development of the Centre region and the Carbonífera remained strongly dependent on AHMSA (Corrales 2004).

To make things worse, the initial success of the new owners of AHMSA did not last long, as AHMSA's steel suffered strongly under the wave of cheap South Korean steel that flooded the world steel market following the Asian crisis of 1997. AHMSA was forced to cut prices in order to boost sales, but thereby rapidly reduced its cash flow and increased the pressure of the loans the company had obtained from (foreign) banks to finance the modernisation process. Efforts to renegotiate AHMSA's debts did not succeed, and efforts to find a strategic national or international partner also failed (Simón and Ramírez 2001, pp. 201–204). In the beginning of 1999, AHMSA unilaterally suspended payments to its debtors, although continuing production. With AHMSA's debtors and much of the local economy left on hold, new companies have become even more reluctant to invest in this sub-region.

Cyclical Shocks

Following the strong performance in the late 1990s, the growth of Mexico's trade with NAFTA partners has fallen significantly since 2001. This was primarily the result of the slowdown of consumer demand in the United States after a prolonged period of expansion between 1995 and 2000. The U.S. being the principal market for most of Mexico's exports, many export-oriented assembly industries immediately responded by (temporarily) reducing production and number of workers. A series of dramatic international events, the terrorist attacks on the United States and subsequent 'wars-on-terror', prevented a quick recovery of the U.S. and NAFTA partners' economies.

At a time when U.S. demand had slumped, Mexico also faced increased competition from other emerging market economies elsewhere in Latin America and Asia. The preferential treatment of Mexico with respect to U.S. investments was negatively affected by new negotiations on (bilateral) free trade agreements within the western hemisphere, such as the Central American Free Trade Agreement (CAFTA) and the Free Trade Area of the Americas (FTAA). Since 2001, an important number of U.S. companies, in particular the lower value-added and labour intensive segments of Mexico's export sector, such as garments, have shifted production from Mexico to cheaper alternatives in Central America. The most important competitor for U.S. investments and threat to Mexico's market share in the United States, however, comes from China. Since its entrance to the WTO in December 2001, China has been rapidly expanding its market share in the United States.

According to some observers, about 30% of the jobs that were created in *maquiladoras* in the 1990s have since disappeared (Audley et al. 2003, p. 12), and challenges to Mexico's export position in the U.S. market are likely only to increase further. Although the government of Coahuila at that time maintained that Coahuila has been less affected by the effects of the U.S. recession than other border states, the effects were severely felt in every sub-region. More importantly, the future prospects of Coahuila's respective industrial agglomerations have become a lot less promising, since the main engine of the local economy, the automotive sector, was directly affected by the economic stagnation that started with the worldwide financial crisis in the year 2008.

Structural Problems

As long as the demand of export markets was increasing, governments tended to overlook the negative side effects of Mexico's free market policies, such as the increasing (regional) disparities described above, and instead focused more exclusively on the economic success-stories. As indicated, the success of NAFTA should not be seen in isolation from the impact of the peso-crisis of 1994–1995, resulting in a drop of real wages from which most have still not recovered, the effects of the prolonged boom of the U.S. economy and of the current recession.

By now, the export sector itself is under pressure and its benefits are no longer guaranteed, which raises more structural questions about the nature of Mexico's development strategy that was gradually introduced in the 1980s, and more firmly since the mid-1990s.

The main challenge of promoting clusters is to create an environment that stimulates and supports local learning, innovation and upgrading. The empirical evidence of Coahuila, however, confirms the argument of Altenburg and Meyer-Stamer (1999, p. 1704), who conclude that the number of local companies that manage to become integrated in international production chains is extremely limited. Particularly in Coahuila's most challenged sub-regions, the objectives of the local government were not feasible, and were altered from promoting specialised export clusters to generating as much employment as possible. In practice, most of these companies generally operated within so-called 'buyer-driven commodity chains': labour-intensive production of consumer goods which are vulnerable to fashion (e.g. garments, footwear, toys), and only have very narrow profit margins per unit (Gereffi 1996, p. 66). Since most of these companies predominantly compete on wages, they are more likely to move their operations to regions with more favourable conditions once the market conditions of the international economy become adverse. Since Mexico's economic slump, such 'boom-and-bust'-scenarios have been seen in several of Coahuila's sub-regions.[8]

The Southeast region of Coahuila is perhaps the only sub-region which has predominantly attracted companies operating within the so-called 'producer-driven commodity chain', consisting of capital- and technology-intensive industries (e.g. automobiles, computers, machinery) (Gereffi 1996). In general, these industrial sectors depend strongly on a large number of suppliers and subcontractors, and are generally thought to offer more perspectives for local companies to become integrated into global value chains. Even in the case of Coahuila's automotive industry, however, the number of local companies that have managed to become integrated into the global automotive value chain is exceptionally low. In fact, most supplying firms that established their operations near the GM and Chrysler plants around Saltillo were often global players themselves, encouraged by their principal clients to build up production facilities close to their new production locations. Consequently, Coahuila's most dynamic exporters were foreign-owned companies, with the *Grupo Industrial Saltillo* perhaps as the most notable exception. Many local small or medium-sized entrepreneurs on the other hand only suffered from the increased international competition.

The economic crises have also made clear that development based on ongoing regional economic specialisation can be dangerous in the long run. In fact, most industrial agglomerations tend to become locked-in themselves at some point by the

---

[8] The phase-out of the so-called Multi-Fiber Agreement in 2005, which eliminated quotas on many garment exports, and the prospect of the final elimination of tariffs on garments and textiles under NAFTA at the end of 2008 already resulted in a significant 'reshuffling' in the global garment value chain, which above all favoured China.

exact same socio-economic conditions that once provided their specific competitive advantages. Once the economic circumstances change, it becomes increasingly difficult for specialised clusters to adapt and diversify to compete with new industrial regions. Today, particularly sub-regions like Coahuila's Centre region and the Carbonífera are left with high unemployment rates and few economic alternatives.

Concluding Remarks

Policymakers have frequently hailed Coahuila as an example of the potential benefits of free trade with respect to local or regional development. However, the case of Coahuila has demonstrated that results are often highly mixed. Coahuila's macro-economic successes have long overshadowed the pronounced inequalities in (sub-) regional developments which were both the result of the same policies. Analysis from a local perspective paints a picture in which the 'realities' of free trade policies are far more complex than their 'promises' suggest. The success or failure of local or regional development generally involves a great number of variables. Local experiences in production and the roles and mutual relationships of local governance and the local private sector, to name a few under study here, are also important in determining the outcomes.

The economic success of the Border region and the Laguna was to a great extent the result of a close collaboration between the Montemayor administration and the local private sector. In the Southeast region, Coahuila's economically most successful sub-region, the direct influence of local governance seems to be less obvious since local development is dominated by a large number of world-class companies and a small group of extremely influential local businessmen. The contrast with the economic reality in the Carbonífera and the Centre region of Coahuila on the other hand could hardly be more striking. Both sub-regions continue to be victims of an economic lock-in, which relied on the strong influence of the federal government, in particular during the 1970s. The role of the local private sector was always rather reactive than proactive. Here, modernisation efforts have only resulted in high unemployment, but not in the expected number of (foreign) investments. Government efforts to create a steel cluster failed because those companies that eventually did establish their operations in one of these sub-regions had no direct links to AHMSA or coal mining activities.

Economic recessions have painfully demonstrated that success-stories like those in Coahuila should not be seen in isolation from the effects of the prolonged expansion of the U.S. economy during the 1990s, and the impact of the devaluation of the peso in 1994–1995 on the Mexican wage-levels. Now that Mexico's cyclical economic developments have become more adverse, it also becomes clear that the agreement should not be considered an end to itself, but that additional policies that take the role of other economic variables and actors into consideration remain important in order to contribute to a more balanced and long-term development.

Chapter 12
Tourism and Local Development Strategies; The Mexican Case[1]

Ludger Brenner

In the 1960s and 1970s, tourism promotion policies in developing countries focused primarily on providing infrastructural support for large-scale, enclave-like projects in order to meet the demands of an ever wealthier international clientele. Development banks granted financial aid to foster investments of tourist consortia, especially hotel chains. As a result, numerous coastal resorts showed high growth rates during these decades. However, this development of tourism was rarely based on planning designed to bring about controlled development. Rather, it caused rapid urbanization of the major beach resorts resulting in severe socioeconomic and environmental problems (Burns and Holden 1995; Broman 1996; Gormsen 1997).

In the early 1980s, authorities – at least in some countries – began to take measures to control these unrestrained urbanization processes (Gormsen 1995, pp. 230–31). The results, however, have been limited, as other policies ironically enough continued to promote tourism in the fast-growing beach destinations (Brenner and Aguilar 2002). It is likely that most countries will continue to do so by fostering large-scale tourism development projects, as mass tourism still promises the greatest and fastest benefits in economic terms. It is therefore important to ask whether and how adequate planning can lead to more sustainable regional development.

Mexico provides an ideal case to analyze this question. By the early 1970s, four major luxury resorts had been developed with considerable governmental support. Today these destinations, especially Cancún, are all important international tourist resorts. Soon after their inception however, they began to show clear signs of social marginalization, formation of enclaves, development of shantytowns, and environmental deterioration. In the case of Huatulco, the most recent large-scale tourism project on the southern Pacific coast initiated in 1984, the authorities attempted to take a different approach. A modified planning strategy and different tools were meant to ensure local development that was both socially sound and economically efficient.

[1] The author would like to thank several students of geography at the University of Utrecht (Netherlands), the University of Trier (Germany) and the University of Munich (Germany) who helped complete this study. Special thanks are due to Clemencia Santos for data-processing and map construction.

This article seeks to identify the factors that have led to this innovative approach and the exact strategy that was employed, before turning to an evaluation of the results.

The chapter is structured in four parts: section one briefly discusses the paradigms that have influenced tourism policy in developing countries over the past 4 decades. In section two, attention will be drawn to the factors that have caused modifications in an otherwise consistent tourism policy in Mexico. The third section highlights the ambivalent impact of the modified policy on national and regional development. The subsequently presented case study of Huatulco reveals the planning strategy that was applied and what measures were taken, and also evaluates the outcomes.

Tourism and Development: Looking Back on 4 Decades of Controversial Debate

The discussion on tourism in regional and national development has passed through three different stages in the course of the past 35 years (Vorlaufer 1996). The first phase, from the mid-1960s to the mid-1970s, was characterized by euphoria over the continuous economic growth and technological advances in the field of transport and communication. In line with the ideas of modernization theory, expectations were focused on both economic growth and the reduction of regional disparities (Broman 1996; Clancy 1999, 2001), under the assumptions that: (a) foreign direct investment would solve the bottleneck-problem of scarce domestic capital; (b) foreign exchange earnings would help to reduce notorious balance-of-payment deficits; (c) generation of employment would mitigate social inequalities; and (d) multiplier effects in peripheral areas would lessen regional disparities. During this stage, the lack of infrastructure and domestic capital were considered obstacles to tourism-based economic growth (Vorlaufer 1996, pp. 171–200). In order to overcome these limitations, state authorities provided infrastructure and other supportive measures to prompt international hotel chains to invest in projects that were otherwise too risky or expensive (Clancy 1999, pp. 9–14).

During the second stage, from the mid-1970s to the mid-1980s, the dependency paradigm gained ground, and increased investments by transnational companies in Third-World destinations were seen as a strategy by the North to take advantage of the natural and cultural resources of the South (Britton 1982; Hills and Lundgren 1977; Matthews 1977; Burns and Holden 1995). It was argued that: (a) leakages and repatriation of profits reduced the net benefits for the developing countries; (b) many tourist destinations depended exclusively on a few countries of origin and /or a handful of consortia; (c) due to low skill and income levels, as well as considerable seasonal fluctuations, tourism's potential to generate employment was overestimated; (d) the tourism sector was only barely integrated into regional and local economies; and (e) the spatial concentration of activities related to tourism caused severe environmental damage and social tensions.

The third phase in the tourism-development debate is closely linked to the burgeoning discourse on sustainable development after 1987. Social and ecological dimensions were added to the, until then, mainly economic approach to development (Becker et al. 1996; Job 1996; Hall and Lew 1998; Mowforth and Munt 1998; Brenner 1999; Brenner and Job 2006). In economic terms, the objective of sustainable tourism was to improve the living conditions of the local population and to prevent an exclusive dependence on tourism. In addition, forward and backward linkages with other economic sectors, such as the construction industry and agriculture, had to be strengthened. Social aims were focused on the material and political participation of the local population. Furthermore, tourism-based growth was not to lead to irreversible environmental deterioration or loss of biodiversity.

The concept of sustainable tourism faces serious challenges. First of all, it has proven difficult to define quantifiable and applicable indicators to monitor the development of tourism and evaluate its effects (Nelson 1993; McLaren 1994; Cater 1995a, b; Archer 1996; Job 1996; Mowforth and Munt 1998; Brenner 1999; Brenner and Job 2006). The challenge is to elaborate a set of indicators that covers the complexity of all relevant factors while at the same time allowing a fast and cost-effective data survey (Becker et al. 1996, p. 127). A further core problem lies in the incompatibility of economic efficiency and local participation. As many case studies have indicated, development of tourism based exclusively on local initiative is unlikely to lead to considerable economic growth (Lindberg et al. 1996; Wallace 1996; Sjoholt 1999; Strasdas 2000). Because the locals lack experience, capital, and market access, the most profitable lines of business (marketing, distribution, transport) tend to be controlled by non-local entrepreneurs. Finally, the functional logic inherent in the country's public administration impedes the implementation of sustainable tourism development (De Kadt 1992; Nelson 1993): authorities devoted to promoting tourism development tend to defend their power realm rather persistently. In the past, this led to a sectorial focus of tourism politics that often concentrated on solving technical infrastructural problems rather than social issues (De Kadt 1992).

Mexican Tourism Policy

Since the early 1970s, Mexican tourism policy has been characterized by a notable continuity in terms of institutions, instruments and strategy, whose central goals were to increase foreign exchange earnings, generate employment and integrate peripheral coastal regions into the national economy (Brenner and Aguilar 2002). Nevertheless, shifts in political and economic systems at the national and international levels, the highly problematical development of important tourist destinations, and the increasingly saturated market of sun-and-beach tourism have led to a number of modifications.

From the early 1970s until the debt crisis in 1982/83, tourism development was institutionalized at the highest governmental level. In 1974, the Mexico City-based National Tourism Fund (Spanish abbreviation: FONATUR) was founded (Jiménez 1992). FONATUR is responsible for constructing and maintaining infrastructure, granting loans, attracting investors and selling property, as well as various administrative duties (FONATUR 1999a). The authority holds extensive powers in declared development areas, including control of land use. One of its main tasks is to create so-called "State-Planned Tourism Destinations" (SPTDs). Up to the present, FONATUR, with significant financial support from the Inter-American Development Bank, has managed to build five SPTDs in formerly undeveloped costal areas: Cancún (begun in 1970), Ixtapa-Zihuatanejo (1972), Los Cabos (1974), Loreto (1975) and finally Huatulco (1984). FONATUR has also invested considerable amounts in other destinations along the Mexican Pacific and Caribbean coasts as well as in Mexico City. In addition, between 1974 and 1989 FONATUR subsidized the construction and renovation of more than 100,000 hotel rooms. Figure 12.1 shows the focus of public financial support on luxury-class hotels and accommodation facilities.

After the debt crisis in 1983, FONATUR gradually retreated from offering direct financial support, as the World Bank and the International Monetary Fund began to impose structural adjustment programs on the state. Additionally, most state-owned enterprises were privatized (Jiménez 1992). Nonetheless, the state continued to cultivate the destinations mentioned above, albeit with reduced financial means. In an attempt to foster tourist activities in other parts of the country, the Mexican government began to focus on cultural tourism (Brenner and Aguilar 2002).

After 1995, noteworthy modifications were made to tourism development policy. Centralized state-interventionism continued, but the concepts of sustainable and nature-based tourism gained a certain importance. For the first time federal authorities addressed social, economic and ecological problems. The goal of developing tourist

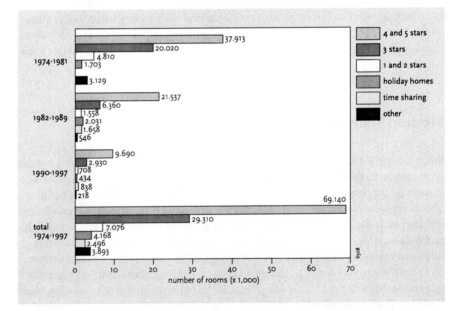

Fig. 12.1 FONATUR-supported construction of accommodation facilities (1974–1997): number of rooms by category (FONATUR 1999a)

destinations along the Pacific and Caribbean coasts was "officially" completed and their further evolution was to be accompanied by supportive measures only (SECTUR 2001).

The Results of State-sponsored Tourism Development

The development of luxury tourism resorts proved to be a good strategy for integrating Mexico into the global tourism market: with 20.6 million international tourist arrivals in 2000 (ca. 3.5% of international tourist arrivals worldwide), Mexico is ranked second only to China (31.2 million) among the developing countries, and is far ahead of Malaysia (10 million) and Thailand (9.6 million) (WTO 2001). This outstanding position is undoubtedly a result of governmental promotion. Between 1975 and 2000, the number of hotel rooms increased from 182,000 to 442,000 (Jiménez 1992), of which 40% are luxury-class. Another reason for this extraordinary growth lies in Mexico's proximity to the USA, whose citizens account for about 80% of all international tourist arrivals in Mexico (SECTUR 1991, 2002). As a result, tourism nowadays is an important sector in the Mexican national economy. Between 1993 and 1998, tourism provided an average of 8.2% of the GDP and 6% of all national employment (INEGI 2000a).

Up to the early 1970s, Mexico faced a bottleneck problem with respect to the accommodation facilities available to meet the demands of international tourists. Only Mexico City, Acapulco, Guadalajara, Mazatlán, Monterrey and Veracruz provided a considerable number of four- and five-star hotels (Jiménez 1992; Brenner 2007). Three decades later, 58% of the 230,000 hotel rooms located in the 52 most important tourist destinations meet international standards (SECTUR 2002). Luxury accommodation is concentrated however in the State-Planned Tourism Destinations, a few traditional resorts such as Acapulco and Puerto Vallarta, and in the country's three largest cities. Figure 12.2 shows the outstanding importance of the SPTDs for incoming tourism, that together host more than 50% of all overnight stays of international tourists (SECTUR 2002). About a third of all foreign exchange generated through tourism derives from activities in the SPTDs (FONATUR 1999a). Another striking fact is the growth in the capacity of the SPTDs and in the number of arrivals, especially in Cancún (see Fig. 12.3). In 2000, these coastal resorts – insignificant or even inexistent up to the late 1970s – offered 35,000 hotel rooms (6% of the national total), while in the same period they received 4.3 million international visitors, equal to 42% of all Mexican incoming tourism (SECTUR 2002).

The spatial concentration of tourism activities and rapid urbanization have led to a wide array of social and ecological problems. Firstly, internal migration to these coastal resorts has resulted in accelerated population growth in these cities. Between 1970 and 1995 for instance, Cancún experienced an annual population increase of 21%. Los Cabos (14%), Ixtapa-Zihuatanejo (12%) and Huatulco (12%) (Brenner and Aguilar 2002, p. 516) have also developed into medium-sized cities, although they lack adequate infrastructure facilities (Bravo 1994; Aguilar et al. 1997; Jiménez 1998).

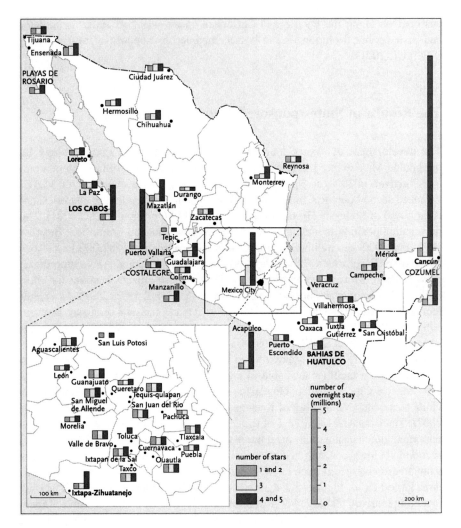

Fig. 12.2 Overnight stays of international tourists in Mexican tourist destinations by category, 2000 (SECTUR 2002)

Shantytowns with no connection to water and sewage systems developed on the outskirts of these urban zones from the very beginning (Bravo 1994).

Secondly, the local population receives only marginal benefits from tourism (Gormsen 1997; Brenner and Aguilar 2002). Communities previously based on subsistence agriculture and fishing have proven to be incapable of coping with the social and economic shifts initiated by tourist activities. A rapid increase in property values, real estate speculation, expropriations and evictions from their lands have forced local populations to give up their traditional activities (Pi-Sunger 2001; Vorlaufer 1996, 1999). Their lack of capital and necessary experience in tourism

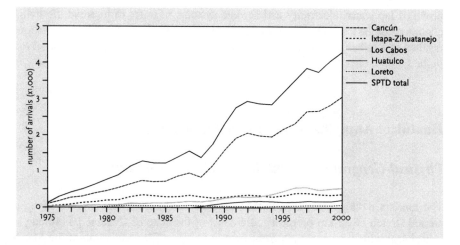

Fig. 12.3 Foreign tourist arrivals in State-Planned Tourism Destinations, 1975–2000 (FONATUR 1999a; SECTUR 2002)

has forced former fishermen and farmers to engage in informal activities to make a living (Arriaga 2000), while formal employers take on more experienced non-local workforces (Bravo 1994).

A third problem is that large-scale tourism development projects have the tendency to form enclaves that are neither economically nor socially linked to their hinterland. Studies in Puerto Vallarta (Müller 1983), Ixtapa-Zihuatanejo (Bravo 1994; Brenner 1999), Cancún (Aguilar et al. 1997; Torres and Momsen 2005) and Los Cabos (López 2002) have demonstrated that very limited linkages exist between the tourism sector and other locally- and regionally-based businesses, which simply cannot meet the demands of large chain hotels.

Fourthly, most tourism-related jobs are characterized by low skill and income levels, even by national standards (Bravo 1994; Sernau 1994; Brenner 1999). What is more, during the off-season employment can decrease by as much as 40% (Aguilar et al. 1997). Although there is no official data, research has indicated a high proportion of informal employment that lacks job security (Arriaga 2000, Madsen Camacho 1996, Sernau 1994).

Finally, the impact of the uncontrolled construction of tourism facilities and urban settlements has led to severe environmental deterioration. In Acapulco and Cancún, for instance, sewage water and intensive marine traffic continue to pollute ground and sea water (Gormsen 1995; Torres and Momsen 2005). The expansion of settlement areas has moreover led to the destruction of mangrove forests, which has already altered the extremely fragile coastal ecosystems (Gormsen 1997; Merino et al. 1993).

Taken together, these problems have had a severe negative effect on the competitiveness of Mexico's major resorts, forcing FONATUR and local authorities to act. They developed land for settlements, initiated housing programs and provided tap water, electricity and sewage systems in order to improve the living conditions of the migrants (Gormsen 1995). However, the lack of building regulations resulted in a rather chaotic process of suburbanization, as the author has observed in the field.

Huatulco: Applying a New Planning Strategy

Physical-Geographical and Socioeconomic Conditions

The tourism development area (TDA) of Huatulco (21,000 ha) extends along a coastal stretch of 35 km on the Pacific coast of the state of Oaxaca. Its climate is subtropical with a rainy season from June to October. The panorama of the Sierra Madre with elevations of up to 3,000 m, the dry tropical forest in the foothills, and the rough coastal landscape alternating with sandy beaches make this area one of the most attractive tourist destinations in Mexico. The ten largest bays offer locations for hotels and club resorts, while the valleys behind the coastline allow for the construction of larger settlements (Fig. 12.4). Until the 1980s this area was characterized by its peripheral location, low population density and high level of marginalization (FONATUR 1982; Orozco 1992).

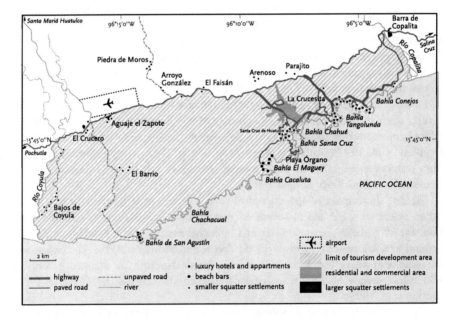

Fig. 12.4 Huatulco – Tourism Development Area

Prior to the construction of the coastal highway in 1982, the bays could only be accessed by boat or unpaved roads. Moreover, until the 1940s, the TDA was largely uninhabited due to the prevalence of tropical diseases. Driven by the increasing scarcity of arable land caused by population growth in the Sierra Madre del Sur, the first settlers arrived in the early 1950s. The largest settlements, Santa Cruz Huatulco and Coyula, were founded 10 years later (Long 1992). At the beginning of the construction phase of the tourism resort in 1984, the local population numbered around 2,500 inhabitants (FONATUR 1999b; Orozco 1992). Their dwellings were built with locally available materials such as wood, bamboo and palm leaves. The use of untreated drinking-water caused gastrointestinal diseases, while malaria and dengue fever were also common (Long 1992, 1993). The locals depended on subsistence agriculture and fishing for a living. Small shops offered a limited range of daily necessities.

In 1982, a presidential decree led to the expropriation of 21,000 ha, which was granted to FONATUR. These lands had previously been used by the indigenous and mestizo populations according to their ancient traditions. Plots of arable land were handed over to recognized members of the community (*comuneros*) for individual use, whereas the remaining land (beaches, forests, lagoons, etc.) was reserved for common use. Though FONATUR assured compensation payments to all 1,523 *comuneros* for the loss of their houses and properties, the process of expropriation and resettlement was a conflict-ridden one (FONATUR 1998, 1999b; Orozco 1992). The main bone of contention was the amount of compensation, which depended on the amount of individual holdings of each *comunero*.

In 1987, after a long negotiation process, representatives of the *comuneros* and FONATUR came to an agreement and the local population was finally resettled in the new residential area *La Crucesita*, located 2 km further inland. So far, only half of the cases has been fully dealt with, as many *comuneros* still demand additional compensation. Moreover, most former farmers and fishermen found it difficult to cope with the new living environment in detached houses made of concrete, unsuitable for the tropical climate (Long 1993).

The Development Process

In October 1984, construction began on the beaches of Santa Cruz, Chahué and Tangolunda, which had been designated as sites for luxury tourism (Fig. 12.4). By December 1987, when the international airport was opened, the first phase of construction had been completed. At the same time, the residential area La Crucesita was divided into lots for 15,000 new settlers. Colonial-style architecture inspired the town centre, where restaurants, souvenir shops, several middle-class hotels, the market and smaller retail shops are located. Moreover, FONATUR offered lots to investors in a fully developed industrial park.

By December 2001, only La Crucesita and the bays at Santa Cruz, Chahué and Tangolunda had been built up. The other zones remained either undeveloped (San Augustín, Cacaluta and Chahacual), unconstructed (Conejos), or used by local people who had built beach shacks (Órgano and Maguey). It is important to mention that more than half of the original TDA (a total of 11,891 ha) was declared a National Park in 1998.[2] It has been administered since by the Mexico City-based National Commission of Natural Protected Areas, a situation which constrains FONATUR's maneuvering space considerably as strict land-use regulations (including a building ban on luxury tourism infrastructure) must be observed.

After rather intensive construction activities from 1988 to 1993, accommodation capacity stagnated (SECTUR 2002) and the number of overnight stays lagged behind those in other SPTDs. In contrast to these destinations, Huatulco is dominated by national investment and domestic tourism. Only two international hotel chains (Club Med and Barceló) have established business there and more than three-quarters of all tourists who go to Huatulco are Mexican. Moreover, the average occupation rate of 50% lags far behind the other SPTDs (ca. 70%) (SECTUR 2002). The initial expectations of creating a second Cancún with a capacity of 22,000 rooms and 300,000 inhabitants by the year 2018 (FONATUR 1982; Bosselman et al. 1999) turned out to be unrealistic. Unofficially, FONATUR is now striving to achieve a final capacity of 12,000 rooms.[3]

Semi-structured interviews with four FONATUR officials, ten managers and owners of high-class tourism businesses and three heads of department of the municipal government of Santa María Huatulco have lead to believe that the stagnating development is the result of several interrelated factors. Due to budget cutbacks after 1983, Huatulco received less public investment than the other SPTDs (Brenner and Aguilar 2002). Furthermore, the resort entered into the global tourism market relatively late, which meant that it never had a chance to compete with the other, better-established national resorts. Widely ignored by the elite of the state of Oaxaca, Huatulco never received major political support at the regional and local levels. Finally, charter flight companies preferred to serve other, more popular destinations, which led to comparatively high-priced fares.

Planning Strategy and Results

In order to avoid the development problems mentioned above, FONATUR decided to strive to (a) foster the participation of the local population; (b) create and support economic linkages between the tourism sector and other branches of the regional economy; and, (c) control urban development in both physical and social

---

[2] www.conanp.gob.mx/anp (accessed: 09/09/2009).

[3] Jorge Arturo López, FONATUR/Huatulco (19.10.2000).

terms (Poder Ejecutivo 1984; Orozco 1992; Convenio del 23 de mayo de 1984[4]). The uniqueness and novelty of this planning approach lie in its highly ambitious attempt to control simultaneously the processes of social, economic, and urban development right from the start, instead of applying belated 'corrective measures' as was the case in Nuevo Vallarta (a luxury resort north of Puerto Vallarta) and in Ixtapa-Zihuatanejo. There FONATUR created new spaces for fishermen in a fruitless attempt to improve their living conditions (Orozco 1992).

In order to evaluate the outcome of these programs, a set of quantitative and qualitative survey methods was applied.[5] Field-based observations and supplementary conversations with La Crucesita residents helped to verify the statements given by the interviewees. The following problems were observed: marginalization of the local population, limited support for regional development, and polarized urban development.

The Marginalization of the Local Population

During the construction phase (1984–1987), a broad-based educational program was implemented. Though it had been designed by professional sociologists and was supposed to meet the specific needs of the local population (Long 1992, 1993; Orozco 1992; FONATUR 1998), locals were never consulted before or during the planning process of the tourism projects. The aim of the more than one hundred educational courses was to improve the literacy rate and to qualify local people for tourism-related jobs such as construction methods and commercial fisheries, so as to ensure participation of the local population from the beginning of tourism development. Later, follow-up courses on jobs in hotels and catering businesses were offered. Apart from that, FONATUR provided facilities to operate beach shacks (run by the wives of former fishermen) and stalls located in two covered markets in order give the locals the opportunity to sell Oaxacan handicrafts.[6]

Despite these measures, social marginalization could not be prevented. Local economic participation is limited to either the less profitable beach shacks or the retail sales selling crafts and souvenirs at the FONATUR-provided stalls (Table 12.1). In both cases revenues are minimal because seasonal fluctuations are high and

---

[4] The Convenio del 23 de mayo de 1984 is a legally binding agreement between the county of Santa Maria Huatulco, FONATUR, the Ministry of Agricultural Reform, the Ministry of Tourism, the Ministry of Urban Development and Environment and the Oaxaca State government.

[5] Methods included: (a) structured and standardized interviews with managers and owners of accommodation facilities, restaurants, beach-shacks, and tourist retail shops; (b) semi-structured, in-depth interviews with senior FONATUR-officials, heads of department of the municipality of Santa María Huatulco and representatives of local non-governmental organizations; and, (c) fieldwork-based observations. In addition, the research area was mapped in order to obtain a complete, up-to-date list of tourism businesses. Fieldwork was conducted during a 15-month period from October 2000 to December 2001.

[6] Patricia Orozco, FONATUR/Mexico-City (28.6.2002).

Table 12.1 Huatulco – Ownership in Tourist Retail Shops

		Owners		
Type of business	Number of businesses	Non-locals living outside Huatulco	Immigrants living in Huatulco	Locals living in Huatulco
Market stalls	44	0	16	28
Shops with officially registered premises	31	2	21	8
Sample size	75	2	37	36
Huatulco total	133	–	–	–

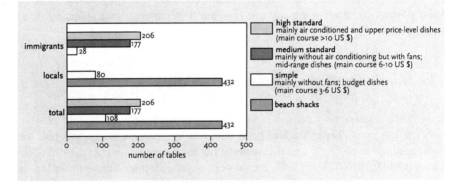

Fig. 12.5 Restaurant ownership in Huatulco

because restaurant owners are obliged to purchase products at relatively expensive retail prices at the local food market, since there are no food wholesalers in La Crucesita. As craft production in the coastal area is limited to carved coconuts, stall owners usually buy commercial souvenirs such as shirts, *sombreros,* pottery and other *airport-art* at relatively high prices from intermediaries based in Oaxaca City and Acapulco.

Mid-level and luxury-class restaurants, as well as the souvenir shops that cater to international and well-off domestic tourists, are owned and run almost exclusively by immigrants from outside of the region (see Fig. 12.5 and Table 12.1). The hotel sector is controlled by several national and two international[7] hotel chains and, to a lesser extent, by wealthy immigrants (see Fig. 12.6). This applies especially to hotels in the luxury class (4 and 5 stars) that together make up 80% of the total capacity. Less than 20% of the total accommodation capacity is owned by middle-class immigrants or entrepreneurs based in Oaxaca City. Former fishermen and farmers own only 2% of all hotel rooms.

When asked about the reasons for the lack of local participation, the key informants interviewed emphasized the following factors: first, the region experienced a

---

[7] *Club Med* (controlled by French investors) and *Barceló* (controlled by Spanish investors).

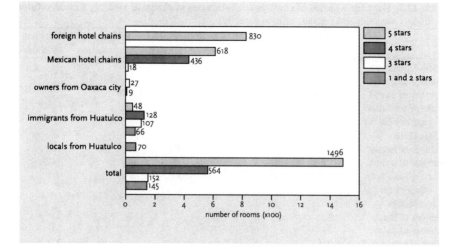

Fig. 12.6 Hotel ownership in Bahías de Huatulco

radical economic and demographic transformation in less than 20 years with which the local population was unable to cope. Within the TDA, only 8% of the population that had previously worked as farmers or fishermen continued to do so in the year 2000, while 73% of the population is now employed in the service sector (INEGI 2002). In the same period, the population increased from 2,500 (FONATUR 1999b) to 14,000 (INEGI 2002), which meant that immigrants quickly outnumbered locals. Second, due to financial cutbacks during the administration of President Carlos Salinas de Gortari (1988–1994), educational programs were suspended after achieving only a minimal transfer of knowledge (Long 1993). Locals have never been able to compete with the better-educated immigrants and were therefore forced to accept almost any salary to earn a living.[8] Third, apart from the beach shacks and souvenir stands, local people failed to start up businesses (FONATUR 1999b). With little or no previous experience and lacking capital, they were unable to take advantage of the opportunities that arose at least during the initial phase (Long 1992, p. 199). Finally, compensation payments were spent quickly on goods which had been unaffordable before (e.g. automobiles, satellite TVs and audio and video equipment).[9]

Limited Support for Regional Development

In order to avoid the formation of enclaves, FONATUR expressed its intention to use "locally available raw materials and products as much as possible in order to raise the

---

[8] Élder Juárez, FONATUR/Huatulco (11.9.2001).
[9] Patricia Orzoco, FONATUR/Mexico-City (28.6.2002).

Table 12.2 Huatulco – Origin of construction companies in charge of building accommodation facilities (Categories and percents of total capacity)

	Mexico City	Other major cities	Oaxaca City	Huatulco	Self-managed construction	Data not available
5-Star-Hotels						
Number of hotels	7	1				
Number of rooms	1.469	27				
Share of total hotel capacity (in %)	*62.3*	*1.1*				
4-Star-Hotels						
Number of hotels	3	3		3	1	1
Number of rooms	228	136		75	13	112
Share of total hotel capacity (in %)	*9.7*	*5.8*		*3.2*	*0.6*	*4.8*
3-Star-Hotels						
Number of hotels	5				2	3
Number of rooms	79				20	53
Share of total hotel capacity (in %)	*3.4*				*0.8*	*2.2*
1- and 2-Star-Hotels						
Number of hotels		1	2	6	2	2
Number of rooms		18	17	53	28	29
Share of total hotel capacity (in %)		*0.8*	*0.7*	*2.2*	*1.2*	*1.2*
Total						
Number of hotels	15	5	2	9	5	6
Number of rooms	1.776	181	17	128	61	194
Share of total hotel capacity (in %)	*75.4*	*7.7*	*0.7*	*5.4*	*2.6*	*8.2*

standard of living of the local population" (Convenio del 23 de Mayo de 1984).[10] To this end, three fishery cooperatives received financial aid and the authorities promised financial support for the irrigation of agricultural land to meet the coming demand for fruits and vegetables (FONATUR 1999b).

These measures, however, proved to be equally unsatisfactory, given the low level of economic development in the region. Due to the lack of major construction firms in the state of Oaxaca (INEGI 2000b), FONATUR had to commission firms based in Mexico City and Puebla to construct the entire urban and tourism infrastructure.[11] Businesses from Oaxaca and Huatulco were contracted only for smaller hotels (see Table 12.2). The demand for building materials also had very little effect on the regional economy, as nearly all materials had to be delivered from Oaxaca or Mexico City.

The economy of the state of Oaxaca is highly dependent on primary sector activities. Therefore, FONATUR intended to bank on stimulating linkages between

[10] See note 4.

[11] Jorge Arturo López, FONATUR/Huatulco (19.10.2000).

Table 12.3 Huatulco – Volume of food products purchased according to place of origin* (Percents of supplied hotel capacities)

Product	Mexico City	Other large cities in Mexico	Oaxaca City	Other cities in the State of Oaxaca	Huatulco	Total
Beef and pork	1.4	43.9	23.2	–	31.5	100.0
Seafood	7.8	–	–	–	92.2	100.0
Dairy products		28.6	–	33.0	38.4	100.0
Poultry	23.2	–	–	–	76.8	100.0
Vegetables	–	–	82.3	–	17.7	100.0
Fruits	–	–	82.3	–	17.7	100.0
Eggs	–	6.5	20.7	–	72.8	100.0
Beer	–	–	–	–	100.0	100.0**
Wine and liquors	46.2	13.4	5.8	–	34.6	100.0
Soft drinks	–	–	–	–	100.0	100.0**

* Suppliers delivering at least 50% of each kind of product
** Consortia with supply depots in Huatulco

the tourism sector and agriculture and fishing.[12] Yet, as Table 12.3 shows, problems similar to those of other tourist destinations such as Cancún (Torres 2002, 2003) can be observed: most of the food consumed in hotel restaurants of a higher standard is purchased directly from non-local sources; soft drinks and alcoholic beverages are supplied by large consortia with supply depots in Huatulco; and only perishables such as fish, crustaceans, poultry and eggs are bought at local markets. However, only fish are caught and delivered by local cooperatives, while nearly all other foodstuffs (perishable and non-perishable) available in Huatulco are delivered from other parts of the country.[13] For this reason, the demand of the over 90 independently managed restaurants and food-stalls has failed to have a positive impact on regional agriculture. Considering these circumstances, it is doubtful whether the irrigation of only 500 ha of land as planned by FONATUR can actually increase agricultural production in a way that would satisfy the needs of tourists and the immigrant population, as intended.

Polarized Urban Development

From 1984 to 1987, La Crucesita was divided into lots and supplied with infrastructure such as roads, electricity, water, and a sewage system in an attempt by FONATUR to accommodate the rapid population growth that was predicted for the region.

---

[12] Patricia Orzoco, FONATUR/Mexico-City (28.6. 2002).

[13] The city of Oaxaca remains the most important supply centre for the majority of foodstuffs consumed in Huatulco due to water shortages, infertile soils, the isolated location and the predominance of subsistence agriculture (Bassols et al. 1994).

Properties were sold to settlers at prices far below those asked for lots designated for commercial purposes.[14] At the same time, FONATUR began a housing program in coordination with other authorities. About 70% of the 3,600 apartments in Huatulco have been built through this program and can be purchased on favorable conditions by employees entitled to national social security.[15] However, 65% of Huatulco's population does not have a right to social security nor an income level low enough to apply for a loan (INEGI 2000b). Thus many apartments remain vacant or have been purchased as objects of speculation. Private investors constructed *inter alia* three housing areas with more than 100 mid-price flats that together resulted in a comparatively large supply in the higher and middle price ranges. High construction costs have also led to higher rents. What remains is a shortage of cheap housing for poorer immigrants, especially as FONATUR has imposed strict building regulations.[16]

Thus, despite its relatively slow population growth, Huatulco is facing polarized urbanization.[17] Social disparities are striking when one compares the upper- and middle-class-dominated La Crucesita with the shantytowns outside the areas developed by FONATUR. La Crucesita has come to be the living space for the better-educated immigrants from the urban centres in Mexico, while migrants from the rural areas in the state of Oaxaca are forced to settle in shantytowns such as El Crucero, El Zapote and El Faisan, along the coastal highway between the airport and La Crucesita.

Our data also provides proof of this spatial and social segregation: in La Crucesita, the share of employed population with incomes below the legal minimum wage is far lower than in other villages and towns inside and outside the TDA. A striking fact is the high percentage of employees earning more than two minimum wages in La Crucesita. There are also noticeable differences with respect to the level of education: adults living in La Crucesita went to school for 7.9 years on average, compared to about only 4 years in other parts of the TDA (INEGI 2002). Moreover, the inequalities regarding access to basic infrastructure are significant. In La Crucesita, nearly all housing units are connected to running water and the sewage system, while percentages in other parts of the TDA are much lower.

Conclusions

So far, most scholars have paid relatively little attention to planning strategies designed to avoid or mitigate the negative social impacts of mass tourism. In this context, Huatulco is a unique example as national authorities have taken a series of

---

[14] Jorge Arturo López, FONATUR/Huatulco (19.10.2000).

[15] Élder Sánchez, FONATUR/Huatulco (11.9.2001).

[16] Jorge Arturo López, FONATUR/Huatulco (19.10.2000).

[17] In 2000, the municipality of Santa Maria Huatulco had a total of 28,000 inhabitants, of whom 13,000 lived in La Crucesita (INEGI 2002).

apparently well-planned measures to foster socially sound regional economic development. However, this attempt cannot be considered successful. First, sustainable economic development based on luxury tourism requires a minimum of regional-based capital, know-how and entrepreneurial initiative, none of which were sufficiently present. Second, authorities had the unrealistic expectations that the local population would be able to cope with the radical social and economic changes involved and become integrated in the development of tourism within a short period of time. Third, while applying coercive measures without prior consultation, FONATUR did not enhance local participation. Moreover, the program lacked steady financial support and monitoring, which could have helped to develop adequate planning tools.

The question thus arises as to which strategies and measures could enhance both local and regional participation and ensure viability in economic terms in the face of the state's diminishing capacity to act. First of all, it is essential to foster small-scale tourism development projects and to focus not only on technical and legal factors, but also on the interests and action-strategies of the stakeholders involved at the local, regional, national and international levels (local population, regional elites, government institutions, tourism companies, tourists, and others). In this regard, existing participant planning approaches which are aimed at 'the locals' (often considered a socially homogenous group) have to be improved in terms of their economic, social and cultural feasibility and be flexible enough to allow adjustments during the process of tourism development.

Additionally, there is a need to integrate the existing coastal resorts more deeply into regional economic production systems, and to make the most of Mexico's enormous natural and cultural potential. In this sense, sun-and-beach tourism should be linked more closely with other emerging types of tourism, such as nature-based and cultural tourism, in order to take full commercial advantage of the country's unique combination of fully-equipped, modern beach resorts, enormous biodiversity and extraordinary cultural heritage. While recognizing the severe problems of development at Cancún, there is no doubt that today it is an important hub of the entire cultural and ecotourism industry in northern Central America, which has fostered economic development in at least some localities in the region. Similarly, other SPTD and traditional resorts such as Huatulco, Los Cabos or Puerto Vallarta could serve as a starting point for trips to their largely unknown but highly attractive hinterlands.

About the Contributors

Leendert de Bell (leendert.debell@hu.nl) obtained his Ph.D. in Human Geography at Utrecht University. His research mainly deals with processes of international economic restructuring, regional economic integration and local development in Latin America. He is lecturer Political Economy of Latin America at the School of Economics and Business in Amsterdam, and coordinator of the Bachelor program of the Kofi Annan Business School at the University of Applied Sciences Utrecht, where he also lectures on entrepreneurship in developing areas and corporate social responsibility.

Axel Borsdorf (axel.borsdorf@uibk.ac.at) is full professor at the Department of Geography, University of Innsbruck, Director of the Institute for Mountain Research of the Austrian Academy of Sciences and full member of this Academy. He acted as the president of the Austrian Geographical Society and is the Vice-President of the Austrian Institute for Latin America. His research is focussed on mountain regions, Latin America, urban and cultural geography. He is editor and member of the editorial board of prestigious journals and taught as visiting professor at the Universities of Berne, Chulalongkorn University Bangkok, Eugene/OR, Tamaulipas/Mexico, UdCh Santiago/Chile and PUC Santiago de Chile.

Ludger Brenner (bren@xanum.uam.mx) is a professor in the Department of Sociology, Universidad Autónoma Metropolitana at Ixtapalapa, Mexico. His current research interests include tourism and regional development and management of Protected Areas. He has published on both topics in national and international journals such as The Professional Geographer, Tourism Geographies, Journal of Latin Geography and the International Journal of Tourism Research.

Karin Fischer (karin.fischer@jku.at) is lecturer at the Johannes Kepler Universität Linz (Institut für Soziologie). Her areas of expertise include: history and theories of development; globalization and urban processes in Latin America. Her current research concerns transnational class formation and elite transformation in Latin America. Her latest publications include "Internationalisms. Transformation of Global Inequality in the 19th and 20th Centuries" (co-editor, Vienna 2008) and "The influence of organized neoliberalism before, during and after the Pinochet dictatorship" (Oxford, forthcoming).

Rodrigo Hidalgo (hidalgo@geo.puc.cl) is professor at the Department of Geography, Pontífica Universidad Católica de Chile. After his Ph.D. from the University of Barcelona, he focussed his research on the changes in the residential districts of large Latin American cities, especially on social housing and gated communities. He published various books and articles in Latin American, North American and European journals and acts as the publisher of the Revista de Geografía Norte Grande and the GEOlibros book series. He is co-editor of some prestigious journals, indicated in ISI, like EURE, Scripta Nova and the Boletín de la Asociación de Geógrafos Españoles. He also taught as a visiting professor in the postgraduate school of the University of São Paulo.

David Hulme (david.hulme@manchester.ac.uk) is Professor in Development Studies and Director of the Chronic Poverty Research Centre at the University of Manchester, UK. His area of expertise includes rural development policy and planning; poverty reduction strategies; sociology of development; role of community organisations and NGOs. His latest books include: "The Chronic Poverty Report 2004–05" (co-authored with U. Grant, K. Moore and D. Sheperd); "The State of the Poorest 2005/2006: Chronic Poverty in Bangladesh – Tales of Ascent, Descent, Marginality and Persistence" (with B. Sen); "Challenging Global Inequality: The Theory and Practice of Development in the Twenty-First Century" (with A. Greig and M. Turner, 2007); and "Social Protection for the Poor and Poorest: Concepts, Policies and Politics" (co-edited with Armando Barrientos, 2008).

Karen Imhof (karen.imhof@univie.ac.at) is lecturer at the Project International Development, University of Vienna. She is also working as a researcher for the research project "The Transformation of Global Financial Governance" sponsored by the Austrian National Bank. Further interests include the history of development economics and theories of trade as well as global financial governance and the interaction of financial structures on the global and local level. She recently co-edited a volume on "Capitalist Development in North and South" (Vienna 2008).

Paul van Lindert (p.vanlindert@geo.uu.nl) is associate professor at the Faculty of Geosciences of Utrecht University, the Netherlands). His main research interests include: regional and local development; rural-urban relations; local governance; sustainable urban development; city networks and city-to-city cooperation; monitoring and evaluation of development cooperation. He published on these topics in World Development, Urban Studies, The Journal of Development Alternatives and Area Studies, TESG, Environment and Urbanization, Habitat International and many other journals.

Dicky de Morrée (d.demorree@zonnet.nl) works at Cordaid, The Hague, a major non governmental development organisation in The Netherlands. She obtained her Ph.D. at International Development Studies at Utrecht University. She carried out her Ph.D. research in Bolivia, as part of a research project on peasant livelihood strategies and development interventions.

Martina Neuburger (martina.neuburger@uibk.ac.at) is assistant professor at the Department of Geography of the University of Innsbruck, Austria. Her work focuses on rural development, peasant and gender issues as well as on vulnerability and political ecology. Her regional specialisation is on Brazil and Bolivia.

Gery Nijenhuis (g.nijenhuis@geo.uu.nl) is assistant professor of International Development Studies at Utrecht University, the Netherlands. Her main fields of interest include decentralization and local participatory governance. Her Ph.D. dissertation dealt with the impact of the participatory governance approach on local economic development in Bolivia. Her current research focus is on the relations between international migration, local development and local governnace.

Cora van Oosten (cora.vanoosten@wur.nl) is a geographer experienced in natural resources governance, regional planning, civil society strengthening and rights based approaches. She worked at the local, regional and national level in Africa (Kenya, Burkina Faso, Ghana), Latin America (Bolivia), and Asia (Cambodia). At present, she is employed as project leader/adviser at Wageningen International, in charge of a portfolio related to natural resources management, landscape/ ecosystems approaches, governance, facilitation of multi-stakeholder processes, and capacity development.

Christof Parnreiter (parnreiter@geowiss.uni-hamburg.de) is professor of economic geography at the University of Hamburg. After receiving his Ph.D. from the University of Vienna, he became post-doc student at the University of Chicago and later research assistant at the Austrian Academy of Sciences. His research interests cover migration, urbanization and development studies, with a regional focus on Latin America. One of his latest publications is his book on Mexico City: "Historische Geographien, verräumlichte Geschichte. Mexico City und das mexikanische Städtenetz von der Industrialisierung bis zur Globalisierung" (Franz Steiner Verlag, Stuttgart, 2007).

Jörg Plöger (joerg.ploeger@ils-forschung.de) is urban geographer, who studied processes of urban transformation in Latin American cities. He received his Ph.D. degree (2006) in geography for his research on residential enclave building in Lima at the University of Kiel, Germany. Currently he is employed as research officer at the ILS Research Institute for Regional and Urban Development in Dortmund, Germany.

Mirjam A.F. Ros-Tonen (m.a.f.ros-tonen@uva.nl) is senior researcher and lecturer at the Amsterdam research institute for Metropolitan and International Development Studies (AMIDSt), University of Amsterdam, The Netherlands. She is engaged in research on forest use, management and governance in the Brazilian Amazon, on which she authored various articles. Recently she co-edited a volume on Partnerships in Sustainable Forest Resource Management: Learning from Latin America (Brill Publishers, Leiden, 2007). Additionally, she coordinates the Dutch Development Policy Review Network (DPRN).

Dörte Segebart (doerte@caju.de) is junior professor at the Institute of Geographical Sciences at the Freie Universität Berlin. Her research focuses on gender sensitive planning and multi-level analysis of governance for sustainable development. Her regional interests are Central Europe and the emerging economies, especially China, Brazil and South Asia. Her PhD research was on participatory monitoring and the strengthening of local (municipal) governance in Brazil.

Otto Verkoren (verko053@planet.nl) is a geographer with a keen interest in the urban geography of Latin America and Africa, more especially in migration and the absorption of migrants in the urban economy, in self-help and public housing, in informal sector development. Together with a growing attention for policy issues, the topics amalgamated into a new research-theme: urban-based local (economic) development. Before his retirement, he chaired the International Development Studies Unit of the Department of Human Geography and Planning, Faculty of Geosciences, Utrecht University.

References

Abastoflor, W. & F. Rivero (1999) *Forjando el Municipio Productivo*. La Paz: AIPE.

Abbot, J., I. Guijt (1999) *Novas visões sobre mudança ambiental. Abordagens participativas de monitoramento*. Rio de Janeiro.

Abers, R. (1998) From Clientelism to Cooperation: Local Government, Participatory Policy, and Civic Organizing in Porto Alegre, *Politics & Society*, 26, 4, pp. 511-537.

Abers, R. (1998a) Learning Democratic Practice: Distributing Government Resources through Popular Participation in Porto Alegre, Brazil. In: M. Douglas & J. Friedmann (Eds) *Cities for Citizens*, pp. 29-65. Chichester: John Wiley and Sons.

Abers, R. (2000) *Inventing Local Democracy: Grassroots Politics in Brazil*. Boulder.

Achilles, G.W. (1989) *Strukturwandel und Bewertung sozial hochrangiger Wohnviertel in Rio de Janeiro. Die Entwicklung einer brasilianischen Metropole unter besonderer Berücksichtigung der Stadtteile Ipanema und Leblon*. Tübinger Geographische Studien 104. Tübingen: Selbstverlag des Geographischen Instituts.

Aguilar, A., B. Graizbord & A. Crispín (1996) *Las ciudades intermedias y el desarrollo regional en México*. Mexico City: UNAM.

Aguilar, A., B. Graiszbord & A. Sanchez (Eds.) (1997) *Política pública y base económica enseis ciudades medias de México*. Mexico City: El Colegio de México.

Alba Vega, C. (1996) Los empresarios y el estado durante el salinismo, *Foro Internacional*, 36, pp. 31-79.

Albuquerque, F. (1999) *Desarrollo económico local en Europa y América Latina*. Madrid: Consejo Superior de Investigaciones Científicas.

Altschuler, B. (2006) Municipios y desarrollo local. Un balance necesario. In: A. Rofman & A.Villar (Eds.) *Desarrollo local. Una revisión crítica del debate*, pp. 131-154. Buenos Aires: Espacio Editorial.

Altenburg, T. & J. Meyer-Stamer (1999) How to promote Clusters: Policy Experiences from Latin America, *World Development* 27, 9, pp. 1693-1713.

Andrews, M. & A. Shah (2005) Citizen-Centered Governance: a New Approach to Public Sector Reform. In: A. Shah (Ed.) *Public Expenditure Analysis*, pp. 153-182. Washington (DC): World Bank.

Apoyo Opinión y Mercado (1999) *Criminal violence: studies in Latin American Cities, the case of Peru*. Lima: Apoyo.

Archer, B. (1996) Sustainable Tourism: an Economist's Viewpoint. In: L. Briguglio (Ed) *Sustainable Tourism in Islands and Small States. Issues and Policies*, pp. 6-17. London/New York: Pinter.

Arriaga, J. C. (2000) Sector informal y economía del turismo en Cancún. In: J. Maerk & I. Boxill (Eds.) *Turismo en el Caribe*, pp. 67-91. Mexico City.

Assies, W. (1997) *Going Nuts for the Rainforest, Non-Timber Forest Products, Forest Conservation and Sustainability in Amazonia*. Amsterdam: Thela Publishers.

Assies, W. (2003) La descentralización a la Boliviana y la économía política del reformismo. In: W. Assies (Ed.) *Gobiernos locales y reforma del Estado en América Latina: innovando la Gestión Pública*, pp. 135-160. Zamora: El Colegio de Michoacán.

Asociación Chilena de Municipalidades (1996) *Desarrollo Económico Local.* Santiago de Chile: ACM-FESUR-DES.

Audley, J. D. Papademetriou, S. Polaski & S.Vaughan (2003) *NAFTA's promise and reality. Lessons from Mexico for the hemisphere.* Carnegie Endowment for International Peace. [www. ceip.org/pubs]

Ayo, D., C. Barragan & O. Guzman Boutier (1998) *Participación Popular: una evaluación aprendizaje de la ley 1994-1997.* La Paz: Ministerio de Desarrollo Sostenible y Planificación.

Bähr, J. (Ed.) (1988) *Wohnen in Lateinamerikanische Städten – Housing in Latin American Cities.* Kieler Geographische Schriften 68. Kiel: Christian Albrechts Universität.

Bähr, J. & G. Mertins (1981) Idealschema der sozialräumlichen Differenzierung lateinamerikanischer Großstädte, *Geographische Zeitschrift,* 69, 1, pp. 1-33.

Bähr, J. & G. Mertins (1995) *Die lateinamerikanische Großstadt. Verstädterungsprozesse und Stadtstrukturen.* Darmstadt: Wissenschaftliche Buchgesellschaft.

Banco Central de Chile (2001) *Indicadores Económicos y Sociales de Chile 1960-2000.* Santiago.

Barajas, I.A. (1993) *Descentralización industrial y desarrollo regional en México.* Mexico City: El Colegio de México.

Barkin, D. & T. King (1970) *Regional Economic Development: The River Basin Approach in Mexico.* Cambridge: Cambridge University Press.

Basombrío, C. (2003) *Perú 2003: Inseguridad ciudadana y delito común.* Lima: Instituto de Defensa Legal.

Bass, S. (2002) Global forest governance: emerging impacts of the Forest Stewardship Council and suggested research questions. *Paper presented at the International SUSTRA Workshop, 9-10 December 2002 on Architecture of the Global System of Governance of Trade and Sustainable Development.* Berlin.

Bassols, A., F. Torres & J. Delgadillo (1994) *El abasto alimentario en las regiones de México.* Mexico City: UNAM.

Becker, C., H. Job & A. Witzel (1996) *Tourismus und nachhaltige Entwicklung.* Darmstadt: Wissenschaftliche Buchgesellschaft.

Bell, P. *et al.* (1996) *Environmental Psychology.* Fort Worth: Wadsworth.

Bell, L. de (2005) *Globalization, regional Development and local Response. The Impact of Economic Restructuring in Coahuila, Mexico.* Amsterdam: Dutch University Press.

Bingham, R. & R. Mier (1993), *Theories of local economic development: Perspectives from across the disciplines.* London: Sage.

Birle, P. (1996) Interne und externe Rahmenbedingungen der bolivianischen Reformpolitik, *Lateinamerika, Analysen, Daten, Dokumentation,* 13, pp. 15-26.

Blair, H. (2000) Participation and Accountability in the Periphery: An Assessment of Democratic Local Governance, *World Development* 28, 1, pp. 21-39.

Blakely, E. J. (1994) *Planning Local Economic Development: Development theory and practice.* Thousand Oaks: Sage.

Blakeley, E. & M.G. Snyder (1997) *Fortress America, Gated Communities in the United States.* Washington (DC)/Cambridge: Brookings.

Boisier, S. (1999) *Teorías y metáforas sobre Desarrollo Territorial.* Santiago de Chile: Cepal.

Bojanic, A. J. B. (2001) *Balance is beautiful: Assessing sustainable development in the rain forest of the Bolivian Amazon.* Utrecht: PROMAB.

Bontenbal, M. (2009a) Cities as partners. The challenge to strengthen urban governance trough North-South city partnerships. Delft: Eburon.

Bontenbal, M. (2009b) Understanding North-South municipal partnership conditions for capacity development: a Dutch-Peruvian example, *Habitat International* 33, 1, pp. 100-105.

Bontenbal, M. & P. van Lindert (2008) Bridging local institutions and civil society in Latin America: can city-to-city cooperation make a difference? *Environment & Urbanization* 29, 2, pp. 465-482.

Bontenbal, M. & P. van Lindert (2009) Transnational city-to-city cooperation: Issues arising from theory and practice, *Habitat International* 33, 2, pp. 131-133.

Booth, J., S. Clisby & C. Widmark (1997) *Popular participation. Democratising the State in rural Bolivia,* Report presented to SIDA, Dept. of Social Anthropology. Stockholm: Stockholm University.

Borsdorf, A. (1976) Valdivia und Osorno. Strukturelle Disparitäten in chilenischen Mittelstädten, *Tübinger Geographische Studien 69.* Tübingen.

Borsdorf, A. (1982) Die lateinamerikanische Großstadt. Zwischenbericht zur Diskussion umein Modell, *Geographische Rundschau* 34, 11, pp. 498-501.

Borsdorf, A.(1998) Vom Casco Colonial zum Barrio Amurallado: Wohnformen in lateinamerikanischen Städten. In: M. Kaller-Dietrich (Ed.) *Recht auf Entwicklung? Atención!* Jahrbuch des Österreichischen Lateinamerika-Instituts, 1, pp. 81-105. Frankfurt/Main,.

Borsdorf, A. (2000) Condominios in Santiago de Chile als Beispiele sozialräumlicher Segregationstendenzen von Ober- und Mittelschicht in lateinamerikanischen Städten, *Peripherie, Zeitschrift für Politik und Ökonomie in der Dritten Welt*, 20, 80, pp. 25-40.

Borsdorf, A. (2002a) Vor verschlossenen Türen – Wie neu sind Tore und Mauern in lateinamerikanischen Städten? *Geographica Helvetica* 57, 4, pp. 278-289.

Borsdorf, A. (2002b) Condominios en Santiago de Chile, Quito y Lima: Tendencias de la segregación socio-espacial en capitales andinas. In: L.F. Cabrales Barajas (Ed.) *Ciudades cerradas – paises abiertos*, pp. 581-610. Guadalajara/Paris: UNESCO.

Borsdorf, A. (2003a) La segregación socio-espacial en ciudades latinoamericanas: el fenómeno, los motivos y las conscuencias para un modelo del desarrollo urbano en America Latina. In: J. L. Luzón, C. Stadel & C. Borges (Ed.) *Transformaciones regionales y urbanas en Europa y América Latina*, pp. 129-142. Barcelona: Publicaciones UBA.

Borsdorf, A. (2003b) Cómo modelar el desarrollo y la dinámica de la ciudad Latinoamericana, *EURE Revista Latinoamericana de Estudios Urbano Regionales* 29, 86, pp. 37-49.

Borsdorf, A. (2004) Landflucht als Teil der Mobilitätstransformation. Das Beispiel lateinamerika, *Praxis Geographie* 34, 7/8, pp. 9-14.

Borsdorf, A., J. Bähr & M. Janoschka (2002) Die Dynamik stadtstrukturellen Wandels in Lateinamerika im Modell der lateinamerikanischen Stadt, *Geographica Helvetica*, 57, 4, pp. 300-310.

Bosselman, F., C.A. Peterson & C. McCarthy (1999) *Managing Tourism Growth: Issues and Applications*, Washington (DC): Island Press.

Bragos, O., A. Mateos & S. Pontini (2002) Nuevos desarrollos residenciales y procesos de segregación socio-espacial en la expansión oeste de Rosario. In: L.F. Cabrales Barajas (Ed.) *Latinoamérica: países abiertos, ciudades cerradas*, pp. 441-480. Guadalajara/Paris: UNESCO.

Braudel, F., (1986) *Sozialgeschichte des 15.-18. Jahrhunderts. Aufbruch zur Weltwirtschaft.* München: Kindler.

Bravo, C. (1994) *La política de impulso turístico en México. Ixtapa-Zihuatanejo como polo de desarrollo turístico.* Master's Thesis, UNA, Mexico.

Brenner, L. (1999) Modelo para la evaluación de la 'sustentabilidad' del turismo en México con base en el ejemplo de Ixtapa-Zihuatanejo, *Investigaciones Geográficas* 39, pp. 139-158.

Brenner, L. (2006) Áreas Naturales Protegidas y ecoturismo: el caso de la Reserva de Biosfera Mariposa Monarca, México, *Relaciones. Estudios de Historia y Sociedad*, 27, 105, pp. 237-265.

Brenner, L. (2007) La política turística mexicana y su impacto en el desarrollo nacional y urbano-regional.- In: Urbanización y turismo, pp. 13-24, ed. Bonnie Lucía Campos Cámera.- Ediciones Pomares: Barcelona/Spain.

Brenner, L. & A. Aguilar (2002) Luxury Tourism and Regional Economic Development in. Mexico, *The Professional Geographer* 54, 4, pp. 500-520.

Brenner, L. & H. Job (2006) Actor-oriented Management of Protected Areas and Ecotourism in Mexico, *Journal of Latin American Geography*, 5, 2, pp. 7-27.

Britton, S. G. (1982) The Political Economy of Tourism in the Third World, *Annals of Tourism Research* 9, pp. 331-58.

Broman, J. (1996) New Directions in Tourism for Third World Development, *Annals of Tourism Research 23*, 1, pp. 48-70.

Brown, E., G. Catalano & P. J. Taylor (2002): Beyond World Cities: Central America in a Global Space of Flows, *Area*, 34, 2, pp. 139-148.

Brown, E., D. Derudder, C. Parnreiter, W. Pelupessy *et al.* (2007) World City Networks and Global Commodity Chains: Towards a World-Systems' Integration. *GaWC Research Bulletin 236* [www.lboro.ac.uk/gawc/rb/rb236.html]

Brown, E., B. Derudder, W. Pelupessy, P. Taylor, & F. Witlox (2010) World City Networks and Global Commodity Chains: towards a world-systems' integration. In: *Global Networks.* 10(1):12-34.

Brown, I. F., S. Brilhante, E. Mendoza & I. de Oliveira (2003) Estrada de Rio Branco, Acre, Brasil aos portos do Pacifico: Como maximizar os beneficios e minimizar os prejuízas para o desenvolvimento sustentável da Amazonia Sul-Ocidental. Rio Branco: Universidad Federal do Acre.

Bulmer-Thomas, V. (1994) *The Economic History of Latin America since Independence.* Cambridge: Cambridge University Press.

Bukes, G. (2000) *Die Zusammenhang von wirtschaftlicher Entwicklung und Demokratisierung. Das Beispiel Bolivien,* Hamburg: Institut für Iberoamerika-Kunde.

Bundesministerium für Wirtschaftliche Zusammenarbeit und Entwicklung (BMZ) (1995) *Ecotourism as a Conservation Instrumen.* Munich: Weltforum Verlag.

Burchell, G., C. Gordon & P. Miller (Eds.) (1991) *The Foucault Effect. Studies in Governmentality.* Chicago: University of Chicago Press.

Burin, D. & A. Heras (Comps) (2001) *Desarrollo local. Una respuesta a escala humana a la globalización.* Buenos Aires: Ediciones Ciccus-La Crujía.

Burki, S. J. & G. E. Perry (1998) *Beyond the Washington Consensus: Institutions Matter.* Washington (DC): World Bank.

Burns, P. & A. Holden (1995) *Tourism: A New Perspective.* London: Prentice Hall.

Bustamante, F. (Comp.) (2004) *Planificación y municipalización en Bolivia. Agentes y Actores, Municipio Productivo y Sistemas Urbanos en Municipios de Cochabamba.* Cochabamba/ Utrecht: PROMEC-UMSS/UU.

Buzai, G. D. (2003) *Mapas sociales urbanos.* Buenos Aires: Lugar Editorial.

Buzai, G. D. (2004) Distribución, segregación y autocorrelación espacial de extranjeros en laciudad de Luján, Argentina. *Avances de Investigación.* Universidad Nacional de Luján.

Cabannes, Y. (2004) Participatory budgeting: a significant contribution to participatory democracy, *Environment and Urbanization,* 16, 1, pp. 27-46.

Cabrales Barajas, L. F. & E. Canosa Zamora (2001) *Segregación residencial y fragmentación urbana: los fraccionamientos cerrados en Guadalaja.* Espiral, Estudios sobre Estado y Sociedad Guadalajara, 7, pp. 223-253.

Cabrales Barajas, L. F. & E. Canosa Zamora (2002) Nuevas formas y viejos valores: urbanizaciones cerradas de lujo en Guadalajara. In: L. F. Cabrales Barajas (Ed.) *Latinoamérica: países abiertos, ciudades cerradas,* pp. 93-116. Guadalajara/Paris: UNESCO.

Caldeira, T. (1996) Building up walls: the new pattern of spatial segregation in São Paulo, *International Sociological Science Journal* 48, pp. 55-56.

Caldeira, T. (2000) *City of Walls. Crime, segregation and citizenship in São Paulo.* Berkeley: University of California Press.

Calderón, J. (2005) *La ciudad ilegal. Lima en el siglo XX.* Lima: Universidad Nacional Mayor de San Marcos.

Campbell, T. (2009) Learning cities: Knowledge, capacity and competetiveness, *Habitat International* 33, 2, pp. 195-201.

Canel, E. (2001) Municipal decentralisation and participatory democracy: building a new mode of urban politics in Montevideo City? *European Review of Latin American and Caribbean Studies* 71, pp. 25-46.

Cardenas Cervera, F. & V. Redonnet (1998) El desempleo en la empresa Altos Hornos de México S.A. en la década de los noventa, *Cuadernos de Investigación. Ciencias Sociales y Humanidades,* 18, pp. 7-29.

Cariola C. & M. Lacabana (2001) La metrópoli fragmentada – Caracas entre la pobreza y la globalización, *Revista EURE,* 27, 80, pp. 9-32.

Carley, M., P. Jenkins & H. Smith (2001) (Eds) *Urban Development and Civil Society. The role of communities in sustainable cities.* London: Earthscan.

Carpio Benalcázar, P. (Comp.) (2006) *Retos del Desarrollo local.* Quito: OFIS/ILDIS/Abya-Yala.

Carroll, T. F. (1992) *Intermediary NGOs. The supporting link in grassroots development.* West Harford (Conn.): Kumarian Press.

Carta de Brazileia-Epitaciolandia (2003) see: http://mapamazonia.net/

Carvalho, M. do C. (2001) Participação social no Brasil hoje. In: J. N. G. de Araújo, Souki, G. Léa, Faria, A. P. de Carlos (Ed.): *Figura Paterna e Ordem Social. Tutela, autoridade e legitimidade nas sociedades contemporâneas*, Belo Horizonte 171-206.

Carvalho, G. O., D. Nepstad, D. McGrath *et al.* (2002) Frontier expansion in the Amazon. Balancing development and sustainability, *Environment* 44, 3, pp. 34-46.

Carvalho, R. (1999) *A Amazônia rumo ao Ciclo da Soja.* Amazonia Papers 1(2). Friends of the Earth/Amigos da Terra, Programa Amazônia. [www.amazonia.org.br]

Cater, E. (1995a) Environmental Contradictions in Sustainable Tourism, *The Geographical Journal*, 161, 1, pp. 21-28.

Cater, E. (1995b) *Ecotourism – A Sustainable Option?* Chichester: John Wiley & Sons.

Chase, J. (2002) (Ed.) *The spaces of neoliberalism: land, place and family in Latin America.* Bloomfield (Conn.): Kumarian Press.

Chavez, A. (2005) *Pensando la Amazonia desde Pando; el MAP, una iniciativa trinacional de desarrollo.* La Paz: PIEB.

Chavez, D. (2004) *Polis & Demos: the left in municipal government in Montevideo and Porto Alegre.* Maastricht: Shaker Publications.

Chavez, D. (2008) The watering down of participation and people's power in Porto Alegre. In: T. Wakeford & J. Singh (Eds.) *Towards empowered participation: stories and reflections*, pp. 57-60. London: IIED.

Clancy, M. (1999) Tourism and Development. Evidence from Mexico? *Annals of Tourism Research* 26, 1, pp. 1-20.

Clancy, M. (2001) *Exporting Paradise. Tourism and Development in Mexico*, Amsterdam: Pergamon.

Cleary, D. (1993) After the frontier: problems with political economy in the modern Brazilian Amazon. *Journal of Latin American Studies* 25, 2, pp. 331-349.

Cook, P. & D. Hulme (1988) The compatibility of market liberalization and local economic development strategies. *Regional Studies* 22, 3, pp. 221-231.

Cooney, P. (2001) The Mexican crisis and the maquiladora boom. A paradox of development or the logic of neoliberalism? *Latin American Perspectives*, 28, 3, pp. 55-83.

Córdova Macías, R. (2003) La participación ciudadana en el gobierno local centroamericano. In: R. Córdova Macías & L. Quiñónez Basagoitia (Eds.) *Participación Ciuidadana y Desarrollo Local en Centroamérica*, pp. 207-251. San Salvador: FUNDAUNGO.

Corragio, J. L. (1998) *Economía Popular Urbana: una nueva perspectiva para el desarrollo Local.* Buenos Aires: Instituto del Conurbano/Universidad General Sarmiento.

Corragio, J. L. (2006) Las políticas públicas participativas: ¿obstáculo o requisito para el desarrollo local? In: A. Rofman & A. Villar (Comps) *Desarrollo local. Una revisión crítica del debate*, pp. 23-36. Buenos Aires: Espacio Editorial.

Corrales, S (2004) *Redes productivas de la industria acerera en Monclova, Coahuila, 1982-2000'.* Unpublished Ph.D. Thesis, Universidad Autónoma de Sinaloa.

Corrêa de Oliveira, M. T. (2002) Multi-sectoral partnerships for low income land development in Brazil. Utrecht: Utrecht Universtity.

Coy, M. & M. Pöhler (2002) Gated communities in Latin American megacities: case studies in Brazil and Argentina, *Environment and Planning B: Planning and Design* 29, pp. 355-370.

Crabtree, J. (Ed.) (2006) *Making institutions work in Peru. Democracy, development and inequality since 1980.* London: Institute for the Study of the Americas.

Cravacuore, D. (2006) La articulación de actores para el desarrollo local. In: A. Rofman & A. Villar (Comps) *Desarrollo local. Una revisión crítica del debate*, pp 183-198. Buenos Aires: Espacio Editorial.

Cravacuore, D., S. Ilari & A. Villar (Comps) (2004) *La articulación en la gestión municipal. Actores y políticas.* Buenos Aires: Universidad Nacional de Quilmes.

Crowley, W. K. (1995) Order and disorder – a model of Latin American urban land use, *APCG Yearbook* 57, pp. 9-31.

Crowley, W. K. (1998) Modelling the Latin American city, *The Geographical Review* 88, 1, pp. 127-130.

Cypher, J. (2001) Developing disarticulation within the Mexican economy, *Latin American Perspectives*, 28, 3, pp. 11-37.

Dean, Mitchell (1999) *Governmentality. Power and Rule in Modern Society*. London.

D'Agostino, T. J. (2005) Latin American Politics. In: R. S. Hillman (Ed.) *Understanding Contemporary Latin America*, pp. 67-116. Boulder (Co): Lynne Rienner.

Dagnino, E. (2002) Sociedade Civil, Espaços Públicos e a Construção Democrática no Brasil: Limites e Possibilidades. In: Dagnino, Evelina (Ed.) *Sociedade Civil e Espaços Públicos no Brasil*, São Paulo 279-301.

Da Silva, M. (1987) *Os trabalhadores na várzea no serviço da madeira: contradições do capital no desenvolvimento e crise do extractivismo no Vale Amazônico*. M.A. Thesis, Universidade Federal do Pará.

Dávila Flores, M. (1998) *Análisis del sector exportador de Coahuila*. Saltillo: Universidad Autónoma de Coahuila.

Dávila Flores, M. (2001) El comercio exterior de Coahuila en 1998, *Cuadernos de Investigación. Ciencias Sociales y Humanidades*, 24, pp. 7-91.

Daughters, R. & L. Harper (2007) Fiscal and Political Decentralization Reforms. In: E. Lora (Ed.) *The State of State Reform in Latin America*, pp. 213-261. Palo Alto/Washington, Stanford University Press & World Bank.

Dean, M. (1999) *Governmentality. Power and Rule in Modern Society*. London.

Dear, M. (2000) *The postmodern urban Condition*. Oxford: Malden.

Deler, J.P. (1989) Quartiers populaires et structuration de l'espace urbain. Un modèle latino-americain. Pauvretés et développement dans les pays tropicaux. Hommage à Guy Lasserre. Bordeaux.

Defensoría del Pueblo (2004) Libertad de tránsito y seguridad ciudadana. Los enrejados en lasvías públicas de Lima Metropolitana, *Informe Defensorial*, 81.

Díaz Orueta, F. (1997) La ciudad en América Latina – entre la globalización y la crisis, *America Latina Hoy*, 15, pp. 5-13.

Dicken, P. (1998) Global Shift: *Transforming the World Economy*. Paul Chapman. London.

Dicken, P. (2003). Global shift. Reshaping the global economic map in the 21st century London: Sage (4th Ed.).

Dicken, P., P. Kelly, K. Olds, H. Wai-Chung Yeung (2001) Chains and networks, territories and scales: towards a relational framework for analysing the global economy, *Global Networks* 1, 2, pp. 89-112.

Dietz, H. & M. Tanaka (2002) Lima: Centralized authority vs. the struggle for autonomy. In: D. Myers & H. Dietz (Eds.) *Capital city politics in Latin America*, pp. 193-225. Boulder (Co.): Lynne Rienner.

Dijck, P. van (Ed.) (1998) *The Bolivian Experiment: Structural Adjustment and Poverty Alleviation*. Amsterdam: CEDLA.

Dijck, P. van (2000): From liberalisation towards deeper integration. In: P. van Dijck, A. Ouweneel & A. Zoomers (Eds.) *Fronteras: Towards a borderless Latin America*, pp 97-118. Amsterdam: CEDLA.

Dijck, P. van & S. den Haak (2006) Troublesome construction; IIRSA and public-private partnerships in road infrastructure, *Cuadernos del CEDLA*, no. 20.

Dooren, R. van (2003) *Garments on the move. The local dynamics of export networks in La Laguna, Mexico*, Amsterdam: Thela Latin America Series.

Dussel Peters, E. (2000) *Polarizing Mexico. The Impact of Liberalization Strategy*. Boulder (Co.): Lynne Rienner.

Eichengreen, B. (1996) *Globalizing Capital*. Princeton: Princeton University Press. EIU (2004) *Chile Country Profile* [www.eiu.com]

EIU Economist Intelligence Unit Chile Country Profile, (2004) [www.eiu.com].

EL DIARIO (2003) Resultados de empresas, 28.3.2003.

Enríquez, A. & E. Gallichio (2003) *Gobernanza y desarrollo local*. Punta del Este: CLAEH.

Eróstegui, T. R. (1996) Die bolivianischen Gewerkschaften: Krisen und Perspektiven, *Lateinamerika, Analysen, Daten, Dokumentation*, 13, 31, pp. 37-42.

Esman, M. & N. Uphoff (1984) *Local organisations: intermediaries in local development*, Ithaca/ New York: Cornell University Press.

Estrategia (2002) Ausencia de Grandes Bancos de Japón y Europa: *el 'Talon de Aquiles' del Sistema*, 12.8.2002.

Evangelisti, B. (2000) *Räumliche Segregation, Gated Communities/Condominios in Santiago de Chile*. Dipl.Th. University of Vienna.

Expansión (2002) *Las empresas mas importantes de México*. México City: CD-Rom.

Fazia, H. (2000) *La transnacionalización de la economía chilena. Mapa de la Extrema Riqueza al año 2000*. Santiago de Chile: LOM Ediciones.

Fearnside, P. M. (1997) Protection of mahogany: a catalytic species in the destruction of rain forests in the American tropics, *Environmental Conservation* 24, 4, pp. 303-306.

Fearnside, P. M. (2001) Soybean cultivation as a threat to the environment in Brazil, *Environmental Conservation* 28, 1, pp. 23-38.

Fedozzi, L. (2001) *Orçamento Participativo. Reflexões sobre a experiência de Porto Alegre*. Porto Alegre/Rio de Janeiro: Tomo Editorial/FASE.

Ferroukhi, L. (Ed.) (2003) *Municipal Forest Management in Latin America*. Bogor: Centre for International Forestry Research / Ottawa: International Development Centre.

Figueroa, A., T. Altamirano & D. Sulmont (1996) Social exclusion and inequality in Peru, Geneva: *International Institute for Labour Studies, Research Series*, 104.

Finot, I. (2001) *Descentralización en América Latina: teoría y práctica*. Instituto Latinoamericano y del Caribe de Planificación Economica y Social – ILPES.

Fiszbein, A. (1997) The emergence of local capacity: lessons from Colombia. *World Development*, 25, pp. 1029-1043.

FONATUR (1979) *Síntesis de la evaluación de los resultados de Cancún* (unpublished document).

FONATUR, (1982) Huatulco, Oaxaca - *Plan Ambiental y Paisajistico* (unpublished document).

FONATUR, (1998) *Protocolo de la sesión no. 167 del Comité de Crédito y Comercialización*, (unpublished document).

FONATUR, (1999a) *Los 25 años del Fondo Nacional de Fomento al Turismo*, Mexico-City: FONATUR.

FONATUR, (1999b) *Propuesta de trabajo para Huatulco, Oax. y su zona de influencia* (unpublished document).

Ford, L. R., (1996) A new and improved model of Latin American city structure, *The Geographical Review* 86, 3, pp. 437-440.

Foucault, M. (1991) Governmentality. In: G. Burchell, G. Colin & M. Peter (Ed.) *The Foucault Effect. Studies in Governmentality*. Chicago 87-104.

Fox, J. & J. Aranda (1996) *Decentralization and rural development in Mexico. Community participation in Oaxaca's Municipal Funds Program*. San Diego: Center for U.S. Mexican Studies, University of California.

Franco, F., S. Gabriele *et al.* (2000) Monitoramento Qualitativo de Impacto – Desenvolvimento de Indicadores para a Extensão Rural no Nordeste do Brasil. (=*SLE-CATAD Studies, No. S 189*, Berlin.

Franko, P. (2003) *The Puzzle of Latin American Economic Development*. Lanham (MD): Rowman & Littlefield.

Freire, P. (1970) *Pedagogy of the Oppressed*. New York.

Freitas, A. de (2003) Sustainable forest management in Brazil and the role of FSC forest certification. *Paper presented at the Congress on 'Globalisation, localisation and tropical forest management in the 21st century'*, Amsterdam, 22-23 October 2003.

Friedmann, J. (1966) *Regional Development Policy: a case study of Venezuela*. Cambridge (Mass): MIT-Press.

Furtado, C. (1970) *Economic Development of Latin America. A Survey from Colonial Times to the Cuban Revolution*. Cambridge: Cambridge University Press.

Gallicchio, E. (2006) El desarrollo local: cómo combinar gobernabilidad, desarrollo económico y capital social en el territorio. In: A. Rofman & A. Villar (Comps) *Desarrollo local. Una revision crítica del debate*, pp. 59-74. Buenos Aires: Espacio Editorial.

Gallego, F. & N. Loayza (1999) Financial Structure in Chile: Macroeconomic Developments and Microeconomic Effects, *Working Papers Central Bank of Chile* 75. Santiago de Chile.

Galtung, J. J.(1971) A Structural Theory of Imperialism, *Journal of Peace Research*, 8, 2 pp. 81-117.

García Delgado, D. (1997) Nuevos escenarios locales. El cambio del modelo de gestión. In: D. García Delgado (Comp) *Hacia un nuevo modelo de gestión local. Municipio y sociedad civil en Argentina*. Buenos Aires, Flacso/Universidad Catolica de Córdoba, pp. 13-40.

Garofolli, (1990) Economic development and local society. *Public Administration* 79, pp. 86-109.

Gaventa, J. (2001) *Participatory local governance: six propositions for development*. IDS: paper presented to the Ford Foundation.

Genro, T., U. de Souza (1997) *Orçamento Participativo. A experiência de Porto Alegre*. São Paulo.

Gereffi, Gary, Miguel Korzeniewicz (Eds.) (1994) Commodity Chains and Global Capitalism. Westport: Praeger.

Gereffi, G. (1996) The elusive last lap in the quest for developed-country status. In: J. Mittelman (Ed.) *Globalization: critical reflections*. Boulder (Co.): Lynne Rienner.

Gereffi, G., J. Humphrey, R. Kaplinsky & T. Sturgeon (Eds.) (2001) The value of value chains: spreading the gains from globalization, *IDS Bulletin* 32, 3.

Gereffi, G. (1994) The Organization of Buyer-Driven Global Commodety Chains: How U.S. Retailers Shape Overseas Production Networks. In: G. Gereffi & M. Korzeniewicz (Eds.) *Commodity Chains and Global Capitalism*, pp. 95-122. Westport: Praeger.

Gereffi, G., J. Humphrey & T. Sturgeon (2005) The Governance of Global Value Chains. *Review of International Political Economy*, 12, 1, pp. 78-104.

Gereffi, G., M. Korzeniewicz (Eds) (1994) Commodity Chains and Global Capitalism. Westport: Praeger.

Gilbert, A. (1974) *Latin American Development. A Geographical Perspective*. Harmondsworth: Penguin Books.

Gilbert, A. (1994) *The Latin American City*. London.

Gilbert, A. (1997) Poverty, regional conversions and development: what kind of relationship? In: A.H.J. Helmsing & J. Guimaraes (Eds) *Locality, State and Development. Essays in honour of Jos G.M. Hilhorst*, pp. 181-204. The Hague: ISS.

Gilbert, A. (2006) Good Urban Governance: Evidence from a Model City? *Bulletin of Latin American Research* 25, 3, pp. 392-419.

Gill, G. (2000) *The Dynamics of Democratization. Elites, Civil Society and the Transition Process*. Basingstoke: MacMillan.

Godfrey, B. J. (1996) Boom towns of the Amazon. *The Geographical Review*, 80, 2, pp. 103-117.

Goedeking, U. (2001) CONDEPA und UCS: Zwei Parteien und ihre Erbfolgeprobleme. Einst Hoffnungsträger vieler nicht-weißer Bolivianer, befinden sich beide Parteien nach dem Tod ihrer Caudillos in der Krise. *Lateinamerika, Analysen – Daten – Dokumentation*, 17, 45, pp. 24-32.

Golte J. & M. de la Cadena (1983) La codeterminación de la organización social Andina, *Allpanchis* 19, pp. 7-34.

Gonzales de Olarte, E. (1998) *El neoliberalismo a la peruana – economía política del ajuste structural, 1990-1997*, Lima: Instituto de Estudios Peruanos (IEP).

Gormsen, E. (1981) Die Städte in Spanisch-Amerika. Ein zeit-räumliches Entwicklungsmodell der letzten hundert Jahre, *Erdkunde* 35, 4, pp. 290-303.

Gormsen, E. (1995) *Mexiko. Land der Gegensätze und Hoffungen*. Darmstadt: Perthes/Klett.

Gormsen, E. (1997) The Impact of Tourism on Coastal Areas, *GeoJournal*, 42, 1, pp. 39-54.

Goumas, A. (2002) *Sozialräumliche Segregation in lateinamerikanischen Städte am Beispiel der barrios cerrados in Lima, Peru*. Dipl.Th. University of Innsbruck.

Greig, A., D. Hulme & M. Turner (2007) *Challenging Global Inequality. Development Theory and Practice in the 21st Century*. Houndmills: Palgrave MacMillan.

Griffin E. & L. Ford (1980) A model of Latin American city structure, *Geographical Review* 70, 4, pp. 397-422.

Griffin E. & L. Ford (1993) Cities of Latin America. In: S. Brunn & J. Williams (Eds) *Cities of the World. World Regional Urban Development*, pp. 225-265. New York: Harper Collins.

Gros, C. (2005) *Indigènes et Politique en Bolivie. Les Stratégies Chiquitanas dans le Nouveau Contexte de Décentralisation Participative.* Paris: IHEAL (Thése de Doctorat).

Grupo de Trabalho Amazônico (2002) *Pelo Futuro da Amazônia/For the Future of the Amazon.* Brasília: GTA.

GTZ (2003) Capacity Development for Sustainable Development. (*=Policy Paper No.1*) Eschborn.

Guimaraes, J. (1997) Local economic development: the limitations of theory. In: B. Helmsing & J. Guimarães (Eds.) *Locality, state and development. Essays in honour of Jos G. M.*

Gwynne, R. (1999) Globalization, commodity chains and fruit exporting regions in Chile, *Tijdschrift voor Economische en Sociale Geografie,* 90, 2, pp. 211-225.

Gwynne, R. (2004) Structural reform in South America and Mexico: Economic and Regional Perspectives. In: R. Gwynne and C. Kay (Eds.) *Latin America transformed: Globalization and Neoliberalism,* pp. 39-66. London: Arnold.

Gwynne, R. & C. Kay (2004) Latin America transformed: Changing paradigms, debates and Alternatives. In: R. Gwynne and C. Kay (Eds.) *Latin America transformed. Globalization and modernity,* pp. 2-30. London: Arnold.

Hilhorst, pp. 281-283. The Hague: ISS.

Hall, M. & A. Lew (1998) *Sustainable Tourism. A Geographical Perspective.* Harlow: Longman.

Harper, R. & A. Cuzán (2005) The Economies of Latin America. In: R. Hillman (Ed.) *Understanding contemporary Latin America,* pp. 145-177. Boulder (Co): Lynne Rienner.

Harris, D. & D. Azzi (2006) ALBA, Venezuela's answer to 'free trade': the Bolivarian alternative for the Americas, Focus on the Global South, *Alianza Social Continental, Occasional Papers.* São Paulo.

Harvey, D. (1996) *Justice, Nature and the Geography of Difference.* Oxford/Cambridge: Blackwell.

Helmsing, A. H. J. (2000) *Decentralisation and enablement. Issues in the local governance debate.* Utrecht: Faculty of Geographical Sciences, Universiteit Utrecht.

Helmsing, A. H. J. (2002) Partnerships. Meso-Institutions and Learning: New Local and Regional Economic Development Initiatives in Latin America. In: I.S.A. Baud & J. Post (Eds.) *Realigning Actors in an Urbanizing World: Governance and Institutions from a Development Perspective,* pp. 79-100. London: Ashgate.

Helmsing, A. H. J. (2005) Local economic development in Africa: new theory and policy practices. In: T.G. Egziabher & A.H.J. Helmsing, *Local economic development in Africa. Enterprises, communities and local government.* Maastricht: Shaker Publishing.

Helmsing, A. H. J. & J. Guimaraes (Eds) (1997) *Locality, State and Development. Essays in honour of Jos G.M. Hilhorst.* The Hague: ISS.

Henkemans, A. B. (2001) *Tranquilidad and Hardship in the Forest, Livelihoods and Perceptions of Camba Forest Dwellers in the Northern Bolivian Amazon.* Utrecht: PROMAB.

Hidalgo, R. (1999) Continuidad y cambio en un siglo de vivienda social en Chile (1892-1998). Reflexiones a partir del caso de la Ciudad de Santiago, *Revista Geográfica Norte Grande* 26, pp. 69-77.

Hidalgo, R. (2004) Condominios y urbanizaciones cerradas en comunas del sector oriente. Tendencias de localización y morfología urbana. In: G. Cáceres & F. Sabatini (Eds) *Barrios cerrados en Santiago de Chile: entre la exclusión y la integración residencial,* pp. 59-82. Santiago: Lincon Institute e Instituto de Geografía, Pontífica Universidad Católica de Chile.

Hidalgo, R. *et al.* (2003) *Los condominios y urbanizaciones cerradas como nuevo modelo de construcción del espacio residencial en Santiago de Chile (1992-2000).* Paper presented at the 5th Coloquio Internacional de Geocrítica (La vivienda y la construcción del espacio social de la ciudad) Barcelona, May 26-30. [www.ub.es/geocrit/sn/vhidal.htm]

Hillman, R. (Ed) (2005). *Understanding contemporary Latin America.* Boulder (Co): Lynne Rienner.

Hills, T. & J. Lundgren (1977) The Impact of Tourism in the Caribbean: A Methological Study, *Annals of Tourism Research* 4, pp. 248-67.

Hoefle, S. W. (2006) Twisting the knife: Frontier violence in the central Amazon of Brazil. In: *Journal of Peasant Studies* 33, 3:445-478.

Huisman, H. (2006) Stylishing switches: Paradigm shifts in mainstream rural development policy. In: P. van Lindert, A. de Jong, G. Nijenhuis & G. van Westen (Eds.) *Development Matters: Geographical studies on development processes and policies.* Utrecht: Utrecht University.

IBAM (2000) Avaliação do Programa Nacional de Fortalecimento da Agricultura Familiar (PRONAF) no estado do Pará. Rio de Janeiro/Belém.

IDB (2000) *Making decentralisation work in Latin America and the Caribbean; a background paper for the subnational development strategy*. Washington: IDB/Sustainable Development Department.

IFAM (1999) *Cinco años de gestión*. Buenos Aires: Editorial IFAM.

IFAM (2003) *Programma de Desarrollo Productivo Local. Relevamiento Diagnóstico Productivo Municipal*. Buenos Aires: Secretaría de Asuntos Municipales de la Nación. IMF (1997) *Good Governance. The IMF's role*. [www.imf.org/external/pubs/ft/exrp/govern/govindes.htm]

IMF (2002) The IMF's Approach to Promoting Good Governance and Combating Corruption A Guide [www.imf.org/external/up/gov/guide/eng/index.htm]

INE/Instituto Nacional de Estadísticas (2002) Censo 2002 [www.censo2002.cl]

INE (1999) *Atlas estadístico de municipios*. La Paz: INE.

INEI (1998) *Encuesta de victimización en Lima Metropolitana*. Lima: INEI/Comisión especial para estudiar las causas y consequencias de la violencia cotidiana.

INEGI (2000a) *Sistema de Cuentas Nacionales de México. Cuenta Satélite de Turismo de México 1993-1998*. Aguascalientes: INEGI.

INEGI (2000b) *Anuario Estadístico del Estado de Oaxaca 2000*. Aguascalientes: INEGI

INEGI (2002) *XII Censo general de población y vivienda. Resultados definitivos por localidad*. Aguascalientes: INEGI.

Jacobi, P. (2000) *Políticas Sociais e Ampliação da Cidadania*. Rio de Janeiro.

Janoschka, M. (2002a) Stadt der Inseln. Buenos Aires: Abschottung und Fragmentierung als Kennzeichen eines neuen Stadtmodells, *RaumPlanung* 101, pp. 65-70.

Janoschka, M. (2002b) Urbanizaciones privadas en Buenos Aires: hacia un nuevo modelo de ciudad latinoamericana? In: L.F.Cabrales Barajas (Ed.) *Latinoamérica – Países abiertos, ciudades cerradas*, pp. 287-318. Guadalajara/Paris: UNESCO.

Janoschka, M. (2002b) Wohlstand hinter Mauern. Private Urbanisierungen in Buenos Aires. *ISR-Forschungsbericht* 27. Vienna.

Janoschka, M. & A. Borsdorf (2004) Condominios fechados and Barrios privados: the rise of private residential neighbourhoods in Latin America. In: G. Glasze, C. Webster & K. Frantz (Eds.) *Private Neighbourhoods. Global and local perspectives*. London: Routledge.

Janoschka, M. & G. Glasze (2003) Urbanizaciones cerradas: un modelo analítico, *Ciudades*, 59, pp. 9-20.

Janvry, A. de & E. Sadoulet (2004) Fitting the facts and capitalizing on new opportunities to redesign rural development programs in Latin America, *Revista de Economia e Sociologia Rural* 42, 3, pp. 399-430.

Jaramillo, S. (1999) El papel del mercado de suelo en la configuración de algunos rasgos Socio-espaciales de las ciudades latinoamericanas, *Territorios*, pp. 107-129.

Jiménez, A. (1992) *Turismo: estructura y desarrollo*. Mexico-City: McGraw-Hill.

Jiménez, A. (1998) *Desarrollo turístico y sustentabilidad: el caso de México*. Mexico-City: Porrúa.

Job, H. (1996) Model zur Evaluierung der Nachhaltigkeit im Tourismus, *Erdkunde*, 50, pp. 112-32.

Johnson Ceva, K. (1998) Business-government relations in Mexico since 1990: NAFTA, economic crisis and the reorganization of business interests. In: R. Roett (Ed.) *Mexico's private sector. Recent history, future challenges*, pp. 125-157. Boulder (Co.): Lynne Rienner

Joseph, J. (2004) Los jardines que se bifurcan: segregación e integración en Lima, *Center for Migration and Development Working Papers*, 04-04c.

Jost, S. (2003) *Bolivien: Politisches System und Reformprozess 1993 – 1997*. Opladen: Leske & Budrich.

Kadt, E. de (1992) Making the Alternative Sustainable: Lessons from Development for Tourism. In: V. L. Smith & W. R. Eadington (Eds) *Tourism Alternatives. Potentials and Problems in the Development of Tourism*, pp. 47-87. Philadelphia: University of Pennsylvania Press.

Kanitschneider, S. (2002) Condominios und fraccionamientos cerrados in Mexiko-Stadt. Sozialräumliche Segregation am Beispiel abgesperrter Wohnviertel, *Geographica Helvetica*, 4, 57, pp. 253-263.

Kanitscheider, S. (2004) *Condominios und Fraccionamientos cerrados in Mexiko-Stadt. Neue Formen sozialräumlicher Segregation unter dem Einfluss der Globalisierung*. Dipl.Th. University of Bonn.

Kauneckis, D. & K. Andersson (2009) Making Decentralization Work: A Cross-national Examination of Local Governments and Natural Resource Governance in Latin America. *Studies in Comparative International Development* 44, pp. 23-46.

Kent, R.B. (2006) *Latin America. Regions and People*. New York: The Guilford Press.

Kirby, P. (2003) *Introduction to Latin America: Twenty-first Century Challenges*. London/ Thousand Oaks: Sage Publications.

Klauda, F. (2001) Bolivien auf dem Weg zum HIPC-Schuldenerlass. In: R. Sevilla & A. Benavides (Eds.) *Bolivien. Das verkannte Land?* Bad Honnef: Horlemann.

Kohl, B. & L. Farthing (2008) New spaces, new contests: appropriating decentralization for political change in Bolivia. In: V.A Beard, F. Miraftab & C. Silver (Eds) *Planning and decentralization. Contested spaces for public action in the global south*, pp. 69-85. London: Routledge.

Kohler, P. (2002) Geschlossene Wohnkomplexe in Quito. Naturraum und rechtliche Rahmenbedingungen als Einflußgrößen für Verbreitung und Typisierung, *Geographica Helvetica* 57, 4, pp. 278-289.

Kohler, P. (2003) Vom öffentlichen zum privaten Raum. Naturräumliche und rechtliche Rahmenbedingungen für bewachte Wohnviertel in Quito/Ecuador. *GW-Unterricht* 91, 2.

Kose, A., G. Meredith & C. Towe (2004) How has NAFTA affected the Mexican economy? Review and evidence, *IMF Working Paper*, 59.

Köster, G. (1995) Bevölkerungsstruktur, Migrationsverhalten und Integration der Bewohner von Mittel- und Oberschichtsvierteln in der lateinamerikanischen Stadt. Das Beispiel La Paz (Bolivien). *Aachener Geographische Arbeiten 30*. Aachen.

Krebsbach, K. (2003) The new Mexican Revolution, *US Banker*, 113(11) 67-69.

Kross, E. (1992) Die Barriadas von Lima. Stadtentwicklungsprozesse in einer lateinamerikanischen Metropole, *Bochumer Geographische Arbeiten 55*. Paderborn.

Lambert, J. (1971) *Latin America. Social Structures & Political Institutions*. Berkely: University of California Press.

Latin America Monitor (2004) 'Banking & Insurance', Southern Cone Monitor, 21(6): 2-7.

Lathrop, G. (1997) Local development, social contract and institutional thickness. In: A.H.J. Helmsing & J. Guimaraes (Ed.) *Locality, state and development. Essays in honour of Jos G. M. Hilhorst*, pp. 95-105. The Hague: Institute of Social Studies.

Laurance, W., M. Cochrane, L. Bergen *et al.* (2001) Environment: the future of the Brazilian Amazon, *Science* 291, pp. 438-439.

Larraín, J. (2004) Identity and Modernity in Latin America. In: R. Gwynne & C. Kay (Eds) *Latin America transformed. Globalization and Modernity*, pp. 22-38. London: Hodder Arnold.

Lederman, D., W. Maloney & L. Serven (2003) Lessons from NAFTA for Latin America and Caribbean countries. Washington (DC): World Bank [www.worldbank.org/laceonomist]

Lehmann, D. (Ed) (1982) *Ecology and exchange in the Andes*. Cambridge: Cambridge University Press.

Lentini, M., D. Pereira, D. Celentano & R. Pereira (2005) *Fatos florestais da Amazônia 2005*. Belém: IMAZON.

Lentini, M., A. Veríssimo & L. Sobral (2003) *Fatos florestais da Amazônia 2003*. Belém: IMAZON.

Leroy, J.-P. (2003) *Relatório brasileiro para o direito do meio ambiente*. Rio de Janeiro. (unpublished).

Lima Ramires, J. C. & B. Ribero Soares (2002) Os condomínios horizontales em cidades médias brasileiras. In: L. F. Cabrales Barajas (Ed.) *Latinoamérica: países abiertos, ciudades cerradas*, pp. 373-396. Guadalajara/Paris: UNESCO.

Lima, E. & F. Merry (2003) Views of Brazilian producers; increasing and sustaining exports. In: D. J. Macqueen (Ed.) (2003) *Growing Exports: the Brazilian Tropical Timber Industry and International Markets*, pp. 82-105. IIED Small and Medium Enterprise series No. 1. London: IIED.

Lima E., A. Leite, D. Nepstad, K. Kalif *et al.* (2003) *Florestas Familiares: um Impacto Sócio ambiental entre a Indústria Madeireira e a Agricultura Familiar na Amazônia*. Belém: Instituto de Pesquisa Ambiental na Amazônia.

Lindberg, K., J. Enriquez & K. Sproule (1996) Ecotourism Questioned. Case Studies from Belize, *Annals of Tourism Research*, 23, 3, pp. 543-562.

Lindert, P. van (2005) Local Government. In: T. Forsyth (Ed.) *The Encyclopedia of International Development*, pp. 415-417. London: Routledge.

Lindert, P. van (2008) The evolution of the urban development agendas since the 1970s, *Journal of Development Alternatives and Area Studies* 27, 3-4, pp. 70-90.

Lindert, P. van (2009) Transnational linking of loal governments: The consolidation of the Utrecht-León municipal partnership, *Habitat International* 33, 2, pp. 173-180.

Lindert, P. van, A. de Jong, G. Nijenhuis & G. van Westen (Eds) (2006) *Development Matters. Geographical Studies on Development Processes and Policies*. Utrecht: Utrecht University.

Lindert, P. van & G. Nijenhuis (2002) Popular Participation and the Participatory Planning Practice in Latin America: Some Evidence from Bolivia and Brazil. In: I.S.A. Baud & J. Post (Eds.) *Realigning Actors in an Urbanizing World: Governance and Institutions from a Development Perspective*, pp. 175-196. London: Ashgate.

Lindert, P. van, Nijenhuis, G. (2004) The challenge of participatory democracy in Latin America. In: D. Kruijt, P. van Lindert, O. Verkoren (Ed.) *State and Development. Essays in Honor of Menno Vellinga*, Utrecht pp. 163-183.

Lindert, P. van & O. Verkoren (Eds.) (1997) *Small Towns and Beyond. Rural Transformations and Small Urban Centres in Latin America*. Amsterdam: Thela Publishers.

Lindert, P. van & O. Verkoren (2004) Planificación del desarrollo local-regional en Bolivia. In: Bustamante, F. (Ed.) *Planificación y municipalización en Bolivia. Agentes y Actores, Municipio Productivo y Sistemas Urbanos en Municipios de Cochabamba*, pp. 353-366. Cochabamba, Bolivia. PROMEC-UMSS.

Lippman, H. & P. Pranke (1998) *Democratic Local Governance in Honduras. Impact Evaluation*. Washington: USAID.

Long, V. H. (1992) Social Mitigation of Tourism Development Impacts: Huatulco, Mexico. In: C. Fleischer-van Rooijen (Ed) *Spatial Implications of Tourism*, Groningen, GeoPers, pp. 185-201.

Long, V. H. (1993) Techniques of Socially Sustainable Tourism Development: Lessons from Mexico. In: J. G. Nelson, R. Butler & G. Well (Eds) *Tourism and Sustainable Development: Monitoring, Planning, Management*, pp. 201-218. Waterloo: University of Waterloo Press.

Lopes de Souza, M. (1993) Armut, sozialräumliche Segregation und sozialer Konflikt in der Metropolitanregion von Rio de Janeiro. Ein Beitrag zur Analyse der 'Stadtfrage' in Brasilien. *Tübinger Geographische Studien* 111. Tübingen.

López, Á. (2002) Análisis de los flujos turísticos en el corredor Los Cabos, Baja California Sur, *Investigaciones Geográficas* 47, pp. 131-49.

Lora, E. (2007) State Reform in Latin America: A Silent Revolution. In: E. Lora (Ed.) The *State of State Reform in Latin America*, pp. 1-56. Palo Alto/Washington: Stanford University Press/World Bank.

Luca, M., M. P. Jones et al. (2002) Buenos Aires: The Evolution of Local Governance. In: D.J. Meyers & H.A. Dietz (Eds) *Capital City Politics in Latin America: Democratisation and Empowerment*, pp. 65-94. Boulder (Co): Lynne Rienner.

Ludeña Urquizo, W. (2002) Lima: poder, centro y centralidad – del centro nativo al centro neoliberal, *Revista EURE*, 28, 83, pp. 45-65.

Macqueen, D. J. et al. (2003) *Growing Exports: the Brazilian Tropical Timber Industry and International Markets*. Small and Medium Enterprise series No.1. London: IIED.

Madanipour, A. (2003) *Public and private spaces of the city*. London/New York: Routledge.

Madsen Camacho, M. (1996) Dissenting Workers and Social Control: A Case Study of the Hotel Industry in Huatulco, Oaxaca, *Human Organization* 55, 1, pp. 33-40.

Manor, J. (1999) *The political economy of decentralization*. Directions in Development, Washington (DC): World Bank.

MAP (1999) Carta de Rio Branco.

MAP (2000) Carta de Puerto Maldonado.

MAP (2001) Carta de Assis Brasil.

MAP (2002) Carta de Cobija.

MAP (2003) Carta de Epitaciolandia/Brasileia.

Marcuse, P. (1989) Dual city: A Muddy Metaphor for a Quartered City, *International Journal of Urban and Regional Research* 13, 4, pp. 697-708.

Marsiglia, J. (1999) (Coord.) *Desarrollo local en la globalización*. Montevideo: CLAEH.

Matos Mar, J. (2004) *Desborde popular y crisis del Estado – veinte años después*, Lima: Fondo Editorial del Congreso del Perú (original 1984).

Matthews, H. (1977) Radicals and Third World Tourism: A Caribbean Focus, *Annals of Tourism Research* 5, pp. 20-29.

Mattos, C. de (1989) La descentralización ¿una nueva panacea para impulsar el desarrollo local? *Cuadernos del CLAEH* 51. Montevideo: CLAEH.

Mattos, C. de (2002) Transformación de las ciudades latinoamericanas – impactos de la globalización? *Revista EURE*, 28, 85, pp. 5-10.

May, P. H. (2002) Forest certification in Brazil: trade and environmental enhancement. *Paper prepared for the Consumer Choice Council.* [www.consumercouncil.org/forest/brazil_forest_english.pdf]

Mayer, E. & M. de la Cadena (1989) *Cooperación y conflicto en la comunidad Andina. Zonas de producción y organización social.* Lima: IEP.

Mayers, J. & S. Bass (1999) *Policy that Works for Forests and People.* Policy That Works Series No. 7: Series overview. London: IIED.

McLaren, D. (1994) Public Involvement in Environmental Assessment of Tourism. In: Goodland & V. Edmundson (Eds) *Environmental Assessment and Development*, Washington (DC): World Bank, pp. 114-124.

Mendoza Cota, J. (1999) Reubicación transnacional como impulso a la formación de distritos industriales. In: C. Ruiz Durán & E. Dussel Peters (Eds.) *Dinámica regional y competitividad industrial*, pp. 79-100. Mexico: Editorial Jus.

Mendoza Cota, J. (2001) Crecimiento y especialización en la región Saltillo-Ramos Arizpe, *Comercio Exterior* 51, 3, pp. 250-258.

Merino, M., J. Sorensen & D. Gutierrez (1993) The Fate of the Nichupte Lagoon System in the Planning of Cancún, Mexico as an International Tourism Center. In: J. Sorenson, E. Gable & J. Bandarin (Eds) *The Management of Coastal Lagoons and Enclosed Bays*, pp. 119-39. New York: American Society of Civil Engineers.

Mertins, G. (2003) Jüngere sozialräumlich-strukturelle Transformation in den Metropolen und Megastädten Lateinamerikas, *Petermanns Geographische Mitteilungen* 147, pp. 46-55.

Meyer, K. & J. Bähr (2001) Condominios in Greater Santiago de Chile and their Impact on the Urban Structure, *Die Erde*, 132, 3, pp. 292-321.

Meyer-Kriesten, K., J. Plöger & J. Bähr. (2004) Wandel der Stadtstruktur in Lateinamerika – sozialräumliche und funktionale Ausdifferenzierungen in Santiago de Chile und Lima, *Geographische Rundschau*, 56, 6, pp. 30-37.

Meyer-Stamer, J. (2002) Paradoxes and Ironies of Locational Policy and how to deal with them. *Paper presented as part of the joint IDS/INEF Project The interaction of Global and Local Governance: Implications for Industrial Upgrading* [www.meyer-stamer.de/2002/JMS-LocParadox.pdf]

Meyers, D. J. & H. A. Dietz (Eds) (2002) *Capital City Politics in Latin America: Democratisation and Empowerment.* Boulder (Co): Lynne Rienner.

Micheli, J. (1994) *Nueva manufactura. Globalización y producción de automóviles en México.* Mexico: UNAM.

Minello, N. & L. Barranco (Eds.) (1995) *El desarrollo de una industria básica: Altos Hornos de México, 1942-1988.* Monclova: Arte y Cultura Monclova.

Ministerio de Desarrollo Social de la Nación (2005) *Plan Nacional de Desarrollo local y economía social*, Documento Institucional. Buenos Aires.

Ministry of the Environment (2002) *Biodiversity and Forests of Brazil.* Brasilia.

Mitlin, D. (2004) Reshaping local Democracy, *Environment & Urbanization* 16, 1, pp. 3-8.

Montemayor Seguy, R. (1994) *Plan estatal de desarrollo, 1994-1999. Coahuila, por un futuro Mejor.* Saltillo: Gobierno del Estado de Coahuila.

Montemayor Seguy, R. (1999) *Sexto informe de gobierno. Rumbo al siglo 21.* Saltillo: Gobierno del Estado de Coahuila.

Molina Monasterios, A. (1997) Historia de la Participación Popular. La Paz: Minsterio de Desarrollo Humano/SNPP.

Morrée, D. de (2002) *Cooperación campesina en los Andes. Un estudio sobre estrategias de organización para el desarrollo rural en Bolivia.* Netherlands Geographical Studies 298. Utrecht: KNAG/UU.

Morris, A. (1981) *Latin America. Economic Development and Regional Differentiation.* London: Hutchinson.

Mowforth, M. & I. Munt (1998) *Tourism and Sustainibility. New Tourism in the Third World.* London/New York: Routledge.

Müller, B. (1983) *Fremdenverkehr und Entwicklungspolitik zwischen Wachstum und Ausgleich.* Mainz: University of Mainz.

Murdoch, J. (1995) Governmentality and the politics of resistance in UK agriculture. The case of the Farmers' Union of Wales. In. *Sociologia Ruralis,* 35, 2:187-205.

Naughton-Treves, L. (2004) Deforestation and carbon emission at tropical frontiers: a case study from the Peruvian Amazon. In: *World Development,* 32, pp. 173-190.

Nelson, G. J. (1993) An Introduction to Tourism and Sustainable Development with Special Reference to Monitoring. In G. J. Nelson (Ed) *Tourism and Sustainable Development: Monitoring, Planning, Managing,* pp. 3-23. New Haven.

Nepstad, D., Azevedo- Ramos, C. & Lima, E. (2005) 'Governing the Amazon timber industry for maximum social and environmental benefits'. *Forest, Trees and Livelihoods* 15:183-192.

Nepstad, D. *et al. (*2002a) Environment: enhanced frontier governance in Amazonia, *Science* 295, pp. 629-631.

Nepstad, D. *et al.* (2002b) *Roads in the Rainforest: Environmental Costs for the Amazon.* Belém: MGM Gráfica e Editora.

Nepstad D., C. Azevedo-Ramos & E. Lima (2003) *Governing the Amazon timber industry for maximum social and environmental benefits.* Paper presented at the GTZ/CIFOR International Conference on Livelihoods and Biodiversity, Bonn, Germany, 19-23 May 2003.

Niekerk, N. van (1994) *Desarrollo Rural en los Andes. Un estudio sobre los programas de desarrollo de organizaciones no-gubernamentales,* Leiden: Leiden Development Studies.

Nijenhuis, G. (2002) *Decentralisation and Popular Participation in Bolivia. The Link between Local Governance and Local Development.* Netherlands Geographical Studies 299. Utrecht: KNAG/UU.

Nijenhuis, G. (2008) Political decentralisation and participatory governance in Latin America, Africa and Asia: an overview. *Journal of Development Alternatives and Area Studies* 27, 3-4, pp. 117-139.

Nijland, E. (1994) Beyond the frontier: the Bolivian Amazon and its inhabitants facing an uncertain future. In: E. Harts-Broekhuis & O. Verkoren (Eds.) *No easy way out: essays on third world development in honour of Jan Hinderink,* pp. 357-363. Netherlands Geographical Studies 186. Utrecht: KNAG/UU.

Nohlen, D. (2001) Die politische Entwicklung Boliviens in den letzten zwei Dekaden. Eine Bilanz. In: R. Sevilla & A. Benavides (Eds) Bolivien, *das verkannte Land?,* pp. 26-42. Bad Honnef: Horlemann.

Ocampo, J. (2003) Las políticas económicas en América Latina y el Caribe, *Anuario Elcano: América Latina,* pp. 260-275.

Odell, P. R. & D. Preston (1973) *Economies and Societies in Latin America. A Geographical Interpretation.* Chichester: Wiley & Sons.

OECD (2002) Challenges in the Mexican Financial Sector, *OECD Economics Department Working Papers 339.* Paris: OECD.

OECD (2003) Chile Survey 2003. Paris: OECD.

OECD (2004) Mexico Economic Survey 2004. Paris: OECD.

Oosten, C. J. van (2004) Fading frontiers: local development and cross-border partnerships in Southwes Amazonia. *Geographical Studies of Development and Resource Use*, 9, 1. Utrecht: KNAG.

Oosten, C. J. van (2005) Fronteras que se decoloran; visión de un proceso de integración regional a traves de las fronteras [www.map-amazonia.net]

Oosten, C. J. van (2009) Globalisation, regionalisation, and regional integration: two cases compared. *Journal of Development Alternatives and Area Studies* 28, 1-2.

Osmani, S.R. (2000) *Participatory Governance, People's Empowerment and Poverty Reduction*. SEPED Conference Series 7. New York: UNDP/SEPED. [http://www.undp.org/seped/publications/conf_pub.htm].

Orozco, P. (1992) Huatulco: reseña de la reubicación, *Alteridades* 2, 4, pp. 95-99.

Pacheco, P. (2004) What lies behind Decentralisation? Forest, Powers and Actors in Lowland Bolivia, *The European Journal of Development Research*, 16, 1, pp. 90-109.

Pader/Cosude (1998) *Municipio Productivo y la promoción económico rural. Aprendiendo la realidad municipal*. La Paz: Pader/Cosude.

Pagiola, S., Bishop, J. & N. Landell-Mills (2002) *Selling Forest Environmental Services. Market-based Mechanisms for Conservation and Development*. London: Earthscan.

Paiva, A. (2003) Relevance of Metropolitan Government in Latin American Cities. Inter-institutional coordination in Caracas, Venezuela and Monterrey, Mexico. Delft: Eburon.

Palomares León, H. (2003) Crecimiento, estructuracion y planeacion interurbana en ciudadades intermedias del Noreste de Mexico. Tijuana: El Colegio de Mexico.

Parnreiter, C. (2002) Mexico: The Making of a Global City? In S. Sassen (Ed.) *Global Networks, Linked Cities*, pp. 145-182. London: Routledge,

Parnreiter, C. (2003) Global City Formation in Latin America: Socioeconomic and Spatial Transformations in Mexico City and Santiago de Chile, *GaWC Research Bulletin 103*, [www.lboro.ac.uk/gawc/rb/rb103.html]

Parnreiter, C. (2004) Entwicklungstendenzen lateinamerikanischer Metropolen im Zeitalter der Globalisierung. *Mitteilungen der Österreichischen Geographischen Gesellschaft* 146, pp. 1-28.

Parnreiter, C. (2007) Historische Geographien, verräumlichte Geschichte. Mexico City und das mexikanische Städtenetz von der Industrialisierung bis zur Globalisierung. Stuttgart: Franz Steiner Verlag.

Parnreiter, C. (2009) Global-City-Formation, Immobilienwirtschaft und Transnationalisierung. Das Beispiel Mexico City. In: *Zeitschrift für Wirtschaftsgeographie, 53*, 3:138-155.

Parnreiter, C. (2010) Global cities in Global Commodity Chains: exploring the role of Mexico City in the geography of global economic governance. In: *Global Networks* 10, 1:35-53.

Pereyra, O. (2003) Del barrio y del crimen. El orden y el pánico frente a la criminalidad en Nuevo Pachacútec, *Working Papers of the Center for the Study of Urbanization and Internal Migration in Developing Countries*. Austin: University of Texas.

Pike, A., A. Rodríguez-Pose & J. Tomaney (2006) *Local and Regional Development*. Abingdon: Routledge.

Pírez, P. (2002) Buenos Aires: Fragmentation and Privatization of the Metropolitan City, *Environment & Urbanization*, 14, 1, pp. 145-158.

Pi-Sunger, Oriol; T.R. Brooke & M. Daltabuit (2001) Tourism on the Maya Periphery.- In: Hosts and Guests Revisited: Tourism Issues of the 21st Century, pp. 122-140, V.L. Smith & M. Bent (eds.).- Cognizant Communication Corporation: Elmsford/USA

Plöger, J. (2006a) Practices of socio-spatial control in the neighbourhoods of Lima, Peru, *Trialog*, 89, pp. 32-36.

Plöger, J. (2006b) Die nachträglich abgeschotteten Nachbarschaften in Lima (Peru) – Eine Analyse sozialräumlicher Kontrollmaßnahmen im Kontext zunehmender Unsicherheiten, *Kieler Geographische Schriften* 112. Kiel: Christian Albrechts Universität.

PNUD (1998) *Informe de DesarrolloHumano en Bolivia 1998*. La Paz: Programa de las Naciones Unidas para el Desarrollo.

PNUD (2000) *Informe de DesarrolloHumano en Bolivia 2000*. La Paz: Programa de las Naciones Unidas para el Desarrollo.

PNUD (2002) *Informe de DesarrolloHumano en Bolivia 200.* La Paz: Programa de las Naciones Unidas para el Desarrollo.

Poder Ejecutivo Federal (1984) *Programa Nacional de Turismo 1984-1988.* Mexico City.

Pöhler, M. (1999) Zwischen Luxus-Ghettos und Favelas. Stadterweiterungsprozesse und sozialräumliche Segregation in Rio de Janeiro: Das Fallbeispiel Barra da Tijuca. *Kleinere Arbeiten aus dem Geographischen Institut der Universität Tübingen.* Tübingen.

Porter, M. (1998) *On Competition.* Boston: Harvard Business Review.

Pradilla Cobos, E. (1998) Metropolis y megalopolis en América Latin, *Revista Interamericana de Planificación,* 119/120, pp. 194-212.

Prévot-Schapira, M. F. (2001) Fragmentación espacial y social: conceptos y realidades, *Perfiles Latinoamericanos,* 19, pp. 33-56.

Pritzl, R. F. (1997) Property rights, Rent-Seeking und 'institutionelle Schwäche' in Latein Amerika. Zur institutionenökonomischen Analyse der sozialen Anomie, *Ibero-Amerikanisches Archiv,* 23, 3/4, pp. 365-407.

PRORENDA/IBAM (2000) *PRONAF e as estruturas institucionais municipais. Estudos de caso em oito municípios do nordeste paraense.* Belém.

PRONAF/IBAM (2000) *Avaliação do Programa Nacional de Fortalecimento da Agricultura Familiar – PRONAF no estado do Pará. Síntese de avaliação.* Belém.

Quintero Ramírez, C. (2003) Intereses nacionales y regionalismo en los sindicatos de Coahuila In: R. Beltrán Enríquez (Ed.) *Coahuila: sociedad, economía, política y cultura,* pp. 149-192. Mexico: UNAM.

Rabach, E. & E. Kim (1994) Where is the chain in the commodity chains? The service sector nexus. In: G. Gereffi & M. Korzeniewicz (Eds.) *Commodity chains and global capitalism,* pp. 123-142. Westport: Praeger.

Ranfla Gonzalez, A. (2000) Crecimento industrial y expansion urbana. *Ciudades,* pp. 25-34.

Rauch, T. (2001) Dezentralisierung ist kein Allheilmittel! - Zur Notwendigkeit einer kontextspezifischen Dezentralisierungspolitik am Beispiel der Kommunalentwicklung in Südafrika. In: *Geographica Helvetica,* 56, 1:13-27.

Rendon Labadan, M. (1996) *Decentralization policies in Guatemala: case studies of citizen participation.* Ann Arbor: UMI.

Rioja, G. (2003) *Diagnóstico Rápido: oportunidades y amenazas del proceso de integración del Norte Amazónico de Bolivia con las regiones vecinas de Madre de Dios-Peru y Acre-Brasil.* Universidad Amazónica de Pando.

Robinson, J. (2002) Global and World Cities: A View from off the Map, *International Journal of Urban and Regional Research,* 26, 3, pp. 531-554.

Robinson, J. (2005) Urban geography: world cities, or a world of cities. *Progress in Human Geography* 29, 6, pp. 757-765.

Roca, J. (2001) *Los Barrios Cerrados en Córdoba.* Córdoba.

Rodriguez Chumillas, I. & M. Mollá Ruiz-Gómez (2002) Urbanizaciones cerradas en Puebla y Toluca. In: L.F. Cabrales Barajas (Ed.) *Latinoamérica: países abiertos, ciudades cerradas,* pp. 511-548. Guadalajara/Paris: UNESCO.

Rofman, A. (2006) El enfoque del desarrollo local: conflictos y limitaciones. In: A. Rofman & A. Villar (Comps) *Desarrollo local. Una revisión crítica del debate,* pp. 37-58. Buenos Aires: Espacio Editorial.

Rogerson, C. (1995) Local economic development planning in the developing world (editorial introduction). *Regional Development Dialogue* 16.

Rogozinski, J. (1993) *La privatización de empresas paraestatales,* Mexico: Fondo de Cultura Económica.

Rojas García, G. (2002) *Ciudad Acuña, Coahuila, Barrio San Antonio,* Unpublished report on urban poverty in Mexico.

Ros-Tonen, M. A. F. (1993) *Tropical Hardwood from the Brazilian Amazon. A Study of the Timber Industry in Western Pará.* Saarbrücken/Fort Lauderdale: Breitenbach Publishers.

Ros-Tonen, M. A. F. (Ed.) (2007) *Partnerships for sustainable forest resource management: learning from Latin America.* CEDLA Latin America Studies 94. Leiden/Boston: Brill Publishers.

Roux, J. C. (2000) *La Bolivie Orientale, Confins inexplorés, battues aux Indiens et économie de pillage*. Paris: L'Harmattan.

Rovira, A. (2002) Los barrios cerrados de Santiago de Chile: En busca de la seguridad y la privacidad perdida. In: L. F. Cabrales (Ed.) *Latinoamérica: países abiertos, ciudades cerradas*, pp. 351-369. Guadalajara/Paris: UNESCO.

Ruiz, J. (2003) Los siete pecados capitales de Iberoamérica: mito, realidad y consecuencias Anuario Elcano: América Latina 2002-03: 276-307.

Ruiz Durán, C., E. Dussel Peters & T. Tanura (1997) Changes in industrial organization of the Mexican automobile industry by economic liberalization. Tokyo: IDE.

Sabatini, F., G. Caceres & J. Cerda (2001) Segregación residencial en las principales ciudades chilenas : Tendencias de las tres últimas décadas y posibles cursos de acción, *Revista EURE*, 27, 82, pp. 21-42.

Saito, F. (Ed.) (2008) *Foundations for local governments. Decentralization in comparative perspective*. Heidelberg: Physica Verlag.

Santana Rodriguez, P. (1995) Local governments, decentralization and democracy in Colombia. In: C. H. Reilly (Ed.) *New paths to democratic development in Latin America*. Boulder/London: Lynne Riener.

Santos, O. Junior A. dos (2001) *Democracia e governo local: Dilemas da reforma municipal no Brasil*. Rio de Janeiro.

Sassen, S. (1991) *The Global City. New York, London, Tokyo*. Princeton: Princeton University Press.

Sassen, S. (1994) *Cities in a World Economy*. Thousand Oaks (Cal.): Pine Forge/Sage Press.

SBIF (2004) Información Financiera. Diciembre de 2004, Superintendiancia de Bancos e Instituciones Financieras de Chile, http://www.sbif.cl/sbifweb/internet/archivos/Info_Fin_708_4032.pdf.

Schejtmann, A. & J. A. Berdegué (2004) *Desarrollo territorial rural*. Santiago: RIMISP.

Scherr, S., White, A. & Kaimowitz, D. (2003) *A new agenda for achieving forest conservation and poverty alleviation: making markets work for low-income producers*. Washington: Forest Trends / Bogor: CIFOR.

Schmukler, S. (2004) Financial Globalization: Gain and pain for Developing Countries, *Federal, Reserve Bank of Atlanta Economic Review* 89, 2, pp. 39-66.

Schneider, H. (1999) Participatory Governance for Poverty Reduction, *Journal of International Development*, pp. 521-534.

Scholz, F. (2000) Perspektiven des 'Südens' im Zeitalter der Globalisierung, *Geographisches Zeitschrift*, 88, 1, pp. 1-19.

Scholz, I. (2001) *Overexploitation or Sustainable Management: Action Patterns of the Tropical Timber Industry. The Case of Pará (Brazil) 1969-97*. London: Frank Cass Publishers.

Scholz, I. (2005) Environmental Policy Cooperation among organised Civil Society, National Public Actors and International Actors in the Brazilian Amazon, *European Journal of Deveopment Research*, 17, 4, pp. 681-705.

Schuurman, F. (1996) Local government in Latin America: some critical notes. In: H. Gans (Hrsg.) *Regionale Entwicklung in Lateinamerika, Erfurter Geographische Studien*, 4, pp. 7-21.

Schwartz, H. (2004) *Urban Renewal, Municipal Revitalization. The Case of Curitiba, Brazil*. Alexandria (VA): Schwartz.

Secretaría de Fomento Económico (1999) *Inversión y empleo, 1994-1999*. Gobierno del estado de Coahuila.

SECTUR (1991) *Compendio Estadístico de Turismo en México, 1990*. Mexico-City: Secretaria de Turimo.

SECTUR (2001) *Programa Nacional del Sector Turismo, 2001-2006*. Mexico-City: Secretaria de Turismo.

SECTUR (2002) *Compendio Estadístico de Turismo en México, 2001*. Mexico-City: Secretaria de Turismo.

Segebart, D. (2007) *Partizipatives Monitoring als Instrument zur Umsetzung von Good Loca Governance – Eine Aktionsforschung im östlichen Amazonien/Brasilien*. Tübingen.

Segovia, L.O. (2003) Balance comparativo de la descentralización en los países de la Comunidad Andina. In: F. Carrion (Ed.) *Procesos de descentralización en la Comunidad Andina*, pp. 65-104. Quito: FLACSO-OEA-Parlamento Andino.

Sen, A. K. (2000) *Ökonomie für den Menschen. Wege zu Gerechtigkeit und Solidarität in der Marktwirtschaft*, München.

Sernau, S. (1994) *Economies of Exclusion. Underclass Poverty and Labour Market Change in Mexico*, Westport & London: Praeger.

Shah, A. & S. Shah (2006) The New Vision of Local Governance and the Evolving Roles of Local Governments. In: Anwar Shah (Ed.) *Local Governance in Developing Countries*, pp. 1-46. Washington (DC): World Bank.

Shaiken H. & S. Herzenberg (1989) *Automatización y producción global. Producción de motores de automóvil en México, Estados Unidos y Canada*. Mexico: UNAM.

Shepherd, A. (1998) *Sustainable rural development*. London: MacMillan.

Sibley, D. (1995) *Geographies of exclusion – society and difference in the West*. London/New York: Routledge.

Sidersky, P., Guijt, I. (2000) Experimenting with Participatory Monitoring in North-east Brazil: The case of AS-PTA's Projeto Paraíba. In: M. Estrella (Ed.) *Learning from Change*. Ottawa, London 68-82.

Simmons, C. S., Walker, R. T., Arima, E. Y., Aldrich, S. P., Caldas, M. M. (2007) The Amazon Land War in the South of Pará. In: *Annals of the Association of American Geographers*, 97, 3:567-592.

Simón Domínguez, N. & D. Ramírez Lugo (2001) Evolución financiera de Altos Hornos de México y su crisis actua. In: I. Rueda Peiro & N. Simón Domínguez (Eds.) *De la privatización a la crisis. El caso de Altos Hornos de México*, pp. 193-221. Mexico: Miguel Ángel Porrúa.

Sjoholt, P. (1999) Eco-tourism and Local Development. Conceptual and Theoretical Framework and Problems in Implementation. Empirical Evidence from Costa Rica and Ecuador, *Fennia* 178, 2, pp. 227-241.

Skidmore, T. E. & P. H. Smith (2005) *Modern Latin America*. Oxford: Oxford University Press.

Smeraldi, R. & A. Veríssimo (1999) *Acertando o Alvo: Consumo de Madeira no Mercado Interno Brasileiro e Promoção da Certificação Florestal*. Belém: Friends of the Earth Amazon Program/ IMAZON/IMAFLORA.

Smeraldi, R. (2003) Expedient plunder? The new legal context for Amazonian logging. In: D.J. Macqueen (Ed.) *Growing exports: the Brazilian tropical timber industry and international markets*, pp. 49-64. IIED Small and Medium Enterprise series No.1. London: International Institute for Environment and Development.

Smith, B.C. (1985) Decentralization: *The Territorial Dimension of the State*. London: George Allen & Unwin.

SNPP (1996) La Participación Popular en cifras. La Paz: Secretaría Nacional de Participación Popular.

Soares, J. A., Gondim, L. (2002) Novos modelos de gestão: lições que vêm do poder local. In: J. A. Soares, S. Caccia-Bava (Ed.) *Os desafios da gestão municipal democratica*. São Paulo 61-96.

Soja, E. (2000) *Postmetropolis: critical studies of cities and regions*. Oxford: Malden.

Souza, C. (2001) Participatory Budgeting in Brazilian Cities: Limits and Possibilities in Building Democratic Institutions. *Environment and Urbanization*, 13, 1, pp. 159-184.

Spink, P. K., R. Clemente & R. Keppke (1999) Governo local: o mito da descentralização e as novas práticas de governança, *Revista de Administração*, 34, 1, pp. 61-68.

Stoian, D. (2000) *Variations and dynamics of extractive economies: the rural-urban nexus of non-timber forest use in the Bolivian Amazon*. Freiburg im Breisgau.

Stöhr, W. (1975) *Regional Development Experiences and Prospects in Latin America*. The Hague: Mouton.

Stone, S.W. (1997) *Growth in the Timber Industry of the Eastern Amazon: Economic Trends and Implications for Policy*. PhD dissertation, Cornell University.

Stone, S.W. (1998) Evolution of the timber industry along an ageing frontier: the case of Paragominas, *World Development* 26, 3, pp. 443-448.

Strasdas, W. (2000) *El ecoturismo en la práctica de proyectos de protección de la naturaleza en México y Belice*. Eschborn: GTZ.

Suttles, G. (1972) The social construction of communities, Chicago: University of Chicago Press.

Svampa, M. (2001) *Los que ganaron - la vida en los countries y barrios privados.* Buenos Aires: Biblos.

Swyngedouw, E. (2004) Globalisation or 'Glocalisation'? Networks, Territories and Rescaling. *Cambridge Review of International Affairs*, 17, 1.

Taylor, P. (2004) *World City Network: A Global Urban Analysis.* London: Routledge.

Toni, F., Souza, C. de A. (2003) Xapuri: Movimentos Sociais no Poder. In: F. Toni, D. Kaimovitz (Ed.): *Municípios e gestão florestal na Amazônia.* Natal 337-372.

Toledo Beltrán, D. & F. Zapata (1999) *Acero y Estado. Una historia de la industria siderúrgica integrada de México.* Mexico: Universidad Autónoma Metropolitana.

Torres, D. (1998) Participación popular y participación campesina: algunas observaciones y Referencias. In: A. Zoomers (comp.) *Estrategias Campesinas en el Surandino de Bolivia. Intervenciones y desarrollo rural en el norte de Chuquisaca y Potosí*, pp. 441-454. Amsterdam/ La Paz: KIT/CEDLA/CID.

Torres, R. (2002) Toward a Better Understanding of Tourism and Agriculture Linkages in the Yucatán: Tourist Food Consumption and Preferences, *Tourism Geographies* 4, 3, pp. 282-306.

Torres, R. (2003) Linkages Between Tourism and Agriculture in Mexico, *Annals of Tourism Research* 30, 3, pp. 546-566.

Torres, R. & J. D. Momsen (2005) Gringolandia: The Construction of a New Tourist Space in Mexico, *Annals of the Association of American Geographers* 95, 2, pp. 314-335.

UCLG (2008) *Decentralization and local democracy in the world. First global Report.* Barcelona/ Washington (DC): UCLG/World Bank [www.cities-localgovernments.org/gold/gold_report.asp]

Ugarteche, O. (1998) *La arqueología de la modernidad – el Perú entre la globalización y la exclusión.* Lima: Desco.

UIA (1998) El proceso social de introducción de demandas. In: UIA (comp.) Participación Popular: una evaluación-aprendizaje de la Ley 1994-1997. La Paz, pp. 69-91.

UNCTAD (2007) *World Investment Report 2007. Transnational Corporations, Extractive Industries and Development.* New York/Geneva: UNCTAD.

UNDP (n.d.) Governance indicators: A Users' Guide. (www.undp.org/oslocentre/docs04/ UserGuide.pdf, assessed on 22.11.2004).

UNDP (1998) *UNDP priorities in support of good governance.* Washington: UNDP.

UNDP (2002) *Human Development Report 2002: Deepening Democracy in a Fragmented World.* New York: Oxford University Press.

UNESCAP (2004) *What is Good Governance?* (http://www.unescap.org/huset/gg/governance. htm, assessed 29.07.2004)

Uphoff, N. (1993) Grassroots Organizations and NGOs in Rural Development: Opportunities with Diminishing States an Expanding Markets. World Development 21, pp. 607-622.

Urendo Díaz, J. C. (1998) *La Descentralización Deficiente.* La Paz: Los Amigos del Libro.

Urioste, U. (2001) *Bolivia: descentralización municipal y participación popular.* La Paz: Fundación TIERRA.

USDA/FAS (2004) The Amazon: Brazil's Final Soybean Frontier. USDA Production Estimates and Crop Assessment Division, Foreign Agricultural Service. [www.fas.usda.gov/pecad/ highlights/2004/01/Amazon/Amazon_soybeans.htm]

USDA/FAS (2005) 'Brazil: 2005/06 soybean area projected to decline'. USDA Production Estimates and Crop Assessment Division, Foreign Agricultural Service, 2005. (URL: http:// www.fas.usda.gov/pecad/highlights/2005/09/brazil_12sep2005/index.htm).

Vellinga, M. (Ed.) (1999) *The dialectics of globalization. Regional responses to world economic processes: Asia, Europe and Latin America in comparative perspective.* Boulder (Co): Westview Press.

Veríssimo, A., M. A. Cochrane, C. Souza Jr. & R. Salomão (2002) Priority areas for establishing National Forests in the Brazilian Amazon, *Conservation Biology* [www.consecol.org/vol6/iss1/art4]

Veríssimo, A., E. Lima & M. Lentini (2003) *Pólos Madeireiros do Estado do Pará.* Belém: IMAZON.

Verkoren, O. (2002) *Terug naar de regio, beschouwingen over regionale/lokale ontwikkeling in Spaanssprekend Latijns-Amerika.* Utrecht: Utrecht University.

Vieira Posada, E. (2008) *La formación de espacios regionales en la integración de América Latina.* Bogotá: Convenio Andrés Bello.

Viera Caetano O'Neill, M. M. (1986) Condominios exclusivos: Um estudio de caso. *Revista Brasileira de Geografia* 48, 1, pp. 63-81.

Villar, A. (2007) *Políticas municipales para el desarrollo económico social. Revisando el desarrollo local.* Buenos Aires: Ediciones Ciccus/Flacso Argentina.

Vorlaufer, K. (1996) *Tourismus in Entwicklungsländern.* Darmstadt: Wissenschaftliche Buchgesellschaft.

Vorlaufer, K. (1999) Bali – Massentourismus und nachhaltige Entwicklung: Die sozioökonomische Dimension, *Erdkunde* 53, 4, pp. 273-301.

Wallace, G. (1996) An Evaluation of Ecotourism in Amazonas, Brazil, *Annals of Tourism Research* 23, 4, pp. 843-873.

Wampler, B. (2007) *Participatory Budgeting in Brazil: Contestation, Cooperation, and Accountability.* University Park (PA): Pennsylvania State University Press.

Watts, M. J. (2003) Development and governmentality. In: *Singapore Journal of Tropical Geography,* 24, 1:6-34.

WCFSD (1999) *Our forests – our future. Summary Report of the World Commission on Forests and Sustainable Development* [www.iisd.org/pdf/wcfsdsummary.pdf]

Wehrhahn, R. (2000) Megastadt São Paulo – Lebensverhältnisse und Umweltbedingungen, *HGO-Journal* 15, pp. 105-118.

Welch, M. (2002) Gartentürme des Wohlstands. Buenos Aires: Projektionen einer Wohnhaustypologie, *RaumPlanung* 101, pp. 71-76.

White, A. & A. Martin (2002) *Who Owns the World's Forests? Forest Tenure and Public Forests in Transition.* Washington: Forest Trends.

Wiersum, K. F. (2000) Forest policy development between globalisation and localisation. *Paper presented at the XXI IUFRO World Congress.*

Wiggins, S. & S. Proctor (2001) How Special Are Rural Areas? The Economic Implication of Location for Rural Development, *Development Policy Review* 19, 4, pp. 427-436.

Wilhelmy, H. & A. Borsdorf (1984) Die Städte Südamerikas. Wesen und Wandel. Urbanisierung der Erde 3,1. Berlin, Stuttgart: Bornträger.

Wilhelmy, H. & A. Borsdorf (1985) Die Städte Südamerikas. Die urbanen Zentren und ihre Regionen. Urbanisierung der Erde 3,2. Berlin, Stuttgart: Bornträger.

Wils, F. (1998) NGOs as a Vehicle for Poverty Reduction: Possibilities and Limitations. In: P. van Dijck (Ed.) *The Bolivian Experiment – Structural Adjustment and Poverty Alleviation,* pp. 205-217. Amsterdam: CEDLA.

Wilson, P. (1995) Embracing locality in local economic development, *Urban Studies* 32, pp. 645-658.

World Bank (1993) World Development Report. Washington.

World Bank (2000) Cities in Transition: A Strategic View of Urban and Local Government Issues. Washington (DC): World Bank.

World Tourism Organization (2001) Yearbook of Tourism Statistics. Madrid: WTO.

Woy-Hazleton, S. & W. Hazleton (1990) Sendero Luminoso and the future of Peruvian Democracy, *Third World Quarterly,* 12, 2, pp. 21-35.

Yáñez Chávez, A. (1994) *Geographical Industrialization in Coahuila and Mexico-U.S. Economic Integration,* Unpublished Ph.D. Thesis Berkeley: University of California.

Zagorski, P. W. (2005) The Military. In: R.S. Hillman (Ed.) *Understanding contemporary Latin America,* pp. 117-144. Boulder (Co): Lynne Rienner.

Ziai, A. (2001) Post-development: Perspektiven für eine afrikanische Debatte? In: *Fokus Afrika, IAK-Diskussionsbeiträge 18,* Institut für Afrika-Kunde, Hamburg.

Ziai, A. (2003) Foucault in der Entwicklungstheorie. In: *Peripherie,* 23, (92):406-430.

Zibechi, R. (2006) IIRSA: la integración a la medida de los mercados. ALAI, América Latina en Movimiento. [www.alainet.org]

Zoomers, A. (Comp.) (1998) *Estrategias Campesinas en el Surandino de Bolivia. Intervenciones y desarrollo rural en el norte de Chuquisaca y Potosí.* Amsterdam/La Paz: KIT/ CEDLA/CID.

Zoomers, A. (1999) *Linking livelihood strategies to development. Experiences from the Bolivian Andes.* Amsterdam: KIT/CEDLA.

Index

A

Access-restricted residential quarters, 25
Accountability, 10, 11, 21, 110, 129, 130
Action research, 129, 135
Agency, 73, 131, 148, 149
Agglomeration process, 32
Agricultural colonization, 13, 103, 113,
   115–116, 118, 142, 145
Agricultural front, 115–117, 139–142, 144,
   145, 151, 152
Agroecological zone, 102–103
Amazonia, 17, 21, 93, 96, 97, 113–127,
   139–153
Andes, 102, 110, 115
Argentina, 6, 8, 17, 24–26, 29, 32
Assembly-based manufacturing, 3
Aviamento, 141

B

Backward linkages, 173
Barrios cerrados, 25
Biodiversity, 146–148, 173, 187
Bogotá, 8, 38
Bolivia, 5, 6, 8, 11, 12, 16, 17, 19, 20, 69–111,
   113, 115–118, 120–123, 125–127
Bottom-up, 10, 14, 73, 126, 127
Brazil, 6, 8, 11, 13, 17, 20, 21, 23, 25, 26, 29,
   38, 93, 94, 113, 115–127, 129–153
Buenos Aires, 8, 23, 24, 29, 32, 38, 53

C

CAFTA. *See* Central American Free Trade
   Agreement
Capacity building, 16, 136
Capacity strengthening, 9
Catraca system, 141, 143
Cattle front, 116–117

CBOs. *See* Community-based organizations
Center, 67
Central America, 5, 167, 187
Central American Free Trade Agreement
   (CAFTA), 167
Central government, 3, 6, 8, 9, 11, 12, 71,
   74, 77, 80, 89, 91, 97, 98, 109, 117
Central Obrera Boliviana (COB), 88, 89
Centre-periphery, 67
Chile, 3, 5, 8, 17, 19, 24, 25, 29, 38, 51–57,
   61–66, 71
Chuquisaca, 20, 69, 74–76, 101, 102
Cities, 1, 4, 8–11, 13, 18, 19, 23–26, 29–33,
   35, 36, 38, 39, 41, 46, 48–67, 70, 73,
   79, 85, 91, 93, 94, 96–98, 103, 113,
   115, 117, 139, 141, 145, 159, 162,
   164, 165, 173–175, 180, 182, 184
Citizen, 8–12, 14, 17, 44, 87, 89, 93,
   132, 158, 175
Citizen-centred governance, 10, 11
Ciudad pobre (poor city), 30
Ciudad rica (rich city), 23
Civil society, 4, 10, 16, 21, 70, 73, 74, 89, 91,
   92, 94–99, 123, 124, 132, 133,
   135–137, 139, 147, 148, 153
Civil society organisations (CSO), 21, 89, 91,
   135, 136, 139, 147, 148, 153
Clientelism, 1, 8, 22, 87, 132
Cluster(ing), 29, 39, 121–123, 159, 161–164,
   166, 168, 169
Co-participación tributaria, 77
Coahuila, 21, 155–169
Coastal resorts, 21, 171, 175, 187
COB. *See* Central Obrera Boliviana
Colombia, 4, 5, 8, 17, 39, 71, 72
Colonization, 13, 103, 113, 115–116, 118,
   142, 145
Comité de Vigilancia (Vigilance Committee),
   74, 76, 80, 91

Commodity chains, 19, 49–67, 168
Community-based forest management, 139,
    145, 148
Community-based development, 15, 16,
    27, 138
Community-based organizations (CBOs), 20
Competitive advantage, 3, 159, 160, 169
Comunidades libres, 94
Condominisation, 19, 35–37, 43–44, 46, 47
Condominiums, 28, 38, 39
Consolidation, 5, 6, 54, 132
Conventillos, 26
Cooperative, 20, 82, 101, 104, 130, 136, 137,
    184, 185
Core, 38, 49, 67, 173
Core areas (regions), 3, 4, 67, 74
Corporate-community partnerships, 149
Cross-border activities, 121–122, 127
Cross-border links, 53
Cross-border networks, 50, 54, 67
Cross-border partnerships, 20, 21, 113–127
CSO. *See* Civil society organisations
Curitiba, 8, 29

D
De-industrialization, 24
Decentralisation, 1, 4–9
    administrative, 1, 73, 89, 109
    fiscal, 6, 9
    functions/responsibilities, 6, 8, 9, 19,
        69, 71–73, 76, 89, 97, 98, 101,
        109, 114, 120
    spatial, 4, 13
Deforestation, 21, 116, 121, 124, 139, 145, 147
Delegation, 6, 109
Democracy, 5, 10–12, 93, 127, 132
Democratic deficits, 5, 6, 12
Democratisation, 6, 14, 16, 21, 96, 98, 99,
    118–120, 132
Densification, 39
Dependency, 39, 67, 85, 94, 172
Deregulation, 26, 155, 156
Desarrollo hacia adentro, 2, 4
Desarrollo hacia afuera, 2
Development, 1–33, 38–40, 48, 50, 52, 54,
    66, 67, 69–99, 101–111, 113–127,
    129, 130, 132–138, 142, 144, 146–149,
    155, 156, 158, 159, 161, 163–166,
    168, 169, 171–187
Development organisation, 87, 101, 103,
    105, 107
Devolution, 6, 21, 139, 145, 149–151, 153
Division of labour (international-, global-), 50

E
Economies of scale, 3, 71, 72, 83, 146
Ecotourism, 187
Ecuador, 5, 8, 17, 24–26, 28
El Salvador, 8, 39, 41
Elections, 4, 5, 10, 46, 73, 82, 109, 110, 160
Empowerment, 10, 14, 132
Enclosed neighbourhoods, 19, 29, 39–41
Equality, 10
Equity, 55, 64, 130
Exclusion, 26, 36, 109
Export enclaves, 4
Export manufacturing, 21, 158, 159, 161,
    162, 165
Export processing zones, 3, 4, 53

F
Farmer, 20, 82, 101–111, 115, 116, 119, 124,
    130, 133, 135, 137, 141, 143, 145, 151,
    177, 179, 182, 183
Farmers organisation, 20, 101–111
Fazendeiros, 141
FDI. *See* Foreign direct investment
Financial service sector, 52, 54–65
FONATUR. *See Fondo Nacional de Fomento
    al Turismo*
Fondo Nacional de Fomento al Turismo
    (FONATUR), 173–175, 177–181,
    183–187
Foreign direct investment (FDI), 21, 24, 52,
    53, 161, 172
Forest management, 21, 81, 139, 142,
    145–153
Forestry, 65, 124, 139–153
Formal, 10, 12, 37, 38, 42, 73, 76, 92,
    105, 124, 127, 133, 135, 138, 177
Formalisation, 42
Forward linkages, 173
Fragmentation, 2, 18, 19, 23–35, 48, 125
Fragmentation of urban space, 30
Fragmented city-agglomeration, 30, 32
Free trade, 52, 117, 155, 158, 161, 169
Free trade area of the Americas (FTAA),
    126, 167
Free-trade area, 122, 126, 155, 167
Frontier, 13, 14, 21, 30, 117, 139–142,
    144–146, 151, 152
FTAA. *See* Free trade area of the Americas

G
Gated communities, 18, 19, 23, 25–30, 32,
    34, 38–40

suburban, 27, 29
urban, 27, 29
Global cities, 19, 39, 49–67
Global commodity chain, 19, 49–52, 54,
    66–67
Globalisation, 1, 21, 35, 49–51, 53–54, 127,
    139, 146, 148, 149, 155
Good governance, 10, 87–89, 92, 98, 99, 129,
    130, 132, 138
Governance, 10, 11, 16, 19, 21, 26, 33, 47,
    49–51, 66, 72, 87, 119, 122, 124, 126,
    127, 129–139, 147, 190
Governance of commodity chains, 19, 49–67
Government, 2–12, 14, 17, 19, 20, 55, 69,
    70–74, 76–80, 82, 83, 89, 91,
    95, 97, 98, 101, 109–111, 115–117,
    119–122, 124, 126, 127, 129–138,
    143, 147, 149, 150, 153, 156, 158–160,
    165, 166, 169, 174, 180, 181, 187
Governmentality, 129–138
Growth centres, 13
Guatemala, 8, 17

H
Honduras, 72, 88
Household economy, 101
Huatulco, 171, 172, 174, 175, 178–187
Human development index (HDI), 74, 88, 134

I
IIRSA. *See Integración de la Infraestructura
    Regional de América del Sur*
IMF. *See* International monetary fund
Import substituting industrialisation, 156, 165
Inclusion, 1, 22
Inclusiveness, 130
Incorporation, 118, 121
Indigenous groups, 94–96
Indigenous territories, 110
Inequality, 3, 13, 17–19, 35, 39, 48
Informal, 10, 20, 32, 37, 38, 42, 44, 47, 48,
    94, 101, 103, 107, 136, 177
Informal networks, 20, 101, 103
Infrastructure, 2, 9, 13, 19, 23, 27, 28, 32,
    38, 39, 45, 73, 80, 86, 87, 89, 98,
    104, 122, 123, 134, 144, 152, 159,
    163, 164, 172, 174, 180, 184–186
*Integración de la Infraestructura Regional de
    América del Sur* (IIRSA), 122, 124
International monetary fund (IMF), 3, 130,
    155, 160, 174
Interventionism, 174

Investment funds
    external, 20, 69, 79, 85
    internal, 79

L
Labour relations, 141
Land rights, 21, 119, 139, 149
Land tenure, 104
Land use, 102, 123, 140, 174, 180
Latin America, 1–36, 38–40, 48–67, 70,
    71, 86, 88, 92, 118, 120–122, 125,
    126, 150, 155, 160, 167
Latin American city (model), 24, 26, 30,
    32, 33, 35, 53
Leakages, 172
Ley de Descentralización Administrativa
    (LDA), 89, 92, 109
Ley de Participación Popular (LPP), 19, 73,
    74, 76–80, 82–86, 91, 92, 109
Liberalisation, 54, 55, 64, 126, 139, 155, 156
Lima, 19, 26, 35–48, 191
Linkages, 50, 53, 126, 173, 177, 180, 184
Livelihood, 15, 21, 102, 139, 146, 152, 153
Livelihood strategy, 102, 152, 153
Local development, 1–22, 66, 67, 69–99,
    113–127, 169, 171–189
Local economic development (LED), 14–16,
    21, 70, 82, 83, 156, 166, 191
Local governance, 1–22, 35–48, 88, 110,
    129, 139, 156, 163, 169
Local government, 2, 4–12, 15–17, 20,
    70–73, 76–80, 82, 83, 89, 101, 109,
    111, 123, 129, 138, 166, 168
Local institutions, 70, 131, 153
Lock-in, 169
Logging, 21, 139–146, 149–153
Lower tier government, 1, 14, 18

M
Madre de Dios, Acre and Pando (MAP),
    114, 123
Mancomunidad, 17
Marginalisation, 22, 171, 178, 181–183
Market economy, 107
Market-led development, 2–4
Metropolitan areas, 8, 18, 25, 38
Mexico, 4, 6, 13, 19–22, 24, 26, 29, 51–58,
    63–67, 71, 155–169, 171–175, 178,
    180, 181, 183–187
Mexico City, 19, 29, 51–53, 63, 64, 66, 67,
    162, 173–175, 180, 184
Modernisation theory, 172

Monterrey, 8, 175
Montevideo, 8, 121
Multiplier effects, 85, 86, 172
Municipal institutional structures, 20, 101, 110
Municipal planning, 95, 96, 101, 110, 111
Municipalities, 71–74, 76–86, 91, 95, 98, 109,
    111, 134, 135, 137, 181
    rural, 8, 10, 69, 74–76, 79, 85, 86, 91,
    97, 109
    urban, 73
Municipio productivo, 16

N
National government, 6, 124
Natural resource management, 150
Natural resources, 8, 21, 52, 96, 104, 118,
    122, 133
Neighbourhood association, 36, 37, 41, 45,
    136
Neighbourhood-based activities, 24, 32, 37, 41
Neoliberalism, 3, 4, 17, 24, 26, 28, 33, 35,
    39, 89, 92, 126, 127
Non-governmental organziations (NGO),
    103, 109–111, 181
Nicaragua, 5
North American Free Trade Agreement
    (NAFTA), 16, 24, 155–169

O
Organizaciones Territoriales de Base (OTB),
    73, 91, 95, 109
Ownership, 54, 119, 132, 150, 182, 183

P
Panama, 5
Pará, 123, 125, 129–139, 142, 143, 145, 149
Paraguay, 5
Participation, 1, 5, 6, 8–12, 14, 16, 19, 20,
    22, 53, 55, 69, 71, 73, 74, 76, 78, 79,
    82, 87, 89, 92, 94–98, 102, 107,
    109–111, 120, 126, 130, 132, 135,
    136, 147, 173, 180–182, 187
Participation rate, 133, 181
Participatory budgeting, 8, 11
Participatory democracy, 10–12, 93
Participatory development, 129
Participatory monitoring, 21, 129, 131,
    133–136, 138
Participatory rural appraisal (PRA), 134
Partnership, 17, 57, 111, 147, 149–153
Patronage, 1, 22, 93

Peasant economy, 103, 105
Peasant household, 101, 103
Peasant organizations, 20, 101, 104,
    107–108, 110, 111
Periphery, peripheries, 1, 3, 27, 32, 33,
    44, 49, 67, 91, 93
Peru, 5, 8, 17, 20, 24, 35–48, 116–118,
    120, 122, 123, 125, 126
Plan de Desarrollo Municipal (PDM), 74, 98
Planning
    of local development, 2, 17, 20
    municipal, 95, 96, 101, 110, 111
    regional, 13, 14, 135
    rural, 129
    urban, 25, 26, 31
*Plano Municipal de Desenvolvimento Rural
    Sustentável* (PMDRS), 134
Polarized city, 23
Polarized urban development, 181, 185–186
Porto Alegre, 8, 11
Poverty, 3, 9, 10, 13, 16, 17, 23, 26, 88,
    92, 94, 121, 133, 134, 155
Predatory logging, 139, 144–145, 150
Primate cities, 1, 13
Private sector, 16, 55, 70, 76, 82, 124,
    149, 156, 159, 164, 169
Privatisation, 18, 19, 33, 52, 54, 64, 98,
    155, 160
Pro-poor, 17
Producer association, 20, 82, 101, 104, 105
Production system, 101, 104, 105, 107,
    115, 187
*Programa Nacional de Fortalecimento da
    Agricultura Familiar* (PRONAF), 133
Property rights, 146, 149, 156
Public sector, 4, 6, 35, 36, 38, 43, 44, 48, 83,
    84, 86, 126

R
Reform, 0, 1, 3, 4, 54, 72, 73, 87–99, 116, 119,
    120, 158, 160, 181
Regional development, 12–15, 73, 78, 91, 97,
    120, 123, 125, 126, 158, 169, 171, 172,
    181, 183
Regional disparities, 167, 172
Regional integration, 20, 21, 113–127
Regional transformation, 30, 52, 118, 126
Regulation, 14, 15, 19, 26, 37, 41–42, 44, 48,
    85, 105, 137, 150, 155, 156, 164, 178,
    180, 186
Regulatory framework, 11, 41, 148
Representative democracy, 5, 10, 12
Residential enclave building, 35–48

Resources, 4, 6, 8, 13–17, 20,
        21, 36, 41, 44, 48, 49, 52, 69–72,
        74, 77–79, 85, 96–98, 101, 103–105,
        107, 109, 115, 118, 122, 133, 134,
        136, 142, 145–147, 149, 150, 172
Road construction, 93
Rural-urban interaction, 73
Rural-urban transformation, 35–48

S
Santiago de Chile, 19, 24, 38, 51, 53, 63, 66
Seasonal migration, 103
Secondary cities, 4, 13, 29
SECTUR (Secretaria de Turismo), 175–177, 180
Security, 10, 19, 30, 35, 37, 39–48, 64, 82,
        124, 177, 186
Segregation, 22, 23, 25–26, 34–36, 39, 186
Self-organisation, 137
Service provision, 6, 35, 39, 44, 53, 70
Sindicatos, 74, 104, 105, 107, 109
Smallholders, 149, 151–153
Social capital, 137
Social disparities, 93, 133, 138, 186
Social mobility, 33
Social movements, 1, 133, 136
Social polarization, 24, 25
Socio-spatial inequality, 39
South America, 126
Soy bean, 139, 144–146, 152
Soybean cultivation, 139, 144–146, 152
Spatial concentration, 53, 172, 175
Spatial mobility, 33
Spatial polarization, 35
Spatial segregation, 23, 25–26, 36
Stakeholders, 1, 6, 10, 11, 14, 20, 21, 113,
        127, 135, 147, 187
State reforms, 88, 89
State-led development, 3, 13
State-sponsored tourism development, 21,
        175–178
Structural adjustment, 14, 39, 89, 155, 174
Structure, 6, 19, 23, 24, 27, 28, 30, 32, 33,
        39, 46–49, 52, 53, 55, 57, 64, 72, 76,

        94, 104, 105, 109, 110, 119, 131, 132,
        137, 163
Subsidiarity, 6, 9
Subsistence agriculture, 74, 176, 179
Suburbanization, 178
Sustainable development, 9, 101, 121,
        123, 124, 133, 172

T
Tax collection, 109
Taxes, 6, 8, 9, 44, 71, 74, 78
Territorio Comunitario de Orígen (TCO), 95
Territory, 4, 16, 35–48, 89, 91, 97, 113–115,
        124, 139, 150
Timber companies, 117, 122, 139, 141,
        143, 145
Timber extraction (exploitation),
        139–143, 149
Timber industry, 21, 139, 141–143, 146
Timber reserves, 123
Top-down, 14, 74, 88, 105
Tourism policy, 172–175
Transparency, 21, 34, 87, 110, 130
Tugurios, 26

U
Uneven development, 50, 67
Urban transformation, 35–48
Urbanisation, 44, 117
Uruguay, 25

V
Venezuela, 4–6, 13, 17, 25
Village organization, 104, 105, 107, 109, 110

W
Washington consensus, 3, 155
World Bank, 10, 70, 130, 147, 155, 174
World economy, 2, 49–53, 67
World system, 50

Lightning Source UK Ltd.
Milton Keynes UK
UKOW03n1943231013

219638UK00001BA/74/P